MW00328416

SOME UNFINISHED CHAOS

Some Unfinished Chaos

The Lives of F. Scott Fitzgerald

Arthur Krystal

UNIVERSITY OF VIRGINIA PRESS
Charlottesville and London

University of Virginia Press
© 2023 by Arthur Krystal
All rights reserved
Printed in the United States of America on acid-free paper

First published 2023

1 3 5 7 9 8 6 4 2

Library of Congress Cataloging-in-Publication Data

Names: Krystal, Arthur, author.
Title: Some unfinished chaos : the lives of F. Scott Fitzgerald / Arthur Krystal.
Description: Charlottesville : University of Virginia Press, 2023. |
Includes bibliographical references and index.
Identifiers: LCCN 2023012236 (print) | LCCN 2023012237 (ebook) |
ISBN 9780813950617 (hardcover) | ISBN 9780813950600 (ebook)
Subjects: LCSH: Fitzgerald, F. Scott (Francis Scott), 1896–1940. | Authors,
American—20th century—Biography. | American literature—20th century—
History and criticism. | United States—History—1901–1953.
Classification: LCC PS3511.I9 Z6734 2023 (print) | LCC PS3511.I9 (ebook) |
DDC 813/.52—dc23/eng/20230523
LC record available at https://lccn.loc.gov/2023012236
LC ebook record available at https://lccn.loc.gov/2023012237

Cover photo: F. Scott Fitzgerald, 1928.
(Everett Collection/Bridgeman Images)

It is not by the direct method of a scrupulous narration that the explorer of the past can hope to depict that singular epoch. If he is wise, he will adopt a subtler strategy. He will attack his subject in unexpected places; he will fall upon the flank, or the rear; he will shoot a sudden, revealing searchlight into obscure recesses, hither-to undivided. He will row out over that great ocean of material, and lower down into it, here and there, a little bucket, which will bring up to the light of day some characteristic specimen, from those far depths, to be examined with a careful curiosity.

—Lytton Strachey

There never was a good biography of a good novelist. There couldn't be. He's too many people if he's any good.

—F. Scott Fitzgerald

CONTENTS

SOME UNFINISHED CHAOS

Some Prefatory Remarks on the Pitfalls of Biography

"FITZGERALD IS A SUBJECT no one has a right to mess up," Raymond Chandler observed. "If the poor guy was already an alcoholic in his college days, it's a marvel that he did as well as he did."[1] But writers *have* messed up the subject, most notably Hemingway, with whom Fitzgerald had a troubled relationship. Critics and biographers are no exception, sometimes overpraising, sometimes maligning him. Fitzgerald was not the hero Lionel Trilling thought he was, or the lout that Jeffrey Meyers makes him out to be. He was simply a man who could not suppress the various facets of his personality. At the mercy of contradictory impulses and prone to self-dramatization, he has led biographers a merry chase. People disagree about Fitzgerald because Fitzgerald often disagreed with himself. He was "all the Karamazov brothers at once," said his teacher Christian Gauss, and he was.[2]

And yes, he was also an alcoholic. "A vicious drunk," Arnold Gingrich, the editor of *Esquire,* called him, "one of the worst I have ever known."[3] Drink made Fitzgerald stupid, loud, truculent. A few shots, and he'd insult his friends, abuse his lovers, and act buffoonish. Alcohol underscored his worst tendencies but did not engender the contradictions in his character. Fitzgerald could be charming, kind, and considerate. He could also be a jerk, a toady, and a boor. Indeed, no one behaved so beautifully when he wasn't behaving so badly. No one was such a loving husband and father when he wasn't being a terrible husband and domineering father. And no one who wanted success so badly was better at sabotaging his own efforts.

Histrionics and mood swings are not exactly unusual for artists, but amid the swirl of contradictions there's usually a temperamental core, a characterological grounding in family, work, or a belief system that defines them. This is what sets Fitzgerald apart: He never quite jells for us because, like a certain Jay Gatsby, he seemed to spring from a Platonic conception of himself. But where Gatsby was faithful to his persona, Fitzgerald was not. Goethe looked out from one eye; Lorenz Hart from the other. Neither by word nor deed did he exhibit a consistent attitude to what drove him.[4]

Nor is it easy to situate him on either a geographical or professional level. There is the midwestern Fitzgerald, the Princeton Fitzgerald, the New York Fitzgerald, the expatriate Fitzgerald, and the Hollywood Fitzgerald. There is Fitzgerald the serious writer, honored by T. S. Eliot and Edith Wharton, and Fitzgerald the hack writer, dismissed by Leslie Fiedler and L. P. Hartley. There is the Fitzgerald who wanted to compose lyrics for show tunes and who, as a friend said, "would rather have written a movie than the Bible, than a best-seller."[5] There is Fitzgerald the humorist, the satirist, the lapsed Roman Catholic, and the spokesman for American youth. More recently there is the historically minded Fitzgerald who, according to David S. Brown, keeps company with Picasso and John Maynard Keynes in a struggle "to make sense of the first unsettled decades of the new century."[6]

As for the guy with the chiseled profile, "he was not a lovable man," John O'Hara said pointedly.[7] Then again, he was, in the words of Alice B. Toklas, "the most sensitive . . . the most distinguished—the most gifted and intelligent of all his contemporaries. And the most lovable."[8] Both assertions are true. One minute you want to hug Fitzgerald, the next you want to wring his neck, not because he was a moralist who behaved like a swine, or a romantic who behaved like a vulgarian—one can chalk that up to booze and false bravado—but because it's difficult to know when to trust him. He seemed to have a compulsion to flog himself in print, yet his sincerity could be suspect. "I've got a very limited talent," he told a friend. "I'm a workman of letters, a professional. I know when to write and when to stop writing."[9]

Fitzgerald was thirty-six when he said this, suffering from both physical and emotional strain. He probably felt he was telling the truth, and it was the truth up to a point. Yet Fitzgerald also had a strong sense of his own worth, planning posthumous editions of his books, designing the volumes, spelling out the contents, estimating the number of pages.[10] Is it a mere "workman" who laments to Maxwell Perkins: "But to die, so completely and unjustly after having given so much. Even now there is little published in American fiction that doesn't slightly bare [*sic*] my stamp—in a *small* way I was an original"?[11]

F. Scott Fitzgerald *was* an original: the first Golden Boy of American Letters and the first to lose a glow that had once dazzled the public. It was an extraordinary life, an improbable life, a life filled with famous people and picaresque details unspooling during a time of social unrest. You can't go wrong writing a book about F. Scott Fitzgerald if you stick to the facts.[12] Then again, those facts have been surveyed, trampled, dug up, patted down, and parceled out by dozens of biographers and critics. What, then, justifies another book about him? The answer to that is the problem that is Fitzgerald. In a phrase, he makes it nearly impossible to state categorically who he was. If he's "all the Karamazov brothers at once," then the books about him (as well as the articles, essays, squibs, and dissertations) may very well arrive at different conclusions. In fact, many do.

After scanning more than a half dozen biographies of Fitzgerald thirty years ago, Jay McInerney commented, "What doesn't emerge from any of these books is the sense of a coherent personality."[13] And John Updike, in his lapidary review of Jeffrey Meyers's biography, feels compelled to note "the cleavages in Fitzgerald's personality—between the spendthrift and the strict accountant, between petty heedlessness and stoic gallantry, between aptitude for chaos and a dream of order, between conceit and insecurity, between, professionally, a hack's opportunism and a pained revision-prone Flaubertian refinement."[14]

Fitzgerald's problem and that of his biographers is the depth and breadth of his polarities, though sometimes the contradictions are situational in nature. It's perfectly normal, after all, to say one thing to one's wife, another to one's editor, and still another to one's daughter. In most cases, however, Fitzgerald's erratic behavior and ricocheting opinions, not to mention the various recollections of people who knew him, make it difficult for *us* to know him. When Michiko Kakutani scolded Meyers for writing a biography that harped on Fitzgerald's "narcissistic self-absorption . . . intellectual pretentiousness . . . self-importance and striving for irresponsibility," she was right to call attention to Meyers's bias.[15] Still, Meyers had reasons to say what he did; it's just that he chose to emphasize the obnoxious and combative Fitzgerald over the loyal and considerate one.

The first biography of Fitzgerald, Arthur Mizener's *The Far Side of Paradise* (1951), was, on the whole, favorably disposed, which makes it a shock to encounter George Jean Nathan's accusation that Mizener's book "is full of distortions of the truth."[16] Yet Nathan, whom Fitzgerald considered a friend, did no better in a portrait of Scott and Zelda that sometimes relied on hearsay.[17] Edmund Wilson also took issue with the biography, as did Hemingway, who described it as "that unspeakable piece of grave robbery."[18] Yet it was Hemingway, more than anyone else, who damaged Fitzgerald's reputation both before and after his death.[19] Fitzgerald's daughter, Scottie Lanahan, also chided Mizener for omitting "the charm, and the goodness, and the . . . heroic side of the man," choosing instead to focus on "the vain, self-indulgent, eternally immature side of him."[20]

Given the scores of books and articles about Fitzgerald, can one portrait be more true to life than another? The short answer is yes, although readers may have to shop around before spying a fair likeness. They can begin by dismissing the unsavory parts of Jeffrey Meyers's book, which hammer away at Fitzgerald's foot-fetishism, womanizing, and fears of sexual inadequacy.[21] Nor should readers accept at face value the tracts claiming that he was responsible for Zelda's madness by delaying her development as a writer, a charge that conveniently overlooks the history of mental illness in the Sayre family. Fitzgerald was neither entirely innocent nor wholly guilty in this regard. Nonetheless, his erratic behavior makes him a perfect vehicle for biographers who unintentionally channel their own ideas about life and art into narratives about Fitzgerald's life and art. No doubt I, too, am guilty of bias, but it is, I like to think, an ecumenical bias: I make it a point not to overlook any of the Karamazov brothers.

As for the discrepancies endemic to biographies in general, what to do about them? I ask not because every variance of fact is significant, but because it makes me wonder what *else* biographers get wrong. Take, for example, Meyers's casual aside that Fitzgerald's first love, Ginevra King, considered his letters to be "clever but unimportant and destroyed them in 1917."[22] Meyers was simply following the lead of Mizener and Matthew Bruccoli, but the truth is somewhat different. According to James L. W. West III, Fitzgerald *asked* Ginevra to destroy his letters, which she obligingly did, which casts a different light on matters.[23] Fitzgerald not surprisingly kept her letters and had them typed up and bound with the title "Personal Letters: Property of F. Scott Fitzgerald (Not Manuscript)."

Or what about a difference of interpretation where no interpretation is necessary? In *Sometimes Madness Is Wisdom,* Kendall Taylor writes that Zelda Sayre was considered southern aristocracy.[24] Yet West emphatically states that the Sayres were not "an old, aristocratic Southern clan."[25] Zelda's parents were not wealthy (like Fitzgerald's mother, they rented), nor was Zelda's father a particularly prominent judge when Scott and Zelda first met. Why there should be confusion about this is hard to fathom.

Mistakes happen—often because anecdotes and incidents are lifted from sources without first checking their accuracy. Some readers, for example, may be under the impression that a particularly pungent exchange once took place between Hemingway and Fitzgerald. When Fitzgerald had supposedly remarked that "The rich are different from you and me," Hemingway had supposedly replied, "Yes, they have more money." Although the first observation occurs near the beginning of "The Rich Boy" and the riposte in "The Snows of Kilimanjaro," no such conversation ever took place, at least not between Fitzgerald and Hemingway, but for many years it was too good an anecdote to let slide.[26]

FOR RICHARD HOLMES, biography is a "handshake across time . . . across cultures, across beliefs, across disciplines, across genders, and across ways of life. It is a simple act of complex friendship."[27] Ideally, yes, but too often biography is motivated by a personal agenda, a political cause, a need to confirm some deeply held belief, or the simple desire to uncover dirt. "The biographer at work," Janet Malcolm writes, "is like the professional burglar, breaking into a house, rifling through certain drawers that he has good reason to think contain the jewelry and money, and triumphantly bearing his loot away. The voyeurism and busybodyism . . . are obscured by an apparatus of scholarship designed to give the enterprise the appearance of banklike blandness and solidity."[28]

Perhaps the best way to view biography's inevitable shortcomings is to imagine one's own life the subject of scholarly interest. How much will be left unsaid? How will the "you" whom *you* know be understood and portrayed? To understand the biographical enterprise, one might first look to the biographer, since every portrait originates in the eye of the beholder, exhibiting whatever shortsightedness or astigmatism already exists. In this sense, biography is always informed bias.

Some Unfinished Chaos is therefore a biographical essay that does not aspire to conclusiveness. Nor is it strictly chronological. The book's tripartite structure—"The Facts of the Matter," "Impressions,"

"Fitzgerald's America"—occasionally blurs as Fitzgerald's story intersects with America's story. Call it an evolving portrait, a layering of impressions that never quite manages to settle. The layers are a bit too wobbly to be strata, but each one, I hope, reflects an evolving relationship between biographer and subject, which gradually coalesces into a living person whose hair needs cutting and clothes need mending, who wakes and sleeps, and who is, like anyone who overthinks existence, a little lost.

For the record, I had no particular expertise about the life or the work. I accepted a job and did my best to fulfill my obligations. Fitzgerald wasn't—to borrow Chandler's term—one of my guys; he wasn't a writer I spent time thinking about. Yes, I loved *The Great Gatsby* when I was a teenager and later a college student. I also liked a good dozen of the short stories, especially "Winter Dreams," "The Rich Boy," and "Babylon Revisited." I had some problems with *Tender Is the Night* the first time I read it, but like Hemingway I found it got better on rereading, much better. As for the first two novels, I couldn't finish them fifty years ago and still have trouble reading them today. What I'm trying to say is that I was neither for nor against Fitzgerald. The truth is, I didn't know much about him other than his tempestuous marriage and his problematic relationship with Hemingway, and, of course, the usual rigmarole about Fitzgerald and the Jazz Age.

It was only when I began to read *about* him and to peruse his writings that I began to get a sense of the man. Which is not to say that I actually "got" him. "No one nature can extend entirely inside another," Fitzgerald counseled.[29] No argument from me. Wholeness is an invention. The best we can take away are partial views, glimmerings of another consciousness alone in a universe that occasionally brushes up against our own.

FEW WRITERS WERE as self-absorbed as F. Scott Fitzgerald, and that's saying something. His narcissism, however, was of a singular kind. Despite deep-rooted insecurities, feelings of failure, and experiences that would rob most men of hope, Fitzgerald pushed ahead. He not only thought he'd succeed, he continued to believe in a more perfect world, a world in which men and women lived by an impeccable code of behavior. Like Gatsby, Fitzgerald possessed "some heightened sensitivity to the promises of life . . . an extraordinary gift for hope."[30]

Calling attention to Fitzgerald's Platonic yearnings in order to illuminate his character may be quixotic, but after examining the letters and *Notebooks,* after taking stock of the opinions of people who knew him, I can only conclude that the dichotomy between the real and the ideal not only informs his best stories but also influenced his behavior. He knew it, too: "The man who blooms at thirty blooms in summer. But the compensation of a very early success is a conviction that life is a romantic matter. In the best sense one stays young. When the primary objects of love and money could be taken for granted and a shaky eminence had lost its fascination, I had fair years to waste, years that I can't honestly regret, in seeking the eternal Carnival by the Sea."[31]

In the end what can you say about a man who said of himself, "In a single morning, I would go through the emotions ascribable to Wellington at Waterloo"?[32] It's a wonderful, preposterous conceit, but somehow it works. Life is a bumpy passage for many people, and each bump may cause a large or small emotional contusion. Fitzgerald, as we know, had a particularly tough time of it, but knowing this doesn't mean we know him.

Perhaps more than any writer since Jean-Jacques Rousseau, F. Scott Fitzgerald acknowledged the contradictions that beset him. And like Rousseau and every other author, he could not confess without shaping that confession. Perfectly capable of extolling his own gifts, he could also admit to being mediocre and unworthy of serious respect: "I am a first-rate writer who has never produced anything but second-rate books," he said of himself.[33] Although determined to live by an honorable code of behavior, he behaved on occasion as no honorable man ever would.

Nothing is black or white when it comes to Fitzgerald; it's always black *and* white. Nor is there much point in trying to pigeonhole him as a writer since the work veers from the ordinary to the exceptional. Joseph Conrad, a writer whom Fitzgerald admired, said something that might serve as a starting point for thinking about him: "The only legitimate basis of creative work lies in the courageous recognition of all the irreconcilable antagonisms that make our life so enigmatic, so burdensome, so fascinating, so dangerous—so full of hope."[34] Fitzgerald was nothing if not a welter of "irreconcilable antagonisms," and to ignore this is to risk not seeing him at all.

Shortly before he died in December 1940, he jotted down a few lines of a poem:

> Your books were in your desk
> I guess and some unfinished
> Chaos in your head
> Was dumped to nothing by the great janitress
> Of destinies.[35]

For Fitzgerald's sake, let's hope he would have changed or excised the last two lines. As for the other fifteen words, they suggest the intense self-awareness typical of all serious writers from the most sensible and down-to-earth to the most sensitive and volatile: there is always some unfinished chaos in their heads. Now all the dutiful biographer has to do is identify, arrange, and pin that chaos to the page. What could be simpler?[36]

The Facts of the Matter: 1896–1920

HE SAVED PRACTICALLY EVERYTHING, everything that had to do with himself. He kept scrapbooks with his reviews and clippings, notebooks in which he jotted down his thoughts, and a ledger that recorded his financial dealings and the dispensation of his stories and novels. He preserved many of the letters he received and often made copies of those he wrote. There are some three thousand letters that we know of, as well as notes and telegrams to friends, publishers, and movie executives. The upshot is that the writer who died practically forgotten in 1940 became, according to Matthew Bruccoli, "the most fully documented American author of the [twentieth] century."[1] If true, it's an appropriate tag for a writer whose third novel has reputedly generated more critical scrutiny than any other work of American fiction.

While all this attention would have surprised and delighted him, he'd be the first to point out the delicious irony of his posthumous fame. Although he published four novels and four collections of short stories (his fifth novel was never finished), it's not the work alone that accounts for his lasting reputation. In hindsight there is something almost archetypal about Fitzgerald's life, though at the time it would have been difficult to predict the dappled glory that would become associated with his name. Somehow the unique combination of the personal and the public—the coming of age of a Scots-Irish writer from the Midwest and the coming of age of America itself—has made the name Fitzgerald a permanent part of our cultural lexicon.

Wherever you look, he jumps out at us. A movie is getting made, a house he rented is being sold, an opera or a play based on *The Great Gatsby* is being performed. An abbreviated list of my own sightings includes: Holden Caulfield's homage to *Gatsby* in *The Catcher in the Rye* ("I was crazy about *The Great Gatsby*. Old Gatsby. Old sport. That killed me"); Bob Dylan's "Ballad of a Thin Man" ("You've been through all of F. Scott Fitzgerald's books"); Richard Yates's short story "Goodbye to Sally" (about a disgruntled screenwriter haunted by Fitzgerald's Hollywood career); Andy Kaufman reading *The Great Gatsby* aloud on *Saturday Night Live;* John Harbison's opera of the same name; Martin Scorsese's fictional production of *Gatsby* on the HBO series *Entourage;* an episode of *South Park* in which the snarky little characters are forced to read *Gatsby* to determine if they have attention deficit disorder; Azar Nafisi's trial of *Gatsby* in *Reading Lolita in Tehran;* and Taylor Swift's "This Is Why We Can't Have Nice Things," which includes the line "Feeling so Gatsby for that whole year." In June 2023, "The Great Gatsby Immersive Experience," which had played first in London, arrived at the Park Central Hotel in New York, where the audience could spend "the evening dancing and clinking glasses with Nick Carraway, Daisy and Tom Buchanan, Myrtle Wilson, and Jay Gatsby himself." And let's not forget the video game based on *Gatsby* that allows you to "Experience the Roaring Twenties first-hand as you uncover secrets behind the richly decadent façade."[2]

There is also something known in economic circles as "The Great Gatsby Curve," which illustrates "the connection between concentration of wealth in one generation and the ability of those in the next generation to move up the economic ladder compared to their parents."[3] *Gatsby* is no longer just a story; it's an industry. Novel after novel features "Gatsby" in the title: *Gatsby's Girl; Gatsby's Last Resort; Gatsby's Vineyard; The Summer We Read Gatsby,* whereas others—Erich Rauchway's *Banana Republican* and Tom Carson's *Daisy Buchanan's Daughter*—simply lean on the original. As for the original itself, around thirty million copies have been sold worldwide, and until 2021, when its copyright expired, more than five hundred thousand copies were sold annually in the United States alone.[4]

And then, with apparently no end in sight, the films: those based on the fiction and those dealing with aspects of Fitzgerald's life.[5] In 2013 Baz Luhrmann's gaudy $125 million production of *The Great Gatsby* opened to much fanfare, and more recently a tepidly received TV series about Zelda with an inane title (*Z: The Beginning of Everything*) ran on Amazon. Just one more sighting: from 2005 to 2012 the Elevator Repair Service theater troupe toured America and Europe with a six-and-a-half-hour word-for-word enactment of *Gatsby* (called *Gatz*), which, according to the *New York Times* theater critic, "captured—in inventively theatrical terms—the unmatchable, heady rush of falling in love with a book."[6]

Historically, though, it was not love at first sight. The novel sold only around twenty-two thousand copies in 1925, and though it received high marks from most critics, it wasn't until the 1950s that *Gatsby* actually became great. Indeed, it is now considered such a remarkable achievement that without it Fitzgerald might have been nothing more than a singular but somewhat minor writer, whose fall from grace in the 1930s would probably not have acquired the mythic overtones it has today. This view is not as blasphemous as might first seem. Gore Vidal, for one, argued that it was Fitzgerald's sad life rather than his work that "continues to provide not only English Departments but the movies with a Cautionary Tale of the first magnitude."[7] But even Vidal would concede that with *Gatsby,* Fitzgerald's stature as both novelist and iconic American writer became unassailable. And since *Gatsby* figures in the minds of many readers as the Great American Novel, it follows that Fitzgerald himself must embody something distinctly American.

Now the pleasantly fuzzy notion of the Great American Novel does not actually require corroboration; like many things about America, it exists more in the imagination than in fact. For many commentators it is embodied in a book of fewer than fifty thousand words, whose action is confined pretty much to Long Island and parts of Manhattan in the year 1922. One year, a specific locale, fifty thousand words. Strictly speaking, however, no consensus about *The Great Gatsby*'s "American-ness" exists. Trilling believed that Gatsby himself inevitably came to stand for America, but this does not necessarily stamp the book with the national seal.[8]

Other critics, however, are not bothered by such niceties. Apparently, *The Great Gatsby* may be, for all of its preemptive melancholy, "the major statement of America realized as world power and imperial presence, as ideologically crucial in its day as Franklin's *Autobiography* had been in its."[9] A ringing endorsement not shared by the critic who wondered if *Gatsby* does not embody "a criticism of American experience—not of manners, but of a basic historic attitude to life—more radical than anything in [Henry] James's own assessment of the deficiencies of his country. The theme of *Gatsby* is the withering of the American dream."[10]

The problem may lie in the implicit conflation of America and the American Dream. They're not the same, except on parchment. Nearly a quarter of a century ago, Thomas Flanagan scoffed at the notion that *Gatsby* is about something called the American Dream: "If you whispered into a reader's sleeping ear the words 'Scott Fitzgerald's *The Great Gatsby*,' she would murmur drowsily 'and the corruption of the American dream.'" There probably is an American dream, Flanagan conceded, "and it probably deserves some of the things that are said about it. But this is not the subject of Fitzgerald's wonderful novel, which is 'about' our entrance into the world 'trailing clouds of glory' until '*At length the Man perceives it die away, And fade into the light of common day.*'"[11]

Well, that might need some pondering. Wordsworth's imprimatur incidentally did not come to Flanagan unbidden. The lines appear in the third and last of the pieces that constitute *The Crack-Up* and do not refer to *Gatsby* but to Fitzgerald's emotional distance from the subjects he writes about. No, it was not the American Dream that Fitzgerald wanted to set down—but what does that matter? There is by now no disputing that he added to the dream both in his own person and in that of Jay Gatsby.

Aside from Fitzgerald's spectacular rise and fall, which set the tone for subsequent American writers who exploded out of the gate but faded toward the end of their careers, there is something quintessentially American about his life. Indeed, one might say that for reasons of heritage, timing, circumstance, and temperament, he, more than any other writer, stood the best chance of producing a novel that would reflect not just the American Dream but also the ineluctable American identity that was then taking shape.[12]

Fitzgerald came along at a moment when the country was entering upon a period of unprecedented growth, when advances in marketing and media were instrumental in disseminating the idea (whether real or not) of a bountiful and culturally cohesive nation. Before he published *The Great Gatsby* in 1925, the times were not ripe for the Great American Novel—how could such a book exist unless the country itself was great?

FRANCIS SCOTT KEY FITZGERALD—the name alone evokes an earlier, more homogeneous America—was born on September 24, 1896, in St. Paul, Minnesota. His mother was Irish, and his father, a scion of two old Maryland families, was equal parts English and Scot. Fitzgerald's great-great-grandfather on his father's side had been a member of Congress during the Jefferson administration; his father's aunt, Mrs. Mary Surratt, had evidently opened her home to the men plotting Lincoln's assassination (she was hanged as an accomplice);[13] and Fitzgerald himself was a second cousin three times removed from Francis Scott Key, the composer of our national anthem.

Fitzgerald's father, Edward, began as a wicker furniture manufacturer in St. Paul in the late 1880s but was forced to close shop in 1898.

In April of that year, he took a salesman's job with Procter & Gamble and relocated the family to Buffalo, New York. It was in Buffalo that Scott's sad sixth birthday party took place. Apparently, the boy wasn't popular enough or his parents important enough for people to bring their children to Fitzgerald's home on that Wednesday in September 1902. If Mizener is correct, Scott waited on the porch all afternoon for children to be dropped off, but no one came. "Sorrowfully and thoughtfully," the boy went inside and "consumed one complete birthday cake, including several candles." Young Scott, it seems, was "a great tallow eater" even into his teenage years.[14]

In 1901, Edward was transferred to Syracuse, where Fitzgerald's sister, Annabel, was born. Two years later, he was sent back to Buffalo. But in March 1908, when Scott was nearly twelve, his father lost his job. "'That morning [Edward] had gone out a comparatively young man, a man full of strength, full of confidence," Fitzgerald would recall. "He came home that evening an old man, a completely broken man. He had lost his essential drive, his immaculateness of purpose. He was a failure the rest of his days."[15]

Forced to return to St. Paul, the Fitzgeralds moved from one rental house to another, settling finally in a row house at the end of one of the smartest avenues in town, which Fitzgerald described as "a house below the average / On a street above the average."[16] According to city directories, Edward Fitzgerald changed residences five times in ten years, and, apparently, the family had at least two other homes during this period.[17] Rent and other expenses were covered by Mrs. Fitzgerald's inheritance, bequeathed by her father, a successful wholesale grocer.

Mary (Mollie) McQuillan (1859–1936) was, biographers agree, a doting, fretful, and eccentric woman who, having earlier suffered the loss of two children, hovered over Scott and his sister. Until the age of fifteen, Scott believed that there wasn't "anyone in the world except me."[18] Mollie was, in Scott's words, "straight 1850 potato famine Irish," but also worth around $300,000, enough money for Fitzgerald to attend the prestigious St. Paul Academy but not enough to make him feel that he belonged. It was in school that he became aware of the distinctions of class within a class, clarifying for him at a tender age his position in the social hierarchy.

Accustomed to his mother's adoration and ashamed of his father's failure (Edward ended up working in the grocery trade out of his brother-in-law's real estate office), young Scott tackled the stratified world of private school in the only way he knew how. From all reports, he was bossy, boastful, and a great know-it-all. "If anybody can poison Scotty or stop his mouth in some way," one of the boys wrote in the school magazine, "the school at large and myself will be obliged."[19]

At thirteen Scotty published a silly detective tale called "The Mystery of the Raymond Mortgage" in the same school magazine that had carried his classmate's letter. He also began to write plays that he directed and acted in, and at fourteen started a "Thoughtbook," in which, according to Matthew Bruccoli, he "chronicled his romantic adventures and logged his campaigns for popularity."[20] The Thoughtbook became his *Notebooks,* and eventually there would also be scrapbooks and a "Ledger."[21] The young writer was, it's fair to say, enthralled with himself; it wasn't necessarily self-love but rather a fascination with his own thoughts and emotions, all of which he felt required expression.

Young Scott was the boy who told you the truth because he knew it, because he wanted you to know that he knew it, and because he thought you should know it, too. He was a teenage pedagogue, a rather peculiar pedagogue. In a letter to his fourteen-year-old sister, written when he was eighteen or nineteen, he advised her on how to win the attention of boys: "A pathetic, appealing look is one every girl ought to have," he wrote. "It is best done by opening the eyes wide and dropping the mouth a little, looking upwards (hanging the head a little) directly into the eyes of the man you're talking to." Continuing in the spirit of brotherly love, he lined up Annabel's good and bad points: she has "good hair, features, and general size." Unfortunately, her figure and teeth are "only fair." She also has "Large hands and feet" (what every teenage girl wants to hear), and he concluded by telling her not to "rub cold cream into your face because you have a slight tendency to grow hairs on it."[22] What kind of eighteen-year-old boy says this to a girl? What kind of teenage boy even knows such things?

In September 1911, Scott's mother packed him off to the Newman School, a middling Catholic boarding school in Hackensack, New Jersey, where he continued to write plays and sketches at the expense of his studies. On a visit to New York, he happened to catch a production of a musical comedy called *The Quaker Girl*. From that moment, as he readily admitted, his "desk bulged with Gilbert & Sullivan librettos and dozens of notebooks containing the germs of dozens of musical comedies."[23]

At Newman he met Father (later Monsignor) Cyril Sigourney Webster Fay, a priest who introduced him to the works of Henry Adams and to the person of Shane Leslie, an Irish writer and first cousin of Winston Churchill. Fay was drawn to the good-looking boy with champagne-colored hair and undertook to broaden his interests, causing him to see the Church as "a dazzling, golden thing."[24] Although born and raised a Catholic, Fitzgerald had little patience with the Church. If not exactly an apostate, he certainly wasn't a believer.[25] Nonetheless, he admired his cousin Thomas Delihunt, a Jesuit priest, whom he listed, along with Theodore Roosevelt and Garibaldi, as one of his heroes. He later dedicated *This Side of Paradise* to Father Fay.

Fitzgerald's Catholicism remains a matter of some dispute. Mizener saw in him a spoiled priest, and certainly the Church plays a role in *This Side of Paradise* and in stories like "Absolution" and "Thank You for the Light," but it's difficult to gauge the depth of Fitzgerald's faith. He married Zelda in New York's St. Patrick's Cathedral and had Scottie baptized, but shortly before his marriage, he wrote to a friend: "You're still a Catholic but Zelda's the only God I have left now."[26] As for the argument that his professed moralism and occasional reference to sin and redemption bear testimony to his faith, who remains untouched by early religious training?[27] Fitzgerald's Catholicism was something deeper and more intangible than Church teaching. "No Irish Catholic ever leaves the Church," Scottie Fitzgerald said. She was referring specifically to her father's sticking with Zelda through "thick and thin," which was "a very Irish Catholic thing to do." It wasn't based on nobility but on "some ancient dark teaching from the past"—an "aching guilt" that is "part of a Catholic upbringing."[28]

Church ritual may have been dazzling to the young student, but theater held the real allure. In his second year at Newman he came across the musical score of *His Honor the Sultan* and learned that the show had been produced by the Triangle Club of Princeton. He entered Princeton in 1913 on a provisional basis and again found himself in an environment where his amour propre was put to the test. Neither wealthy nor socially connected, he had to find a way of standing out. Instead of hitting the books, he began writing an operetta. He also tried out for the freshman football team, but he was even then a shade too small or slow to play.

His one chance to shine was the Triangle Club, and he was heartened to see his librettos accepted and produced. He also occasionally performed and looked great in drag. A photo of him in makeup, wearing a woman's dress and hat, appeared on January 1, 1916, in the *New York Times;* the caption read, "the most beautiful girl in the world." But what he desperately wanted above all else was to become president of the club—*that* would place him among the school's elite. Unfortunately, his poor grades rendered him ineligible for extracurricular activities, including the presidency of the Triangle. It was a setback that haunted him for the rest of his life, the moment when his "career as a leader of men was over."[29]

He did, however, receive an invitation from one of the best eating clubs, the Cottage Club, where he became part of the literary crowd that included Edmund Wilson and John Peale Bishop. He read poetry—Swinburne, Rupert Brooke, Tennyson, Keats—and consumed the novels of Tarkington, Wells, Butler, and Compton Mackenzie, whose *Sinister Street,* a novel about an illegitimate but well-born Englishman matriculating at Oxford, made a deep impression on him.

Academics remained a problem. In November 1915 he dropped out, though he expected to return and repeat his junior year. Before he left, he managed to persuade a dean to write an official statement declaring that he was leaving for reasons of ill-health rather than unfinished work. The dean agreed but couldn't resist a little dig in his cover letter to the young student: "Dear Mr. Fitzgerald," he wrote, "This is for your sensitive feelings. I hope you will find it soothing."[30] Fitzgerald returned as a member of the class of 1918 but decided, in the summer of 1917, to join the army under the condition that he could reenter Princeton when the war was over.

Fitzgerald's one great consolation during these trying times was having won the affections of Ginevra King, a mildly rebellious fifteen-year-old socialite from Lake Forest, Illinois (she'd been caught talking to boys from her dormitory window). He pursued Ginevra during the winter and spring of 1915 and persuaded her to visit him at Princeton. For Scott it was a deathless romance; for Ginevra it was more of a lark. Initially, she found him appealing, and her letters would have made any college freshman happy, but time, distance, and Fitzgerald's temperamental nature dampened her feelings. For the most part, it was an epistolary romance but no less intense for that. Scott was nothing if not a tenacious correspondent. Before long he was picking fights in his letters, finding cause to be jealous, while drawing Ginevra's attention to the small flaws in her character. Eventually, she broke off their affair, as he would note, "with the most supreme boredom and indifference."[31]

He was, of course, devastated, though he may not have been entirely surprised. Ginevra's father was a powerful stockbroker and banking mogul, and on one of the few occasions when Scott and Ginevra actually met—Scott had accompanied her to a party in Lake Forest—he overheard someone say, "Poor boys shouldn't think of marrying rich girls."[32] Into his brain and *Ledger* the statement went. Ginevra was the first girl he had ever loved, and she would thereafter remain the one he could never possess: "High in a white palace the King's daughter, the golden girl."[33] She became for him the model for many of his heroines, including Isabelle Borge in *This Side of Paradise,* Judy Jones in "Winter Dreams," Josephine Perry in *The Basil and Josephine Stories,* and, of course, Daisy Buchanan in *Gatsby.*

Kirk Curnutt, who has written astutely about Fitzgerald, called the rejection "The Snub That Launched a Career."[34] It's a nice phrase, but it didn't really turn Fitzgerald into a writer. Undoubtedly, some yet-to-be-written stories might have had a different patina of sadness to them, but what romantic young man with literary aspirations doesn't write about love?[35] Curnutt overstates the case because Fitzgerald himself overstated it. Twenty years after Ginevra broke his heart, Fitzgerald admitted that most of his heroines were based on "my first girl 18–20 whom I've used over and over and never forgotten."[36]

IN OCTOBER 1917, Fitzgerald received a commission as an infantry second lieutenant and reported to Fort Leavenworth, Kansas, where, working nights in the Officers Club, he completed a first draft of "The Romantic Egoist." That winter he submitted it to Charles Scribner's Sons. Scribner's editor in chief was not impressed, but another editor, the thirty-two-year-old Maxwell Perkins, thought it showed promise. He wrote to the author and encouraged him to revise it. Two months later, another manuscript arrived. But it, too, was deemed too rough around the edges. Disheartened, Fitzgerald put the manuscript away.

In February 1918, Fitzgerald was posted near Louisville, Kentucky, then to Georgia, and finally, in April, to Camp Sheridan on the outskirts of Montgomery, Alabama. It was in Montgomery at a country club dance that he met Zelda Sayre. The daughter of Judge Anthony Sayre, who would later become an associate justice of the Alabama Supreme Court, Zelda was a blond Ginevra with a lot less money but a lot more moxie. Ginevra King might have talked to boys from her window, but Zelda hopped out of the window to attend enlisted men's dances.

Around five feet five inches tall, Zelda was daring, self-confident, gay, and alluring—openly flirtatious but also elusive. She attracted eligible bachelors of every stripe, from privates to senior officers.

Infatuated pilots performed aerial stunts over her house while infantrymen paraded up and down her street, executing drills in her honor. "There were notes in her voice that order slaves around," Scott wrote, "that withered up Yankee captains, and then soft wheedling notes that mingled in unfamiliar loveliness with the night."[37] She was also, apparently, a dab hand with makeup, and was, so it is said, the first of her set to use mascara.

Photographs could not capture her appeal. Ring Lardner insisted that no photo of her "conveyed any real sense of what she looked like, or at least the way she looked to me."[38] Apparently, the camera wasn't able to communicate what her presence did: a vitality heightened by gorgeous coloring and honey-gold hair. Was it Zelda in the person of Gloria Gilbert whom Fitzgerald described in *The Beautiful and Damned:* "the glow of her hair and cheeks, at once flushed and fragile, made her the most living person he had ever seen"?[39]

Instead of being intimidated by her beaux or discouraged by his experience with Ginevra, Fitzgerald waded into the pool of suitors and brazened his way into her affections. He was handsome and his uniform fit, but more dashing officers were also courting Zelda—so why did she choose Scott? A reasonable supposition is that he tried harder and sensed that she liked men who skated on the edge, who were as uninhibited as she was. They became informally engaged in the fall of 1918, just before he was sent to Camp Mills on Long Island to await embarkation. But the war ended in November, and soon he was back in Montgomery. Two months later "the world's worst second lieutenant" received his discharge from the army.[40]

What now? Uncertain about Princeton—his friends had graduated, and no one was pressing him to return—Fitzgerald decided to move to New York and become a writer. He took a job as a copywriter for the Barron Collier advertising agency for ninety dollars a month and moved into a cheap room near Columbia University on Claremont Avenue, which for some reason he thought was in the Bronx.[41] There he began to churn out poems, sketches, jokes, and stories. Soon he had

"122 rejection slips pinned in a frieze about [his] room."[42] His prospects looked grim, and in June 1919 Zelda broke off their engagement. Instead of sulking, he quit the agency, went on a drinking binge, and returned to St. Paul. He moved back in with his parents and once again tackled "The Romantic Egoist." Some months later and with a new title, he resubmitted it to Scribner's.

Scott's luck was about to change.

In September 1919, his first commercial short story, "Babes in the Woods," was accepted by the *Smart Set,* coedited by H. L. Mencken and George Jean Nathan. A few weeks later Maxwell Perkins informed him that Scribner's had accepted his novel. With Scribner's promise as ammunition, he traveled to Montgomery and talked Zelda into renewing their engagement. In March 1920, *This Side of Paradise* appeared in print, and on April 3, Scott and Zelda were married. Two weeks later he woke up to find himself famous.

First Impressions

BEFORE HE WAS SCOTT, he was Scottie. Later he was F. Scott, Fitz, Fitzy, and, to Zelda, "Goofo" or "Do-Do." Scottie was likable enough, if you didn't mind being buttonholed by an enthusiastic teenager who found the world and himself equally fascinating. He was lively, smart, curious, bumptious, and eager to make friends. Oddly innocent (capable of being both surprised and disappointed by people), he imagined himself to be calculating and manipulative. Even as boy, there was a fundamental honesty about him, a tendency to look life squarely in the face. As a man, he refused to pretend, even though he was in the pretend business. He may have downplayed his drinking and blamed others for some of his own mistakes, but generally he told the truth. He claimed to be "probably one of the most expert liars in the world," but, in fact, he was a terrible liar.[1] He could pose but not dissemble; he was too impulsive, too sensitive, too ruthless in his self-regard.

For reasons one can only guess at—an eccentric mother, a deflated father, a keen awareness that his family was not up to snuff—young Scott seemed compelled to take his own measure. And the same blunt honesty that hurt his sister's feelings could just as easily be directed toward himself. Fresh out of college, he listed his good and bad qualities:

> Physically—I marked myself handsome; of great athletic
> possibilities, and an extremely good dancer. . . . Socially . . . I was
> convinced that I had personality, charm, magnetism, poise, and
> the ability to dominate others. Also I was sure that I exercised a
> subtle fascination over women. . . . Mentally—I was vain of having
> so much, of being so talented, ingenuous and quick to learn. . . .
> Morally—I thought I was rather worse than most boys, due to latent
> unscrupulousness and the desire to influence people in some way,
> even for evil. I knew I was rather cold; capable of being cruel; lacked
> a sense of honor, and was mordantly selfish. . . . Psychologically—
> Much as I influenced others, I was by no means the "Captain of my
> Fate." I had a curious cross section of weakness running through my
> character. I was liable to be swept off my poise in a timid stupidity.
> I knew I was "fresh" and not popular with older boys. I knew I was
> completely the slave of my own moods, and often dropped into a
> surly sensitiveness most unprepossessing to others. . . . Generally—
> I knew I had no real courage, perseverance or self-respect.[2]

Although proffered by Stephen Palm, the protagonist of "The Romantic Egoist," the description fits the author to a T. There is humor, as well as the fixation to compare himself to boys who were more self-confident. Naturally, there's also a good deal of embellishment since words have a way of accumulating other words. And because no one ever accused the young author of seeking *le mot juste,* we have to wonder if he meant "ingenious" rather than "ingenuous." Finally there's the inherent contradiction of the boy who can "dominate others" but who is also weak and subject to "a timid stupidity."

At this point, despite his professed lack of "self-respect," Fitzgerald believed that a special destiny awaited him. But at the same time he felt overshadowed by others. His self-proclaimed ability to influence and dominate was a source of satisfaction, but just how real was this pre-sumptive power over people? The truth is, he was more impressionable than his peers. He never forgot, for example, a boy who had played basketball at the YMCA "with a fierce but facile abandon."[3] At Princeton he fell under the spell of football players Hobey Baker and Buzz Law, who represented "an ideal worthy of everything in my enthusiastic admiration."[4] Later he would be thrilled on meeting Gene Tunney at a party and would not leave his side.[5] Encountering James Joyce in Paris, he offered, as proof of his devotion, to jump out of a hotel window. Joyce naturally thought Fitzgerald was touched in the head and worried that he would one day injure himself.[6]

The realization that some men were better and more successful nagged at him. Having seen his father reduced by circumstance, he decided that "life was something you dominated if you were any good" (a recipe for unhappiness, if ever there was one).[7] Thus, he idolized men who exuded boldness and self-assurance, who casually wielded power over others because they had power over themselves. There is no irony in the fact that he admired the very men who would never think to save clippings of themselves, who knew their own value without having to read about it, and who, because they were indifferent to the opinion of others, thereby gained others' good opinion.

For the young Fitzgerald, such men possessed something he did not, which enabled them—no matter their profession—to make something substantial out of their intangible yearnings. So how could he, Scott Fitzgerald, emulate them? Well, he could write and direct plays as he had at St. Paul Academy. Or he could become a football star, or, at the very least, make the team. But he was not asked to join the team, and this haunted him. Hemingway—whose every second or third word about Fitzgerald should be suspect—recalls their walking down Fifth Avenue one afternoon when suddenly Fitzgerald blurted out, "If only I could play foot-ball again with everything I know about it now."[8] Hemingway suggested that they walk in the street against traffic "since [Fitzgerald] wanted to be a back-field man." Other writers have also mocked Fitzgerald's regret at not having played varsity ball, but in truth, the regret had merit. When Fitzgerald unpacked his bags in Princeton in 1913, college football was, as Mizener pointed out, "a deadly serious affair . . . conducted by gentlemen in a kind of Tennysonian Round-Table spirit."[9]

College football, as Fitzgerald later recalled, was "a sort of symbol . . . something at first satisfactory, then essential and beautiful. It became the most intense and dramatic spectacle since the Olympic games."[10] His high regard for the oblong ball and the men who played with it was not unique. In *The Legend of Hobey Baker,* John Davies noted that "football was a sort of civic religion" and that in "the fall of 1912 Governor Woodrow Wilson went down to practice [at Princeton] three times, including the day of his election as President of the United States."[11]

Which left the Triangle Club. If young Scott could become its president, then glory would be his, and for a time it seemed that he might ascend to the presidency. But in his junior year, that, too, would be denied him. No touchdowns, no Triangle presidency, no graduation. College, he said later, had defeated him: "There were to be no badges of pride, no medals, after all."[12] Too much? Perhaps not. One hundred years ago, college figured far more prominently in a young man's life. College wasn't merely a four-year interim leading to something more essential; it *was* essential. The eating clubs, the teams, the theater groups fashioned an identity that accrued to students decades later. Not to distinguish oneself in some way—be it on the stage, in the classroom, or on the gridiron—was to leave no mark, no lasting impression on the minds of teachers and classmates. And for Fitzgerald, who desperately wanted to stand out, who needed to be the most popular boy in class, Princeton reinforced an already acute sense of class distinction.

As a result, he developed what he called "a two-cylinder inferiority complex."[13] Writing to John O'Hara in 1933, he explained that he was "half black Irish and half old American stock with the usual exaggerated ancestral pretensions. The black Irish half of the family had the money and looked down upon the Maryland side of the family who had, and really had, that certain series of reticences and obligations that go under the poor old shattered word 'breeding.'"[14] His Irish half always made him wary. He imagined that even if "elected King of Scotland tomorrow after graduating from Eton, Magdalene to the Guards, with an embryonic history which tied me to the Plantagenets, I would still be a *parvenu*," someone who spent his youth "alternately crawling in front of the kitchen maids and insulting the great."[15]

Yet for all his insecurity, Fitzgerald was hardly a shrinking violet. On the contrary, he liked to be the center of attention, he *demanded* to be the center of attention, especially on those occasions when he felt overshadowed. Self-dramatization was not foreign to him: "If I couldn't be perfect, I wouldn't be anything," he wrote in his *Ledger* at the age of nineteen—a thought that practically begs for a comeuppance.[16] He took solace in the fact that he could write, or, more accurately, in the prospect that his writing might distinguish him. He loved literature, but literature was also a means to impress others. When he exclaimed to Edmund Wilson that he wanted to be one of the greatest writers who ever lived, he was saying, in effect, that he wanted to be famous and respected. Princeton may have wounded him, but it also steadied his gaze: He saw what he *couldn't* have and knew he could write about it. Envy may not produce gravitas, but failure often does; and failure was something Fitzgerald understood long before his writing career stalled. Failure was the shadow that stalked him because anything less than perfection was unthinkable.

IT COULDN'T HAVE been much fun being F. Scott Fitzgerald, always wondering how he appeared to others, always worried about the impression he was making, yet behaving at times to ruin that impression. Nathan, who met Fitzgerald when he and Mencken were editing the *Smart Set,* recalled hearing a story that Fitzgerald, while at Princeton, had sent "questionnaires to prospective feminine dates as to: (1) whether they had had their hair washed during the day and

(2) how many baths they had taken."[17] Nathan also testified "from personal observation that it was [Fitzgerald's] habit . . . to demand of any female companions in taxicabs that they open their mouths so he might determine that the insides of their teeth were free of tartar."[18] Not sure *any* of the Karamazov brothers would have done that.

Fitzgerald at twenty could be obnoxious and clueless, but there was also something appealing about him. Too many irascible and tough-minded people were drawn to Fitzgerald for him to have been such a dolt. Edmund Wilson liked him, as did Christian Gauss, who steered him toward Charles Scribner III. Later on, H. L. Mencken, Van Wyck Brooks, Dorothy Parker, Gertrude Stein, Hemingway, and Gerald and Sara Murphy found him to be good company, though Hemingway would change his mind.

He had a gift for friendship and a gift for alienating his friends. Sara Murphy once told him that "consideration of other people's feelings, opinions, or even time was *Completely* left out of your makeup. . . . [Y]ou haven't the faintest idea what anybody but yourself is like."[19] One may disagree. Fitzgerald seemed genuinely interested in other people and not just as potential material for his fiction. And it was this interest coupled with his earnestness that sometimes made him hard to be around. He stood too close and talked too much. Yet somehow you forgave him because, well, because he was so eager—eager to talk, listen, or throw himself into any activity.

But he lacked, as he admitted, prudence. In his rush to get to know someone, he often asked inappropriate questions. Running into Compton Mackenzie in 1924, Fitzgerald asked him why he "had petered out and never written anything that was as good" as *Sinister Street*.[20] And at their first meeting, according to Hemingway, Fitzgerald had asked him if he had slept with his wife before marrying her. The man seemed unable to bottle up his feelings, often revealing things that others would just as soon not hear. He seemed to have no defenses, which often made him a bore, but also allowed him to respond spontaneously to people and events. On receiving the news that Scribner's would be publishing *This Side of Paradise,* Fitzgerald literally ran into the streets of St. Paul like someone in a Frank Capra film, stopping traffic and telling everyone he met the good news.[21]

"If personality is an unbroken series of successful gestures, then there was something gorgeous about him," Fitzgerald said of Gatsby. Whether personality really manifests in this way is open to question, but Fitzgerald thought it did. He believed in extravagant gestures; the larger the gesture, the greater the man. When Zelda ended their engagement, he didn't collapse; he returned to St. Paul not to lick his wounds but to write a book that would make him rich enough to win her back. And, as it happened, it did. It was a lesson to him: If he committed himself to his work, he could get what he wanted. If he dared greatly, he would be rewarded proportionately. So while obstacles were everywhere and defeat was imminent, all could be saved by the extravagant gesture: you could write a book, or you could buy a mansion across the bay from the woman you love, and happiness would be within your reach. Gatsby didn't just magically appear in Fitzgerald's fiction; he'd been gestating in his imagination for years.

Nonetheless, the man continued to make life difficult for himself. It's as though he purposely set the bar high enough for him to fail, so that when he finally cleared it, the satisfaction would be that much greater. The pattern fell into place during his teens: He aims high, he tries hard, he meets with rejection. He then picks himself up and tries again. He gives in to despair, but there's a resilience to him, a resolve to overcome, which, despite a veneer of self-pity, refuses to let him quit. He loses hope, but never for long.

WHEN WE'RE YOUNG we tend to believe that life will deliver what we want, if not immediately, then soon. And what Fitzgerald wanted was to live life on a higher plane. Not content to be content, he approached things with an intensity that probably made his friends squirm. Yet, as a writer, he also had to step back from experience. According to his Princeton classmate John Peale Bishop, Fitzgerald had "the rare faculty of being able to experience romantic and ingenuous emotions and half an hour later regard them with satiric detachment."[22] Malcolm Cowley, building on Bishop's point, contended that Fitzgerald "took part in the ritual orgies of his time, but he also kept a secretly detached position, regarding himself as a pauper living among millionaires, a Celt among Sassenachs and a sullen peasant among the nobility."[23]

Cowley's elaborate juxtapositions derived from Fitzgerald's own self-professed attitude toward the leisure class, which he disliked not with "the conviction of a revolutionist but the smoldering hatred of a peasant."[24] Fitzgerald may have been an outsider, but he was hardly a peasant. Meanwhile, both Mizener's and Cowley's fixation on "the doubleness of Fitzgerald's perception" seems to me a pronunciamento of less than lofty significance. What conscientious novelist works differently? One dances with the girl, then one goes home to write about it. Even writers to the "manor" born who choose to focus on manners, such as Edith Wharton and Louis Auchincloss, write as outsiders. Writers at their desks *are* outsiders; it's why they so often sit at their desks.

Novelists aren't issued manuals of instruction; no rules of prosody apply as they might to a poem. They can write what they want, how they want—but if they're worth our time, it's because their voice makes us believe their words. Fitzgerald tried his hand at satire ("The Diamond as Big as the Ritz") and fantasy ("The Curious Case of Benjamin Button"), both interesting failures in this reader's estimation. He also wrote young adult stories about Basil and Josephine and half-humorous, cynical stories about Pat Hobby, as well as many fanciful tales of young romance, but what he was really good at and knew he was good at was capturing a feeling that had once touched him.[25] His best stories, as he noted, were always fueled by a specific emotion; the others consisted of "plots without emotions, emotions without plots."[26]

When young he didn't have much to write about except himself and his friends, but he knew what mattered to him. His gift was not only the ability to describe the sweetness of experience but also the knowledge that the sweetness stems from impermanence. Whether it's the first flush of love, the first scent of fall in the air, or the joyous calm of a snowy field at midnight, the sensation of happiness is always tinged with melancholy. The snow will melt, love will die, beauty fades, and life is but a moment in a blind and careless eternity. Life thus needs to be reclaimed with the same lyrical tenderness with which Keats imbued the figures on a Grecian urn, a poem that Fitzgerald returned to again and again.

But it wasn't enough to be a stylist or storyteller. Fitzgerald also fancied himself a man of affairs, a Richelieu-like figure, skilled in the art of manipulation. It wasn't enough to feel deeply; one also had to be a man of the world, a sharp-eyed observer of men and manners, whose purpose was to record the changes in American society, some of which he himself was bringing about. It was a delusion that Alfred Kazin picked up on. After calling him "one of the most naturally sentient novelists we have ever had," Kazin adds, "he had to think like a salesman . . . to show that he was on to every smart perception that was a condition for survival in the world he loved."[27]

Hence the "wised-up" articles that he wrote in his early twenties, as well as the satiric stories that he felt showed off his analytical side. Nothing was going to get past him, not even himself. If he had faults and limitations, he would acknowledge them: "I didn't have the two top things: great animal magnetism or money. But I had the two second things: good looks and intelligence. So I always got the top girl."[28] Which is sort of true. He got Ginevra—until he lost her. But in losing her, he gained a valuable insight. Her rejection not only cemented his station in life; it was also a signal that happiness, as an element in fiction, as in life, was best left to the imagination. It was Ginevra who doomed Gatsby, becoming the ideal he could never possess. And, in a way, Fitzgerald preferred the unattainable. As he wrote to his daughter in October 1937, on the eve of seeing Ginevra again after a span of more than twenty years, "She was the first girl I ever loved and I have faithfully avoided seeing her up to this moment to keep that illusion perfect."[29]

Before he was twenty, Fitzgerald seemed to have found his theme: loss of love and the nurturing of illusion. Ginevra may not have delivered the snub that launched him as a writer, but she certainly gave him something to write about, and few other writers have written so tenderly and persuasively about the poignancy of youth and the cost of its passing. "Everything you are and do from fifteen to eighteen is what you are and will do through life," he counseled Scottie when he was forty-two and she seventeen.[30] What he didn't tell her, though, is that not *everyone* falters under the burden of the past. It takes a writer, and a particular kind of writer—one always watching himself, as if he were a character in a play—who bends under the weight of accumulated indignities.

Far more than most people, Fitzgerald kept close the humiliations of youth as well as the youthful hopes that had once made life seem so full of promise. He was an adolescent dreamer whose attachment to dreams prolonged adolescence long after it was gone. And like any romantic poet (whether he's seventeen or twenty-seven), he was sure that he felt more intensely than others, vibrating to every burgeoning friendship, every romantic encounter, every well-wrought poem—but he was also something of a performer, even with an audience of one: "Taking things hard—from Ginevra to Joe Mank [movie producer Joseph Mankiewicz]," he wrote when he was in his forties. "That's the stamp that goes into my books so that people can read it blind like brail [*sic*]."[31]

All the hurts and slights remained until the end. He felt himself outmatched in private school, at Princeton, in New York, in the South of France, and in Hollywood, yet he continued to gravitate toward men he considered his betters—either because they were better born, or better at games, or better in business—as if only in their presence could he take the full measure of himself. Intrigued by his own nature, he wrote not so much to share his experience as to get a grip on how *he* felt about it. This may not make him different from other writers, but in Fitzgerald's case the interest was so consuming that fiction alone could not encompass it—hence, the *Notebooks,* the *Ledger,* and the stream of letters. Jeffrey Meyers, in his occasionally brutal biography, accuses him of a "narcissistic self-absorption."

But what writer is not self-absorbed? "We have two or three great and moving experiences in our lives," Fitzgerald once observed. "Then we learn our trade, well or less well, and we tell our two or three stories—each time in a new disguise—maybe ten times, maybe a hundred, as long as people will listen."[32] In his best stories there is a blend of lyricism and melancholy, a sense of time passing, of emotions fading, of chances missed, of a happiness always just out of reach. "I was reminded of something," Nick Carraway thinks, "—an elusive rhythm, a fragment of lost words, that I had heard somewhere a long time ago."[33]

Admittedly, nostalgia is an easy trap to fall into—lost loves, dead friends, roads not taken—but that isn't what makes Fitzgerald important. He may have been obsessed with his own history, but nostalgia is neither cheap nor sentimental; it is, in fact, as Camus suggests, what all thought comes down to. All we have is life and what we infer from experience, and experience occurs sequentially. We build on what we learn, so that memories viewed with detachment may guide us to self-knowledge. What Meyers doesn't get is that Fitzgerald was painfully honest in his self-absorption, that it entailed as much self-criticism as self-regard. And if he sometimes absolved himself of blame with regard to Zelda, he also recognized that he had a hand in the dissolution of their marriage.

Young men, if nature takes its course, grow into old men and become less and less susceptible to dreams. Although Fitzgerald didn't reach a ripe old age, he lived long enough to know that he was not the man he had hoped to be. All he wanted was to be greater than he was, and for the longest time he could not regard this aspiration with the wistful resignation it deserved. How could he? He was a romantic and an impressionable fool who was wise only when he stepped away from the world and re-created it in his imagination.

Fitzgerald's America I

FITZGERALD WAS BORN JUST as the Gilded Age was ending. Stretching roughly from 1870 to the Panic of 1893, the last quarter of the nineteenth century saw a boom in American manufacturing that surpassed the combined production of Britain, Germany, and France. Ruthless entrepreneurs, such as Cornelius Vanderbilt, Henry Clay Frick, Jay Gould, and John D. Rockefeller, gobbled up locally owned businesses and replaced them with conglomerates that monopolized steel, railroads, oil, and banking. With the expansion of railroads (tracks tripled between 1860 and 1880), coal and steel became indispensable to the economy and created the beginnings of a national marketplace. As the country became more connected, the federal government extended its power over both morals and business practices, passing antitrust laws alongside legislation outlawing polygamy and obscenity.

Entrepreneurship, however, was seen in Darwinian terms, and success as survival of the fittest. The rich embodied values that helped build the country: hard work, ambition, individualism, and self-reliance. Horatio Alger didn't write novels about the rich, but his titles—*Do and Dare, Strive and Succeed, Shifting for Himself, Bound to*

Rise—pointed the way to wealth. Alger knocked off two dozen of these inspirational tales between 1867 and 1899, celebrating the kid who came from the wrong side of the tracks and who, by dint of hard work and pluck, came to own those tracks and much of the cargo that ran on them. (Who is James Gatz if not a Horatio Alger figure?) In Alger's novels, the poor boy who makes good is a walking testimonial to the goodness of America itself.

To be sure, unionists and clergymen railed against unfair business practices and the evils of money (between 1877 and 1880 the number of national labor unions increased from three to eighteen),[1] but in general the rise of banking moguls like J. P. Morgan and James J. Hill (who presided over Fitzgerald's hometown of St. Paul) dovetailed nicely with the American ethos of success.[2] Naturally, a reaction set in. The preoccupation with success was seen by some to be psychologically damaging, as well as antithetical to democratic values. In a 1906 letter to H. G. Wells, William James famously made reference to "the bitch-goddess Success." A decade or so later, the theater critic and essayist William Winter didn't mince words: "The spirit of our country is and long has been one of pagan Materialism, infecting all branches of thought, and of unscrupulous Commercialism, infecting all branches of action. . . . Our methods of business, approved and practised, are not only unscrupulous but predatory."[3]

While the concurrent spurts of economic growth and social unrest figure prominently in histories of the Gilded Age, Jackson Lears's *Rebirth of a Nation: The Making of Modern America, 1877–1920* targets a more subtle transformation. For Lears, the energy required to sustain rapid economic growth also helped to create societal institutions of an increasingly rigid kind, which, in turn, sapped the energy of the people these institutions were designed to assist. A fear had arisen that America was becoming overcivilized. The frontier was vanishing, and machinery was taking the place of man. As a consequence, Americans began presenting with neurasthenia (a weakening of the nerves), manifested by lassitude, insomnia, tooth decay, dyspepsia, and nocturnal emissions. Neurasthenia, Lears believes, represented "an extreme version of a broader cultural malaise—a growing sense that the Protestant ethic of disciplined achievement had reached the end of its tether, had become entangled in the structures of an increasingly organized capitalist society."[4]

Apparently, the Puritan values that spurred economic growth were now being suborned by a complex and soulless capitalist economy, creating in its wake a pervasive psychic implosion. Aptly, Lears quotes Emerson's dialectical aperçu: "Every spirit makes its house; but afterwards the house confines the spirit."[5] If Lears's appraisal is correct, then Fitzgerald was born when America suffered from "the dis-ease of the fin de siecle"—that is, an ebbing of our natural vitality that, in turn, fostered a search for regeneration and spiritual rebirth, thus making us ripe for the militant expostulations of evangelical Protestantism and the more earthbound tenets of muscular Christianity. Hence, the upper-class male's interest in boxing, physical health, and improbable adventure stories.

In short, the Gilded Age was laden with contradictions. Industrialization may have contributed to a national neurasthenia, but who could deny that a strong work ethic and an entrepreneurial spirit were also necessary for the very situation that Lears contends contributed to the ebbing of vitalism? Indeed, the social Darwinist struggle to survive (inherent in capitalism) makes no sense *without* vitalism—unless one calls it by another name: the will. If, in fact, something vital in the American character was weakening, then another trait had to be advanced that would enable individuals to overcome societal challenges.

Who then should enter upon the stage but Teddy Roosevelt? Here was the exemplary American who, despite the encumbrances of modern civilization, had built himself up with exercise and manual labor. Industrialization didn't cause *him* to waver. Listen to him sing the praises of "the man who is actually in the arena, whose face is marred by dust and sweat and blood; who strives valiantly; who errs, who comes short again and again . . . who spends himself in a worthy cause;

who at the best knows in the end the triumph of high achievement, and who at the worst, if he fails, at least fails while daring greatly, so that his place shall never be with those cold and timid souls who neither know victory nor defeat."[6]

Whether the nation experienced a loss of vitalism around the turn of the twentieth century is a question for social scientists to ponder. *Theories* about vitalism, however, *were* taking root in America during Fitzgerald's teenage years. After 1900, Nietzsche's works began showing up on college campuses, as did Henri Bergson's *L'Evolution créatrice* (1907), which introduced the concept of the *élan vital,* and Oswald Spengler's *Decline of the West* (1918), with its theory of nations' cyclical rise and fall. Fitzgerald appears to have read articles about Spengler's book in the summer of 1924 and became infatuated with the idea that civilization requires the ascendancy of the critical over the creative.[7] Spengler's emphasis on organic historical growth and decay, according to some current scholars, seems to mirror Fitzgerald's own opinions about the decline of European culture.[8]

As to how much Fitzgerald was influenced by talk of vitalism, it's impossible to know. We know that he admired Roosevelt (both men when young had spent time in Montana), and we also know that Fitzgerald believed that his own vitality would see him through life (wasn't Gatsby sustained by "the colossal vitality of his illusion"?).[9] And it's certainly possible that Edward Fitzgerald's feckless nature accounted in some measure for his son's often reckless behavior. Whatever the case, Fitzgerald decided around 1933 that his own vitality was being sapped. "Of all natural forces, vitality is the incommunicable one," he noted in one of the essays that would become *The Crack-Up.* "You have it or you haven't it, like health or brown eyes or a baritone voice."[10] Indeed, vitality's most salient characteristic seems to be its loss. Fitzgerald sometimes refers to this as "emotional bankruptcy," a thought that occurs frequently in his books and letters.

In an early story, "Winter Dreams," the protagonist is stunned to realize that he has lost more than the girl he once loved; he has lost the capacity to care about that loss. In *Tender Is the Night,* Dick Diver also fears he may become incapable of feeling, and indeed he does end up an *"homme épuisé"* (a man exhausted or worn out). It's a fine subject, the loss of vitality, and Fitzgerald made good use of it for a while: "Horror and waste—Waste and horror—what I might have been and done that is lost, spent, gone, dissipated, unrecapturable. . . . The horror has come now like a storm."[11]

Still, it feels a bit much, this investiture of emotion in the possible diminution of emotion. But then Fitzgerald was never one to shy from the overly dramatic when describing the arc of his own life. Wringing tragedy out of what is essentially melancholia has its appeal. Of course, one runs into a spot of trouble here. After all, it's the vitality which Fitzgerald brings to the theme that enables him to write so well about it.

IF, INDEED, A spiritual anemia characterized American society around 1915, it certainly wasn't prevalent in those circles where the idea of America was fomenting vigorous debate. Perhaps because it was a new century, or because a reaction had set in to the Gilded Age, or because writers thought it high time that culture took its cue from America rather than Europe, a good deal of attention began to be paid to the nature of our democracy. What was our national character? What made us different from other nations? Would America be corrupted by immigration? By race? By opportunism? By a loosening of morals? Naturally, opinions varied, and as is often the case, the same cluster of events had pundits declaring that America was either losing its way or else reaping the benefits of material progress.

Among those who subscribed to the first view was Fitzgerald's friend Van Wyck Brooks. In 1918, Brooks wrote, "It seems to me symbolic of our society that the only son of Abraham Lincoln should have become president of the Pullman Company, that the son of the man who liberated the slaves politically should have been the first, as *The Nation* pointed out not long ago, to exploit them industriously."[12] Brooks was echoing John Jay Chapman, who three years earlier had noted: "Our age has been an age of management, not of *ideas* or of men. Our problems have been problems of transportation and housing, *not* of thought."[13] What was bothering Chapman and Brooks? As Brooks put it: "The gradual commercialization of all the professions, meanwhile, has all but entirely destroyed the possibility of personal growth. . . . [T]he more sensitive minds of the younger generation drift almost inevitably into a state of internal anarchism that finds outlet, where it finds outlet at all, in a hundred unproductive forms."[14]

Something was in the air. It may not have been evident to everyone, it may not have been as dire as some made it out to be, but a sense of unease—of decline and fall—seemed to weigh on the minds of our cultural arbiters. Gazing westward from London in 1920, George Santayana worried that "civilisation is perhaps approaching one of those long winters that overtake it from time to time. A flood of barbarism from below may soon level all the fair works of our Christian ancestors, as another flood two thousand years ago leveled those of the ancients."[15]

It's a fear not exactly alien to most periods in our history. That it seemed part of the cultural malaise after the turn of the last century brooks no dispute, but culture is never less than a cross-hatching of diverse and often contradictory attitudes and opinions, and it would be irresponsible to define in an absolute sense the predominant spirit of a decade, much less an age. While some social commentators expressed dismay and anxiety over trends occurring in the first two decades, others like Irving Babbitt and H. L. Mencken took a more sanguine view (if one can apply such a word to Mencken). In *Democracy and Leadership* (1924), Babbitt suggested that America had the capacity to accommodate differences and that different peoples will be incorporated in a national orchestra, resulting in "a richer harmony . . . providing they can be properly led. Otherwise the outcome may be an unexemplified cacophony."[16]

As for Mencken, he, of course, assailed the very thing the naysayers were fearful of. In fact, he was dismissive of the Anglo-Saxon ideal and of the people who worried that its passing would mean the end of civilization: "Of the Americans who have come into notice during the past fifty years as poets, as novelists, as critics, as painters, as sculptors in the minor arts, less than half bear Anglo-Saxon names."[17] By 1917, he was arguing that the multifarious nature of our democracy was at the core of our prosperity; the system worked not despite but because of "the essential conflict of forces among us."[18]

Was the nation losing its way? Was unrestricted immigration altering more than just the complexion of the populace? Underscoring the fear that America was in ethnic danger, a specious "scientific" eugenics movement (a term coined in 1883 by Darwin's half cousin Francis Galton) emerged that advocated the genetic superiority of the white race. Its tenets were "taught in schools, celebrated in exhibits at the World's Fair, and even preached from pulpits."[19] For William Winter, "Foreign elements alien to our institutions and ideas as to our language and our thoughts,—seditious elements, ignorant, boisterous, treacherous, and dangerous,—have been introduced into our population in immense quantities, interpenetrating and contaminating it in many ways." Like other observers, Winter felt the peril was self-evident: Despite "iterated warnings and protests, immigration into the United States has been permitted during the last twenty years of about 15,000,000 persons—including vast numbers of the most undesirable orders."[20] Sometimes the predictable needs stating: *Plus ça change, plus c'est la même chose.*

Indeed, for many Americans, the country looked as if it were going to ruin. In the early 1920s, the *Saturday Evening Post* ran a series of articles titled "Why Europe Leaves Home," in which the author Kenneth Roberts speculated that "if a few more million members of the Alpine, Mediterranean and Semitic races are poured among us, the result must inevitably be a hybrid race of people as worthless and futile as the good-for-nothing mongrels of Central America and Southeastern Europe."[21] If readers missed the articles, they were likely to chance upon Hendrik Willem Van Loon's popular *The Story of Mankind,* which postulated that our culture could meet the same fate as Rome's when "unknown hordes from unknown parts of Asia and Eastern Europe broke through the barriers of Rome and installed themselves amidst the ruins of the old Augustan cities."[22]

So prevalent was the concern about the influx of people from southern and eastern Europe that in 1921 Congress passed the Quota Act and, three years later, the even more restrictive Immigration Act of 1924. "Thank God we have in America perhaps the largest percentage of any country in the world of the pure, unadulterated Anglo-Saxon stock," said South Carolina senator Ellison DuRant Smith. "And it is for the preservation of that splendid stock that has characterized us that I would make this not an asylum for the oppressed of all countries."[23]

Concerns about ethnicity were, of course, inseparable from race. One hundred years ago, many educated people found nothing reprehensible in thinking that people of color were genetically and morally inferior to Caucasians—in which case, a mingling of the races was detrimental to both whiteness and civilization. It wasn't only the philistines or the "booboisee" voicing these concerns. In 1916, the historian and anthropologist Madison Grant published *The Passing of the Great Race: Or, The Racial Basis of European History*, which put in academic language an already articulated fear. Grant's book (published by Scribner's) came out not long after the release of D. W. Griffith's *The Birth of a Nation,* which, as moviegoers know, presented the Ku Klux Klan as heroic defenders of white maidenhood and traditional values. The Klan, almost dormant by the end of the nineteenth century, now experienced a resurgence of popularity, spurred by the northward migration of African Americans.

And because race-mixing was a real fear, Lothrop Stoddard's *The Rising Tide of Color Against White World-Supremacy* (1920) even caught the attention of President Harding: "Whoever will take the time to read and ponder Mr. Lothrop Stoddard's book . . . must realize that our race problem here in the United States is only a phase of a race issue that the whole world confronts," he proclaimed on October 26, 1921.[24] Stoddard's book makes an appearance in *Gatsby,* though Tom

Buchanan butchers both the title and the author's name. When Tom blurts out, "Nowadays people begin by sneering at family life and family institutions, and next they'll throw everything overboard and have marriage between black and white,"[25] he is taking part in a public dialogue that in 1922 would not have seemed unreasonable to most Americans.

ALTHOUGH *THE GREAT GATSBY* is openly contemptuous of Buchanan and his views, Fitzgerald himself bought into racial and ethnic stereotypes. On his first trip to Europe he sent a letter to Wilson that read in part: "The negroid streak creeps northward to defile the Nordic race. Already the Italians have the souls of blackamoors." Although he soon backpedaled, calling his reactions "philistine, anti-socialistic, provincial and racially snobbish," he quickly segued into another preposterous stance: "I believe at last in the white man's burden. We are as far above the modern Frenchman as he is above the Negro. Even in art!"[26] It's hard to know how serious he was about the French, but no matter, he tossed off racist remarks without a qualm.

A casual, unself-conscious racism runs throughout "The Diamond as Big as the Ritz," and a downright nasty racism ("some n—scrap") mars a chapter or two in *Tender Is the Night*.[27] George Nathan recounts a dubious anecdote about how Fitzgerald aroused "the wrathful indignation of colored elevator boys in a New York hotel where he was staying by confining their tips at Christmastime to fancily wrapped bottles of a well-known deodorant."[28] Nathan provides no evidence, but once read, it's hard to forget.

What makes such blatant racism even more shameful is the fact that offenders knew they would not be vilified for it. Antipathy toward African Americans was as pervasive as ever. After Jack Johnson soundly beat Jim Jeffries for the heavyweight title on July 4, 1910, riots broke out from St. Louis to New York. Blacks could celebrate, but only in secret. As is amply documented, lynchings in the Jim Crow South were commonplace, invariably unpunished, and photographs were sold as souvenirs. In 1918 Congressman Leonidas Dyer of Missouri introduced an Anti-Lynching Bill—the Dyer Bill—which was finally passed by the House of Representatives on January 26, 1922, but was stopped in the Senate by filibuster conducted by southern Democrats.[29] Lynchings, they argued, were a state matter.

In the summer of 1919 approximately twenty-five race riots occurred throughout the nation, the most violent in Chicago, Boston (Roxbury), New York, Washington, DC, and Tulsa, Oklahoma.[30] In Chicago, the stoning death of a young Black swimmer led to seven days of shootings, arson, and beatings, resulting in the deaths of fifteen whites and twenty-three Blacks, with an additional 537 people of both races injured. In Tulsa, Oklahoma, although it was not bruited at the time, hundreds of African Americans were murdered on May 31 and June 1, 1921, when white residents burned down homes, a library, a hospital, churches, hotels, and stores in the city's Black community.[31] Fitzgerald was in all likelihood aware of many of these horrific events but makes no mention of them as far as I know.

As for Fitzgerald's vaunted anti-Semitism, that's rather more complicated. Although Fitzgerald met and admired Irving Thalberg, who, at twenty-six, headed up production at MGM, he spent very little time among Jews before moving to Los Angeles.[32] No surprise, then, that Jewish characters in his early work do not come off well. In some stories derogatory terms for women and minorities had to be excised by the magazines that accepted them; for example, "Sheeny" was changed to "Jewess." But, as James L. W. West III points out, "the antisemitic slurs in these stories are spoken by reprehensible characters. . . . It's the characters who are antisemitic, not Fitzgerald."[33] That, however, can be a distinction without a difference.

It's hard to forget the "small flat-nosed" Meyer Wolfsheim in *The Great Gatsby* with his tiny eyes, molars for cuff links, and "two fine growths of hair" inhabiting his nostrils. Or "a fat Jewess, inlaid with diamonds" in "Echoes of the Jazz Age." Nonetheless, one has to allow a writer to speak as a man of his times speaks. Raymond Chandler also peppered his fiction with racial, ethnic, and anti-Semitic slurs but claimed "the right to call a character called Weinstein a thief without being accused of calling all Jews thieves."[34]

One has to wonder, in fact, if such obvious stereotyping constituted true animus. The caricatures of Jews propagated by the Dreyfus Affair around the turn of the twentieth century and by the German press in the 1930s were driven by pure hatred. Fitzgerald, however, was simply reiterating a familiar physiognomic code. He was provincial but not malicious and made similar attributions about various nationalities, including the Irish. "Jews lose clarity," he jotted in his *Notebook*. "They get to look like old melted candles, as if their bodies were preparing to waddle. Irish get slovenly and dirty. Anglo-Saxons get frayed and worn."[35] Still, we have to admit that his portrayal of Wolfsheim, if not triggered by anti-Semitism, certainly emboldens it.

Fitzgerald would have thrown up his hands at this. According to Frances Kroll, his private secretary for the last eighteen months of his life, he was stung by accusations of anti-Semitism and insisted that Wolfsheim "fulfilled a function in the story and had nothing to do with race or religion."[36] (Even the off-putting fact that Wolfsheim works out of "The Swastika Holding Company" might be irrelevant. Although the Nazi party adopted the swastika in 1920, the symbol meant nothing sinister at the time.) Wolfsheim's "function," however, is precisely what riles a reader like Ron Rosenbaum. By purposefully identifying Wolfsheim with Arnold Rothstein, the gambler who fixed the 1919 World Series, Fitzgerald makes him, in Rosenbaum's opinion, the Jew who "violated the innocence and despoiled the purity of an iconic American institution."[37]

But we already knew that going in, didn't we? There were plenty of Jewish gangsters around in the 1920s, as well as Jewish boxers. Murder, Inc. was run by Jews, and the young Meyer Lansky and Dutch Schultz were carving out territory in New York when *Gatsby* was percolating in France. In short, it was perfectly reasonable to make a mobster Jewish. The fact is, Fitzgerald just didn't think very much about Jews—that is, not until he found himself writing a novel about one, the very novel that would be typed up by Frances Kroll, herself a *maidel* from the Bronx.

In Kroll's charming, unself-conscious memoir, *Against the Current,* Fitzgerald comes off as a polite, sickly, appreciative, middle-aged man who seems genuinely interested in Kroll and her family.[38] He apparently pestered her about Jewish characteristics and customs and seemed fascinated by "the Passover feast" and the practice of keeping *kosher.* If Kroll's memoir is any indication, she and her family were the first Jewish people Fitzgerald had ever spent time with. At their first meeting, it should be noted, this self-styled man of the world immediately confided to Kroll that he was working on a new novel about the motion picture industry and wanted no word of it to leak out. Is this what you tell someone you haven't hired yet? "Do-do," Zelda had called him. "Do-do" is right.

In any event, Fitzgerald's curiosity about Jews also stemmed from self-interest. He was now at work on *The Last Tycoon,* whose hero, Monroe Stahr, is based on Thalberg, a man whose intelligence, sensitivity, and passionate commitment to the movies had very much impressed Fitzgerald. Stahr's Jewishness is alluded to but never disparaged. At one point, a director gazes consideringly at Stahr and muses, "He had worked with Jews too long to believe legends that they were small with money."[39]

Stahr is admirable in almost every respect, and only a determined political correctivist would be bothered by another character, "a middle-aged Jew who alternately talked with nervous excitement or else crouched as if ready to spring." It might be that Fitzgerald was now compensating for his distasteful portrayal of Wolfsheim, or maybe he didn't want to be labeled anti-Semitic in an industry populated by Jews, or maybe he was mindful of what was going on in Europe in 1939.

Anyway, accusations of anti-Semitism rankled in him. His *Notebooks* contain the following entry: "Hell, the best friend I have in Hollywood [Eddie Mayer] is a Jew—another of my best dozen friends is a Jew. Two of the half dozen men I admire most in America are Jews and two of my half dozen best men in History are Jews. But why do they have to be so damned conceited. That minority conceit—like fairies."[40] Had Fitzgerald more feet to shoot off, he'd probably run out of bullets.

It would be nice to report that he eventually rid himself of anti-Semitic feelings, but it wouldn't be true. Sheilah Graham, his mistress for the last three years of his life, reported that when he was drunk he might occasionally sing out her real name ("Lily Shiel") and chant, "She's a Jew." And he sometimes confided to Kroll that Graham was "part Jewish" as though he and Kroll were in cahoots. But surely the fact that he was spending the greater part of his days and nights with two Jewish women contributed to his portrait of Stahr. One likes to think that it made him feel warmer toward Jews in general—but who knows? People are complicated; they can harbor ethnic and racist feelings but also struggle against them. It was nothing more than a tic, but Fitzgerald apparently liked going to delicatessens and ordering knishes because he liked saying "knish."[41]

IN 1896, THE year of Fitzgerald's birth, a kiss was recorded on film for the first time. The forty-second-long scene, produced by Thomas Edison, was described in his catalogue as, "They get ready to kiss, begin to kiss, and kiss and kiss and kiss in a way that brings down the house every time." The film not only signified a change in mores (smooching in public was not customary); it also heralded a technological revolution that forever changed the way Americans viewed themselves.[42] Writers, scholars, legislators, and judges may have been busy rehashing the nation's raison d'être around 1900, but without a mass communication system delivering homiletic or patriotic messages honed by advertising and public relations firms—and without radio and film presenting a commonly held, if impressionistic, view of the nation—the idea of America largely depended on what part of America you hailed from.

In 1900, one could live one's entire life without running into someone from another state, especially from a state in a distant part of the country. People were Vermonters or Kentuckians before they were Americans, as the Civil War sadly attested. Even five decades after the war ended, how united was the United States? The railroad and telegraph notwithstanding, many citizens, even as late as 1915, still identified themselves regionally rather than nationally. They may have loved their country, but only because they loved that part of it in which they were raised.

The "indivisible" nation heralded in 1892 in our Pledge of Allegiance (originally "The Pledge to the Flag") was more a wishful sentiment than a commonly held view. As for "The Star-Spangled Banner," composed in 1814 by Fitzgerald's distant cousin, it was recognized by the US Navy in 1889 and by President Wilson in 1916, but it became the national anthem only when adopted by a congressional resolution in 1931—the year that Zelda noted, "Nobody knew the words to the Star-Spangled Banner."[43]

It's a tricky proposition, trying to determine when a people form a sense of themselves as a national entity, or to what extent this entity represents the beliefs and ideals of most people. The conception of "country" or "nation," however amorphous, always hinges on the recoverable past, on the myths and images available to a large part of the population. Americans at the turn of the twentieth century shared the Founding Fathers, the Declaration of Independence, the Constitution, the flag, the Alamo, the Gettysburg Address, Custer's Last Stand, and the War with Spain. But was this enough? The popular culture borrowed liberally from such well-known sources as the Bible and Shakespeare, but "Americana," coined in 1841, was still very much a work in progress. What we take for granted today—the stories, songs, and iconographic images that signify America—did not become widespread until the electronic media, aided by new marketing techniques, began to partially dissipate America's ingrained sectionalism.

Therefore, talk of a national culture around 1910 seems somewhat overblown given the sectarian and inchoate nature of the Union at the time. True, there were popular books and major newspapers, as well as illustrations and daguerreotypes, but such materials were local and didn't travel easily. Visiting America in 1831 and 1832, Alexis de Tocqueville noticed many differences between Americans and Europeans, but commented that our bookshelves—except for pamphlets and religious treatises—contained the same books found in England. Some ninety years later, when Fitzgerald began writing, he could have picked up James Fenimore Cooper's *Leatherstocking Tales,* Hawthorne's *House of the Seven Gables,* Emerson's "American Scholar," Whitman's *Leaves of Grass,* the *Education of Henry Adams,* novels by Twain and Henry James, and the poems of Longfellow. But these writers, with the exception of Twain and Longfellow, were read by the educated middle class, not by ordinary Americans, and the esteem in which they were held was nothing compared to the adulation reserved for Dickens, Thackeray, and Tennyson.

Henry James, who could detect innuendo in a circle, found the idea of Americanness to be exceedingly nuanced while also feeling that American writers suffered from "a paucity of materials." In his 1879 essay on Hawthorne, James listed our shortcomings: "No sovereign, no court, no personal loyalty, no aristocracy, no church, no clergy, no army, no diplomatic service, no country gentlemen, no palaces, no castles, nor manors, nor old country houses . . . no great universities, or public schools,—no Oxford, nor Eton, nor Harrow; no literature, no novels, no museums, no pictures, no political society, no sporting class . . . no Epsom nor Ascot!"[44]

Forty years later, Fitzgerald felt differently. Flying straight toward the emotional heart of complex issues, he decided not only that the nation's "materials" were plentiful but that they were also being done to death by American writers. This difference of opinion says more perhaps about two writers' respective temperaments than about their reading habits, but it also serves to remind us that separating ourselves politically from England was relatively easy compared to loosening England's *cultural* hold on us.

Without a strong national identity, how could we have a representative literature? Whatever our native genius, a distinctive literary identity had to wait until there were aspects of ordinary life that were distinctly American or at least recognizably different from comparable behaviors and practices in Europe. This is what Emerson hoped for in 1844 when he envisioned a poet who could take the measure of America: "a genius . . . with tyrannous eye, which knew the value of our incomparable materials . . . logrolling, our stumps and their politics, our fisheries, our Negroes, and Indians, our boasts, and our repudiations, the wrath of rogues, and the pusillanimity of honest men, the northern trade, the southern planting, the western clearing, Oregon, and Texas, are yet unsung. Yet America is a poem in our eyes; its ample geography dazzles the imagination, and it will not wait long for metres."[45]

In short, we were waiting for an American Dickens to come along, and though he never arrived (though Dickens himself twice set foot here), forceful writers did emerge, most notably Whitman, soon followed by Twain, London, William Dean Howells, Frank Norris, Theodore Dreiser, and Sinclair Lewis. Not only did we have to distance ourselves from Europe, we also needed Europe to acknowledge an indigenous American literature. But aside from the French symbolist poets' fascination with Poe, or England's gracious acceptance of Henry James, Europeans did not rush out to read American writers. That would come about only after Dos Passos, Hemingway, Faulkner, and Fitzgerald began publishing, all of whom, with the exception of Faulkner, spent a good deal of time abroad before fashioning the literature that would come to be seen as uniquely American.

The Facts of the Matter:
1920–1930

ONE FINE DAY IN the fall of 1920, elated by the publication of his first novel and his marriage to Zelda Sayre, F. Scott Fitzgerald, while riding in a New York taxi, suddenly began to bawl. He sobbed because he had everything he wanted and because he knew he would "never be so happy again."[1] He was twenty-four years old and *This Side of Paradise* was about to catapult him to the top of the literary pyramid. It was a celebrity unprecedented in American letters. England had Chatterton, who died at eighteen, and Byron, who awakened famous one morning when he was also twenty-four, but never in America had such a young writer burst so spectacularly on the scene. Harriet Beecher Stowe's *Uncle Tom's Cabin* sold well in 1852, but its author was forty-one. Stephen Crane was also twenty-four when *The Red Badge of Courage* was published in 1895, but his book, needless to say, did not become a rallying cry for disillusioned youth. Fitzgerald, however, was "not so much a novelist as a new generation speaking."[2]

He seemed to come out of the blue, trailing after him clouds of newsprint. It wasn't just that *This Side of Paradise* sold forty thousand copies in its first year (other novels sold equally well), it was, as such phenomena tend to be, a combination of subject, timing, looks, and personality. The age may not have demanded a book like *This Side of Paradise,* but once published it seemed so true a portrait that Matthew Bruccoli praised it as "an iconoclastic social document—even as a testament of revolt."[3]

Of course, by our standards it's rather tame. Its shocking secret? Girls just want to have fun. "None of the Victorian mothers—and most of the mothers were Victorian—had any idea how casually their daughters were accustomed to being kissed," the book's hero, Amory Blaine, thinks to himself. Not only did they kiss, they were "doing things that even in his memory would have been impossible: eating three-o'clock, after dance suppers in impossible cafes, talking of every side of life with an air half of earnestness, half of mockery, yet with a furtive excitement that Amory considered stood for a real moral let-down. But he never realized just how widespread it was until he saw the cities between New York and Chicago as one vast juvenile intrigue."[4]

But beneath the juvenile intrigue—the "depravity" of bobbed hair, cocktails at noon, and petting parties—lay a serious fault line. Civilization was ailing. The First World War had brought about a devastation so complete in Europe that everything leading up to it was ipso facto wrong. Society's conventions, its moral assumptions, its leaders were all flawed. For many young men and women, the world was now spoiled, ruined by the very people—parents, teachers, officials—who remained in authority. For the first time in our history—at least since the American Revolution—maturity was not sufficient to command respect. Age had become a disqualification so severe that anyone over forty was suspect.

Youth may have rebelled in England at the beginning of the nineteenth century and in France in 1820 and again in 1848, but these protests were prompted by repression and economic hardship. For Fitzgerald's generation, protest in America—labor strikes aside—did not take the form of barricades but in acts of cultural defiance. The values of the older generation had become suspect, and youth now possessed the authority of the disillusioned or, as Fitzgerald put it: "all Gods dead, all wars fought, all faiths in man shaken."[5]

As with most first novels, *This Side of Paradise* is largely autobiographical. Amory Blaine spends a portion of his teenage years in Minneapolis/St. Paul, attends prep school and Princeton, writes the book for a college musical, and has friends very much like John Peale Bishop and Father Fay. For Isabelle Borgé, read Ginevra King; for Rosalind Connage, Zelda Sayre. Very much a young man's novel, *This Side of Paradise* had a brashness that almost dares you to disapprove of its motley elements. What's more it awoke America to the news that college students not only could think but also constituted a segment of society with its own music, slang, style of dress, and ideas. Seemingly overnight a generation gap opened up in America. Fitzgerald hadn't just documented the culture of youth and disaffection; he had helped to create it, much as Salinger and Kerouac would do two generations later.[6]

It didn't matter that *This Side of Paradise* was a mess, a narrative pastiche of poems, letters, lists, and a three-act play. Indeed, more than a few critics thought the clutter added to the novel's vitality. William Rose Benét declared it "amazing in its excitement and gusto, amazing in phrase and epithet, amazing no less for all sorts of thoroughly bad writing pitched in with the good."[7] Other reviewers also felt that the book's energy and exuberance forgave any number of expository sins, including an undergraduate solemnity that must have grated even in 1920. Less understandable is how the usually clear-thinking Mencken convinced himself that the novel was "original in structure, extremely sophisticated in manner, and adorned with brilliancy."[8]

Fitzgerald's other great literary friend Edmund Wilson was less enthusiastic: "The story itself, furthermore, is very immaturely imagined: it is always just verging on the ludicrous. And, finally, *This Side of Paradise* is one of the most illiterate books of any merit ever published (a fault which the publisher's proofreader seems to have made no effort to remedy). Not only is it ornamented with bogus ideas and faked literary references, but it is full of English words misused with the most reckless abandon."[9] With friends like these . . . Only a spiteful stranger could inflict more hurt: "As a novel, it is rather tiresome; its values are less human than literary, and its characters, men and women alike, with hardly an exception, a set of exasperating *poseurs,* whose conversation, devoted largely to minute self-analysis, is artificial beyond belief," wrote the critic for the *London Times Literary Supplement.*[10]

It was an opinion shared by the American columnist and sportswriter Heywood Broun: "There is too much footwork and too much feinting for anything solid and substantial being accomplished."[11] Broun was an established figure on the New York literary scene, and Fitzgerald impulsively invited him to lunch. How well he succeeded in changing Broun's mind can be gleaned from another of Broun's columns. After reprinting an interview Fitzgerald had given to another reporter, Broun noted: "Having heard Mr. Fitzgerald, we are not entirely minded to abandon our notion that he is a rather complacent, somewhat pretentious and altogether self-conscious young man."[12] But even Broun would come to admire some of the stories in *Flappers and Philosophers,* and when he read *The Great Gatsby,* he unhesitatingly proclaimed that Fitzgerald was a writer who mattered.

As for *This Side of Paradise,* it is to anyone over the legal drinking age this side of untenable.[13] Fitzgerald's diverse narrative devices glance off a self-conscious prose that is both overbaked and underthought. In 2000 Thomas Flanagan put it more delicately: "Reading it today, one blanches at its emotional and rhetorical excesses. . . . It is the autobiographical first novel of a very young writer who took himself very seriously, and who had not provided for his hero those escape hatches of irony which Joyce had built into *A Portrait of the Artist.* But it was not, by any stretch, the work of a man who planned a career as a writer of commercial fiction."[14] The novel was, for all its faults, an attempt at seriousness.

Staunch admirers of Fitzgerald's fiction continue to support his debut not only because it is a first novel, but also because they don't see

Some Unfinished Chaos

the borrowings beneath its excited literary patina. Anthony Powell was not one to miss such things. Writing in the *Times Literary Supplement* in 1950, he notes Compton Mackenzie's *Sinister Street*'s influence on the young author. Amory Blaine, Powell writes, is "an American edition of the English dilettante, half-aristocrat, half-bohemian, lover, scholar, and man-of-the-world, nearing disintegration.... *This Side of Paradise* cannot be called a good book."[15] Whatever its merits or demerits, the novel was not entirely responsible for its own success. Had it been written by someone older, less attractive, and less personable, it might not have caused such a ruckus. It was Fitzgerald, or, more accurately, the combination of Scott and Zelda, which elevated the book to news-event status. Except for Mark Twain, it's hard to think of another author, up to that point, capable of selling books through sheer force of personality. The more copy that Scott and Zelda generated with their antics, the faster his books sold.

NOT LONG AFTER the publication of the novel, Scott and Zelda rented a house in Westport, Connecticut, where he began working on *The Beautiful and Damned*. Six months later they moved into an apartment on West Fifty-Ninth Street in Manhattan. They threw parties and attended parties. People wanted to meet the handsome young writer with the Barrymore-esque profile and his smart, attractive, southern wife with her sly sense of humor. They made a nice-looking couple, and they knew it. They were, in fact, the first literary show-business couple in America. Zelda's yearning for sophistication and glamour rivaled Fitzgerald's own: "If ever there was a pair whose fantasies matched, it was Zelda Sayre and Scott Fitzgerald," Wilson remarked.[16] Lillian Gish recalled being in a restaurant with them, thinking, "They were both so beautiful, so blond, so clean and so clear—and drinking strait [*sic*] whiskey out of tall tumblers."[17]

The pair delighted in and cultivated celebrity. They rode down Fifth Avenue on tops of taxis, jumped into the fountain at Union Square and the Pulitzer fountain in front of the Plaza, and tried to undress during a showing of *The Scandals*. Ruth Prigozy makes the nice point that the very carelessness of their existence, the exuberance with which they seemed to greet the day, contributed to their appeal.[18] They were a more madcap pair than Nick and Nora Charles (whom Dashiell Hammett invented a decade later), and their air of conspiratorial self-mockery made them even more endearing. Giddy and boisterous, they were also media savvy, pouncing on every picture of, and article about, themselves. Painful though it is to contemplate, the young Scott and Zelda would probably have entertained doing a reality TV show. Even toward the end of his life when his books were ignored, Fitzgerald continued pasting the occasional clipping into a scrapbook, though he had the grace to put them under the heading "The Melody Lingers On."

Between 1920 and 1924 there were many clippings, not only because he churned out a large number of short stories but also because he was seen as an expert on whatever was new and fashionable. Reporters and editors requested his opinion on sex, courtship, marriage, parenting, manners, morals, and the longings of teenage girls. He sat for interviews and answered written queries and was paid good money to do so. He even appeared as a judge of a beauty contest in 1926 along with Cornelius Vanderbilt Jr. and John Barrymore—not something one can imagine Hemingway or Faulkner doing.[19]

Sometimes he was serious, sometimes not: "I'm very much interested in the state of the nation," he told one reporter. "Personally—I think it's entirely too big ever to be managed properly. I think it ought to be cut up in six independent political sections."[20] Years later, when things were tough, his sense of humor survived: "When I reached the port of embarkation," he quipped in a 1937 letter, "the Germans decided they'd better quit. That's the true story of the armistice. Have ever since suffered from non-combatant shell-shock in the form of ferocious nightmares. . . . My favorite American authors are Dreiser, Hemingway and the early Gertrude Stein. I am an admirer of Mencken and Spencer Tracy, but not of Benny Goodman or Father Coughlin. I would like to be a G-Man but I'm afraid it is too late."[21]

A mercurial nature is going to register changes in the air's vibrations even when alone. Imagine, then, Fitzgerald's reaction when he becomes a celebrity, when everything he says is dutifully recorded by eager journalists. A pedagogue manqué from adolescence, he has no qualms about telling people how the world works. (At Princeton, he informed one of his teachers, a Pulitzer Prize–winning playwright, how his play could have been improved.[22]) And as the self-appointed chronicler of his generation, he veers between sage and hedonist. "Don't you know I am one of the most notorious drinkers of the younger generation?" he announced to reporters.[23]

He also liked to tell journalists that he was a literary prodigy—a habit that his friend Ring Lardner remarked on: "Mr. Fitzgerald sprang into fame with his novel *This Side of Paradise* when only three years old and wrote the entire book with only one hand."[24] With his other hand, Fitzgerald wrote articles and stories that, it might be said, took some of the sheen off his genius. But then he had no choice. He *had* to write and keep writing since he spent money like a lord, and Zelda was no better. "Scott was extravagant, but not like her," Maxwell Perkins said; "money went through her fingers like water; she wanted everything; she kept him writing for the magazines."[25]

Magazine writing, however, was not what *he* wanted, but since he and Zelda were spending more than thirty-six thousand dollars a year (about $636,000 in today's dollars), he could not turn down offers from the *Saturday Evening Post* and *Collier's,* which often paid him between two and four thousand dollars per story. (His agent Harold Ober later called him a virtual employee of the *Post.*) Debts are what accounted for what he termed in "The Lees of Happiness" as "passably amusing stories, a bit out of date now, but doubtless the sort that would have whiled away a dreary half hour in a dental office."[26]

Then again, he would also go on to write a number of very fine stories—"The Ice Palace," "Winter Dreams," "Absolution," "The Rich Boy," "Babylon Revisited," "Crazy Sunday"—the best of which rival the work of all but a few American writers. In all, depending on how one chooses to regard some of the autobiographical pieces, he eventually produced around 180 stories; so many, in fact, that he claimed they sapped him of the creative juices necessary to compose novels.[27] This bitterness, Bruccoli contends, "was generated by the effort—not the ease—of writing fiction for the mass-circulation magazines."[28] Fitzgerald seems to uphold this view: "I have asked a lot of my emotions—one hundred and twenty stories," he wrote in a *Notebook*. "The price was high, right up with Kipling, because there was one little drop of something not blood, not a tear, not my seed, but me more intimately than these, in every story, it was the extra I had. Now it has gone and I am just like you now."[29]

Even if we accept this, it still sounds as if he's playing to an audience. Did he really spend so much time working on tales best read in a dentist's waiting room? Did they really use up his "literary capital"? He certainly felt bad about having written so many and in 1925 told John Peale Bishop, "I now get $2000 a story and they grow worse and worse and my ambition is to get where I need write no more but only novels."[30] That said, no anthology of great American stories would be complete without at least one or two of Fitzgerald's stories.

A week shy of his twenty-fourth birthday, Fitzgerald had the gall to complain that his life so far had consisted of "the struggle between an overwhelming urge to write and a combination of circumstances bent on keeping me from it."[31] This would became an anthem: cruel fate conspiring against him, time and troubles robbing him of his powers—his talent "lost, spent, gone, dissipated, unrecapturable"—as though he had nothing to do with it.[32] The truth is, most writers—Anthony Trollope and Aleksandr Solzhenitsyn aside—are notorious for slacking off. Few, however, ever leapt so readily from their desks as did Fitzgerald. The man liked being lionized, and he liked to have a good time: "A month of 1000 parties and no work" is how he described June 1925.[33] People who knew him in the early 1920s recalled his infectious enthusiasm, his love of playacting, his drinking, his liking of games and practical jokes. In short, he created the very circumstances that prevented him from writing the kind of fiction he wanted to write; and because he and Zelda lived beyond their means, he basically remained in debt his entire life.[34]

IN MAY 1921, Scott and Zelda sailed to Europe. In London he had dinner with John Galsworthy. They visited France and Italy and returned to America in July. In August they moved to St. Paul, where on October 26, 1921, Frances Scott "Scottie" Fitzgerald was born. Giddily, the new father wired Zelda's parents: "LILLIAN GISH IS IN MOURNING CONSTANCE TALMADGE IS A BACK NUMBER A SECOND MARY PICKFORD HAS ARRIVED."[35]

In March 1922, *The Beautiful and Damned* was published to much fanfare. But from its charmless and rather stupid epigraph, "The victor belongs to the spoils," to its clichéd handling of a disintegrating marriage, the book's weltschmerz never adds up to gravitas. As Fitzgerald ploddingly traces the lives of Anthony and Gloria Patch and their friends, one might be forgiven for recalling the old joke about existential posturing: "You know, like Kierkegaard but without the humor." Gilbert Seldes, for one, took exception to the novel's "pretensions as a work of art" and to the author's "overburden of sentiment and his really alarming seriousness."[36]

The one grace note was Zelda's mock review in the *New York Tribune,* which urged readers to purchase the book so that she could afford a new dress and the diamond ring she had her eye on. She also recognized in the book "a portion of an old diary . . . and also scraps of letters which, though considerably edited, sound to me vaguely familiar. In fact, Mr. Fitzgerald—I believe that is how he spells his name—seems to believe that plagiarism begins at home."[37]

The Fitzgeralds returned East in the fall of 1922 and rented a house in Great Neck, Long Island, not far from Ring Lardner's home. The two men, who shared a passion for books and gin, became great friends and spent uproarious evenings drinking and talking. One night they danced on the lawn of the Doubleday estate to impress the visiting

Joseph Conrad. The Fitzgeralds liked Great Neck. There were dinners and cocktail parties with Groucho Marx, Lillian Russell, George M. Cohan, and Florenz Ziegfeld. Being around theater people gave Fitzgerald the idea to write a play, a political satire. He called it *The Vegetable* and thought it would make him rich, especially after Wilson pronounced it a great American comedy. It wasn't. The play tried out in Atlantic City in November 1923, and bombed.

Disappointed but undeterred, Fitzgerald continued spending lavishly and writing stories to cover his expenses. In one six-month period between November and April he produced eleven short stories. But it wasn't enough. He was in debt to Scribner's for more than five thousand dollars, and he began thinking about writing for the movies. A few years earlier, Ober had sold the screen rights to one of his stories to Metro Pictures and later did the same for *The Beautiful and Damned*. Ober's success gave Fitzgerald the idea that if all else failed, Hollywood would come to the rescue.

In the spring of 1924, the couple decided that living in Great Neck was both too hectic and too expensive. In April, with Scottie in tow, they set sail for France. For the next two and a half years they lived abroad, shuttling between Paris and the Riviera, with stops in Rome and Capri. Their first summer in the South of France, they met Gerald and Sara Murphy and became part of their eclectic social circle, which included Cole Porter, Archibald MacLeish, the playwright Philip Barry, and various painters, designers, and dancers. The Murphys organized picnics and dinner parties and carried them off with tact and precision. Unfortunately, Fitzgerald sometimes thought the parties too tame and livened things up by smashing wineglasses and throwing food at the guests. After one such incident, Gerald Murphy informed him that he would not be welcome for the next three weeks. Murphy made good on his threat, so at the next dinner party Fitzgerald tossed a can of garbage onto the Murphys' patio.

It was around this time that Zelda may have had a brief affair with a French aviator. His name, according to Arthur Mizener, was Réné Silvé, though in subsequent biographies he's identified as Edouard Jozan. All of Fitzgerald's biographers—Mizener, Bruccoli, Meyers, et al.—take for granted that Zelda and Jozan slept together at least once. Updike follows their lead,[38] as did just about anyone looking into Fitzgerald's life until 2003, when Zelda's biographer, Sally Cline, determined that no substantive evidence of a physical affair existed.[39] Zelda, after all, flirted as a matter of course. She liked Townsend Martin, John Peale Bishop, and George Nathan but didn't sleep with them, whereas Scott, according to Cline, probably had an affair as early as 1920 with a woman by the name of Eugenia Bankhead.[40]

Whatever happened between Zelda and Jozan only highlighted the problems in the Fitzgeralds' marriage. For Scott, Zelda's actions were a form of betrayal regardless of sexual intimacy.[41] For all his bravado, Fitzgerald was puritanical about sex and thought physical intimacy had moral ramifications. If Zelda had been unfaithful, then love itself could not be pure. "That September 1924 I knew something had happened that could never be repaired," he wrote in his *Ledger*.[42] Something *had* happened, but he never (to my knowledge) wrote at length about having been cuckolded. It was Zelda who, in her own novel, *Save Me the Waltz,* would write about the affair.

IN THE FALL of 1925, Scott and Zelda traveled to Rome, where they hung around the set of *Ben-Hur,* further stoking Fitzgerald's interest in the movies. Two unpleasant incidents marred the visit: one night they were ordered from their table in a hotel to make room for a Russian aristocrat; on another night, Fitzgerald, probably drunk, got into a fistfight with a group of taxi drivers because one of them demanded an extortionate fare. During the scuffle Fitzgerald managed to punch a plainclothes policeman who had waded into the melee. He was hauled off to jail, where, bruised and humiliated, he waited until Zelda and a friend arrived to bail him out. (A similar scene occurs in *Tender Is the Night.*) Zelda did not behave much better. At an inn in St. Paul de Vence, she wordlessly threw herself down a flight of stairs because Scott and Isadora Duncan were flirting. On another occasion she attempted to drive their car off the road.[43]

While in Capri during the spring of 1925, Fitzgerald met Compton Mackenzie, who introduced him to other British writers visiting the island: F. Benson, Norman Douglas, and Somerset Maugham, thus prompting Fitzgerald's note to Perkins: "this place is full of fairies."[44] Zelda, however, liked the company. "Zelda painting, me drinking," Fitzgerald noted.[45] In a letter sent to Bishop from Rome that winter, he wrote: "The cheerfulest things in my life are first Zelda and second the hope that my book has something extraordinary about it. I want to be extravagantly admired again. Zelda and I sometimes indulge in terrible four day rows that always start with a drinking party but we're still enormously in love and about the only truly happily married people I know."[46] There is something sadly characteristic about these sentences: the admission of fighting and drinking, the hopefulness he has in their love, the unabashed desire to be admired—and no mention at all of Scottie.

The book to which he was referring was called "Trimalchio," or "The High-Bouncing Lover," or "Among the Ashheaps and Million-aires," or sometimes "Gold-Hatted Gatsby." In April, while Scott and Zelda were still in Italy, *The Great Gatsby* was published. Anxious about the book's reception since he no longer considered his age to be a mitigating factor should it be coolly received (he was now twenty-eight), Fitzgerald remained in Europe. But except for one or two unfavorable notices, including the absurd headline in the *New York World*, "F. Scott Fitzgerald's Latest a Dud," *Gatsby* was respectfully, if not enthusiastically, received.

The British were the least effusive. The short-story writer L. P. Hartley declared that "Mr. F. Scott Fitzgerald deserves a good shaking. . . . *The Great Gatsby* is an absurd story, whether considered as romance, melodrama, or plain record of New York high life."[47] William Collins, Fitzgerald's English publisher, refused to print it since it was likely to "reduce the number of [Fitzgerald's] readers rather than to increase them."[48] In a farcically odd way, it was an understandable reaction. *Gatsby* was so perfectly executed that even its admirers couldn't quite take it in. Nothing had really prepared them for it. Despite his great debut, Fitzgerald was mainly regarded as a magazine writer whose second novel was only passable. So the majority of reviewers, while liking the novel, never suspected that a classic had landed on their desks.

More gratifying to the author were the congratulatory letters he received from Van Wyck Brooks, Willa Cather, and T. S. Eliot, who hailed *Gatsby* as "the first step American fiction has taken since Henry James."[49] Edith Wharton also wrote Fitzgerald a flattering letter and followed up with an invitation to tea at her house in Saint-Brice-sous-Forêt, about forty miles from Paris. The Fitzgeralds had moved to Paris in April, and Scott naturally wished to go. Zelda, however, declined, fearing that the elegant Wharton would condescend to her.

On the appointed day, Fitzgerald and the composer Ted Chanler arrived a little tipsy at Wharton's home. After being shown into the sitting room where Wharton and her guests waited, Fitzgerald launched into a cockamamie story about how he and Zelda had once lived in a Parisienne bordello for two weeks. Intending to shock or amuse Wharton, he succeeded only in arousing her curiosity. What, she wondered, went on in the bordello—to which Fitzgerald could give no satisfactory reply. After returning to Paris, he moaned to Zelda, "They beat me. They beat me! They *beat* me!"[50]

This story, as I've summarized it, appears in Mizener's biography of Fitzgerald and R. W. B. Lewis's biography of Edith Wharton, though certain details vary. Mizener includes an endnote acknowledging that the incident is hearsay, though he also says that as far as he was "able to check it, it appears quite accurate."[51] But when Jeffrey Meyers retells the story, *his* endnote simply mentions the relevant page in Mizener's book without mentioning Mizener's own qualification.[52] Although Meyers refers to Lewis's book, he doesn't substantially deviate from Mizener's version. As for Lewis's biography of Wharton, the incident with Fitzgerald is fleshed out but not substantiated. According to Lewis,

Fitzgerald told some "rather rough stories," which caused Wharton to remark dryly, "lacks data."[53]

As for Wharton, she simply noted in her diary: "To tea, Teddy Chanler and Scott Fitzgerald, the novelist—awful."[54] And that is all she wrote. Although hardly a career-altering moment for either writer, the anecdote calls attention to how unconfirmed stories become wrapped in the mantle of fact. Indeed, without Bruccoli's detailed and nuanced biography, which addresses the ambiguities involved in the incident, Mizener's and Meyer's versions would stand as fact.

IN PARIS IN May 1925, Fitzgerald met Hemingway in the Dingo Bar. He'd already read some of Hemingway's stories and had touted him to Perkins. So when he found himself beside the husky, broad-shouldered writer with his dark, bristling mustache and fierce commitment to art, he became his usual worshipful self.[55] The two quickly formed a friendship, drinking and discussing their respective projects, even taking a trip together to Lyons. Fitzgerald missed the train going down but managed to drive back with Hemingway on their return.

The Fitzgeralds stayed in Europe for another nineteen months. In 1926, the year he should have capitalized on the critical success of *Gatsby,* he wrote two undistinguished stories and worked sporadically on another novel. His income was still around twenty-five thousand dollars from his share of a play based on *Gatsby* and the sale of the movie rights. Money wasn't the problem; liquor was. Everyone drank too much, though not everyone raided a small restaurant in Cannes, stole the silverware, kidnapped the proprietor and waiters, and held them hostage near a cliff. His partner in crime, the playwright Charles MacArthur, later helped Fitzgerald lure some orchestra musicians to a house, lock them in a room with a bottle of whiskey, and demand that they play their favorite songs.

In June 1926 at a party given by the Murphys for Hemingway, Fitzgerald threw ashtrays at other tables and goaded Murphy until the host left his own party. At another soirée he pushed a fig down the back of a princess's dress.[56] In his *Ledger* Fitzgerald described 1925–26 as "Futile, shameful useless but the $30,000 rewards of 1924 work. Self-disgust. Health gone."[57] There were also fights with Zelda, more arguments with the Murphys, and a cooling of relations with Hemingway. Fitzgerald's self-disgust was evident in a letter to Perkins. Whether he was plastered or sober seems almost irrelevant: "If you see anyone I know tell 'em I hate 'em all, him especially. Never want to see 'em again. Why shouldn't I go crazy? My father is a moron and my mother is a neurotic half insane with pathological nervous worry. Between them they haven't and never have had the brains of Calvin Coolidge. If I knew anything I'd be the best writer in America."[58]

To make matters worse, Zelda could not conceive again. Although a botched 1924 operation in Rome had probably damaged her ovaries, Zelda decided that her failure to become pregnant was a function of Scott's sexual inadequacy.[59] She even accused Scott of being sexually attracted to Hemingway. This, along with Hemingway's unverifiable anecdote in *A Moveable Feast* concerning Fitzgerald's anxiety about the size of his penis, did much to put into question Fitzgerald's virility. According to Sally Cline, "Scott had always exhibited a rigid Midwestern Puritanism in the face of Zelda's Southern sexual openness. Wit and charm, but not virility, were his strong suits."[60] Cline based her remarks on an article, "My Friend Scott Fitzgerald," by Elizabeth Beckwith MacKie, who found Scott not to be "a very lively male animal."[61] The probability that Scott didn't find MacKie attractive, or that he was full of pills and booze, doesn't seem to matter.

Although hardly a rake, Scott probably began seeing other women before Zelda's breakdown. Interestingly, none of his or Zelda's biographers hold his feet to the fire about this.[62] Bruccoli, in fact, suggests that he was driven to see other women to counteract Zelda's charges of homosexuality.[63] Whatever the case, Scott kept from Zelda his affairs, his drinking, and his health problems. Both, however, felt the marriage was foundering.

THE FITZGERALDS RETURNED to America in December 1926 intending to lead a more orderly life. "We were back in America—further apart than ever before," Zelda later wrote.[64] Scottie was now five, and her parents felt she needed stability. As for Scott, he needed to earn more money. But first they visited Fitzgerald's parents in Washington, DC, and the Sayres in Montgomery. In Montgomery they learned that First National Pictures (later Warner Bros.) wanted Fitzgerald to write a treatment for the actress Constance Talmadge about a magic lipstick that made any woman desirable. He would receive $3,500 and another $12,000 if the screenplay was accepted. Fitzgerald didn't hesitate. He'd been submitting treatments to Hollywood since 1922 and had even told Perkins that if fiction could not support him, he would "come home, go to Hollywood and learn the movie business."[65]

As early as 1923 in "Dice, Brassknuckles & Guitar," he wrote:

> if this were a moving picture (as, of course, I hope it will some day be) I would take as many thousand feet of her as I was allowed—then I would move the camera up close and show the yellow down on the back of her neck where her hair stopped and the warm color of her cheeks and arms. . . . Then I would hire a man named Israel Glucose to write some idiotic line of transition, and switch thereby to another scene that was taking place at no particular spot far down the road.[66]

Ronald Berman speculated that Fitzgerald's knowledge of moviemaking is what enables Nick Carraway to be "as coldly objective as the eye of the camera."[67] Berman takes his cue from Frederick Karl's *Modern and Modernism,* which insists that "early film techniques—montage, rapid cutting, freezing, speeding up and slowing down, the long shot, the close-up, even flashback and crosscutting—were developing parallel to comparable techniques in the major art forms."[68] Berman identifies Ford Madox Ford, James Joyce, and Pound as writers particularly influenced by the movies, and maintains that Fitzgerald belongs in their company.

I would argue, however, that close-ups, long shots, dissolves, and flashbacks existed figuratively almost as long as the novel has and that Fitzgerald did not seriously think about camera angles while working on *Gatsby*. He may have *visualized* scenes and thought about continuity and momentum, but that's not the same as applying cinematic technique to prose. Indeed, I doubt that he bothered much about the similarities between film and fiction. Even after he went to Hollywood for the third time in 1937 and began studying scripts in earnest, he didn't resort to film terminology when it came to novel-writing.[69] Serious novelists don't think like screenwriters, and Fitzgerald was in his own mind first and foremost a novelist.

Screenwriting, however, paid well, and in January 1927 the Fitzgeralds traveled to Los Angeles, where they were much fussed over. At a luncheon given for them by Douglas Fairbanks and Mary Pickford, Fitzgerald met the seventeen-year-old silent-screen actress Lois Moran. They struck up a friendship, and Moran even arranged a screen test for him, though nothing came of it. Moran (with whom Fitzgerald might or might not have dallied) became the model for Rosemary Hoyt in *Tender Is the Night*.[70]

Zelda, naturally, was stung by Scott's interest in the younger woman but understood her appeal for him. Scott, as he freely acknowledged, wanted "to be liked, to be reassured not that he was a man of a little genius, but that [he] was a great man of the world."[71] In any event, Scott and Zelda cut a wide swath through Hollywood. At a party hosted by Lois Moran's mother, they collected all the purses, boiled them in tomato sauce, and served the concoction as soup. On another occasion, they showed up uninvited at a party for Sam Goldwyn and barked like dogs until they were let in.

Such antics aside, Fitzgerald completed his "magic lipstick" treatment, which was summarily dismissed. After being paid, he and Zelda stacked all the furniture in the middle of their hotel room and crowned the pile with unpaid bills.[72] Then they skedaddled. Back East, they rented an enormous twenty-seven-room house near Wilmington,

Delaware, called Ellerslie, where Scott planned to work and where Zelda took to practicing ballet before a huge mirror that Fitzgerald thought belonged in a brothel. They lived at Ellerslie for a year and threw lavish parties that, according to Meyers, were dreaded by their guests for their strident attempt at gaiety and the conspicuous absence of food. James Thurber, after visiting the huge house, remarked, "There were four or five Zeldas and at least eight Scotts so that their living room was forever tense with the presence of a dozen desperate personalities, even when they were alone in it."[73]

By the middle of May 1928, they were back in Paris, where Zelda enrolled at the Diaghilev Ballet School. Too old to launch a balletic career, she hoped to land a small role somewhere. Fitzgerald, put out by her zeal, thought there was something neurotic about her wanting to dance professionally. In September, they returned to Ellerslie, bringing with them a former boxer and taxi driver named Philippe, who acted as manservant, chauffeur, sparring partner, and drinking buddy. Fitzgerald now fancied himself a pugilist, further irking Hemingway, who scoffed there was "no distinction in punching Scott on the nose. Every taxi driver in Paris has done it."[74]

Zelda, though, probably wanted to take a poke at him. As in Capri, there were terrible fights. He accused her of being jealous of his fame; she retorted that he was an inadequate lover with a crush on Hemingway. She had never liked the outdoorsy writer, whom she described as a "professional he-man" and a "pansy with hair on his chest."[75] Fitzgerald may have admired the bigger man's physique, but there is no evidence to suggest latent homosexual feelings. Like many men of his day, Fitzgerald referred to homosexual men as "fairies," and on one occasion had to retract the term and apologize. "I'm sorry that I used the word fairy and that you found it offensive," he wrote to a friend of Zelda's who had visited them at La Paix. "It is a lousy word to anyone who is not a member of the species. I offer you my sincere apologies and put it down to the fact that I was half asleep when you came and subsequently a little tight."[76]

As for Hemingway, he felt that Fitzgerald was running his talent into the ground. He had liked him at first and was grateful for his support, but eventually he found both Fitzgeralds impossible. Zelda, he thought unstable and deliberately trying to sabotage Scott's writing. He even believed she encouraged Fitzgerald's drinking in order to keep him from working. Zelda, in turn, blamed Hemingway for the same offense. The two men continued to share a certain camaraderie, joking and exchanging warm and sometimes silly letters, but the relationship began to sour.

Perhaps it was inevitable. They had little in common except a qualified respect for each other's work. Fitzgerald spent money freely, staying at the best hotels and renting large apartments in swanky neighborhoods, whereas Hemingway, who wasn't nearly as poor as he liked to make out, lived in *pensions* and small apartments. An English nanny looked after Scottie; a French peasant woman minded Hemingway's son. Soon enough, Hemingway grew tired of Fitzgerald's insecurities and inability to hold his liquor. He disliked Scott for talking too much, for mistreating servants and taxi drivers, and for his willingness to write for the slick magazines. He later characterized Fitzgerald as a man whose idea of heaven was "A beautiful vacuum filled with wealthy monogamists, all powerful and members of the best families all drinking themselves to death."[77]

Not that Hemingway was above reproach. He could be callous, even cruel, and though physically courageous (he'd been hit by shrapnel while serving as a Red Cross volunteer in Italy), he also loved to pose as a boxer, although as soon as he fought anyone more skilled than Ezra Pound, he got flattened. It was because of his self-styled mastery of boxing that his relationship with Fitzgerald became even more strained.

By the spring of 1929 the friendship had deteriorated to such a point that Hemingway, upon learning that the Fitzgeralds were returning to Paris, instructed Perkins not to give Scott his address.[78] Fitzgerald knew he was being snubbed—he said so in his *Notebooks*—but chased after Hemingway regardless.[79] Such, anyway, is the impression given by Morley Callaghan, a Canadian writer who had known Hemingway when both men had worked for the *Toronto Star*. When Callaghan and his wife arrived in Paris in the summer of 1929, he introduced himself to Fitzgerald and renewed his friendship with Hemingway. Since Callaghan was an amateur boxer, he and Hemingway began sparring together. Callaghan, though shorter and somewhat pudgy, had a good deal of experience and easily handled the slower, clumsier Hemingway.

Fitzgerald, of course, was desperate to join in these sparring sessions and begged to attend. He was made timekeeper; his job was to shout out when a three-minute round was over and to allow one minute for the men to rest. The first round went by without a hitch. During the second round, Callaghan opened a cut on Hemingway's lip. Hemingway, seeing the blood on his glove, sprang forward and threw one of his typical roundhouse punches. Callaghan stepped inside and caught Hemingway with a punch of his own, and Hemingway went down. He lay on his back a moment and started to get up when Fitzgerald cried, "Oh, my God. I let the round go four minutes." Hemingway said nothing for a few seconds and then: "All right, Scott. If you want to see me getting the shit knocked out of me, just say so. Only don't say you made a mistake."[80]

Hemingway's accusation stung. "[Scott's] eyes looked sick," Callaghan recalled in his likable memoir, *That Summer in Paris*.[81] Although written some thirty-four years after the disputed incident, the memoir is quite specific that Fitzgerald had not purposely let the round go on too long; he had simply been surprised by Callaghan's dominance and couldn't take his eyes off the ring. Hemingway, who lied with impunity, remembered it differently. In a letter to Perkins a few months after the fight, he emphasized the amount of alcohol he'd consumed that afternoon. The rounds, he went on to say, were two minutes long, and other than getting his lip cut and his face "mushed up," he'd performed adequately except for a slip in the later rounds.[82] By 1951 he was identifying the first round as the long round, which he said lasted for "thirteen minutes"—a preposterous claim. In addition, he had given Callaghan all he could handle and was "pretty sure [he] could have knocked him out. . . . But [he] did not want to knock him out."[83]

After 1930, Fitzgerald and Hemingway drifted apart and saw each other only sporadically. They attended a Princeton football game in October 1931 and had an awkward dinner with Edmund Wilson in New York in January 1933. By then they were communicating mainly through Perkins. As Fitzgerald's stock fell, Hemingway's rose, and by the mid-1930s their respective positions in the literary world had been reversed. Both men naturally thought they deserved their fates. But while Fitzgerald rarely spoke ill of his friend, Hemingway was often contemptuous. In *A Moveable Feast,* he's both laudatory and dismissive: "The mouth worried you until you knew him and then it worried you more."[84]

THE SUMMER OF 1929 wasn't pleasant for either Scott or Zelda. His work wasn't going well, and her ballet lessons were taxing; she seemed to dance with an intensity inversely proportional to her talent. To escape Paris, they traveled to the Riviera and, in the winter of 1930, to North Africa. By now they were an old married couple who knew how to apply the scalpel at the precise point where the nerve was exposed. Robert Penn Warren, who saw them in Paris that year, remembered one "frightful hissing quarrel, well laced with obscenities, which went on between them."[85] They still engaged in public displays, but now the hilarity and the high jinks seemed less the release of youthful energy than a desperate attempt to stave off boredom. In Cannes, Zelda nearly drove off a cliff. On another occasion, she lay down on the road and ordered Scott to drive over her, and he might have had not someone prevented him.[86]

Stress, frustration, and anxiety colored their daily existence. According to Jeffrey Meyers, Zelda was now suffering from asthma, severe flare-ups of eczema, fainting spells, and auditory hallucinations.[87] She formed the notion that she was in love with her ballet teacher, Lubov Egorova, and the prospect disturbed her. She could still be jaunty and amusing, but increasingly there were long moments of an eerie self-absorption. She continued to see her friends but often went missing in full view. In April 1930 she checked herself into the Malmaison Clinic outside Paris. Two weeks later, however, she discharged herself. In May, she needed to be hospitalized again and entered a clinic in Gilion, Switzerland. From there she was transferred to Les Rives de Prangins in Nyon. Fitzgerald moved to Switzerland to be near her.

At Prangins, where she remained between June 1930 and August 1931, Zelda was diagnosed with schizophrenia and later manic depression. Her self-professed lesbianism continued to frighten her, and she was often delusional. Although there were periods of remission, she slipped in and out of a despair that made Scott's seem mild by comparison. In retrospect, it's apparent that her disorderly behavior was evidence of mental instability rather than weakness of character. Her feverish dancing was probably a symptom, but her desire to write was not. She could also draw, paint, and design furniture; and her letters, occasionally full of neediness and sorrow, are also full of intelligence, wit, and fine observations.

In one exchange, the year after her breakdown, they assessed what had happened to their marriage. Whether it was the influence of psychoanalysis, then coming into vogue, or the fact that they simply could not hold back, their letters have a harsh and vulnerable honesty that makes you want to weep for them.

SCOTT: I know this then—that those day [*sic*] when we came up from the south, from Capri, were among my happiest—but you were sick and the happiness was not in the home. By the time we reached the beautiful Riviera I had developed such an inferiority complex that I couldn't face anyone unless I was tight. . . . [Y]ou were going crazy and calling it genius—I was going to ruin and calling it anything that came to hand. . . . Toward the end nothing much mattered. The nearest I came to leaving you was when you called me a fairy in the Rue Palatine. . . . We ruined ourselves—I have never honestly thought that we ruined each other. . . .

Some Unfinished Chaos

ZELDA: We lived in the Rue Vauginard. You were constantly drunk. You didn't work and were dragged home at night by taxi-drivers when you came home at all. You said it was my fault for dancing all day. You made no advances toward me and complained that I was un-responsive. You were literally eternally drunk the whole summer. You left me more and more alone, and though you complained that it was the apartment or the servants or me, you knew the real reason you couldn't work was because you were out half the night and you were sick and you drank constantly.[88]

Marriage is more complicated than the public or even private remonstrances of husbands and wives. Nonetheless, people naturally take sides. Who suffers the most? Who's the wronged party? Among writers, only the marriage of Ted Hughes and Sylvia Plath has met with as much scrutiny. Lately a new rash of books, including two novels and a graphic novel, remind us that Zelda deserves more consideration than was granted during her lifetime.[89] Rightly so. Only her instability, over which she had no control, prevented her from becoming a productive artist and writer. And it's chastening and sad to think what might have been, had the proper drugs and therapy been available to her ninety years ago.

Second Impressions

JOHN PEALE BISHOP, WHO met Fitzgerald at Princeton, once complained that "he took seventeen as his norm, making everything later a falling off." According to Bishop, Fitzgerald had replied, "If you make it fifteen, I'll agree with you."[1] This obsession with youth is usually viewed as another one of Scott's shortcomings, but as Kirk Curnutt observed, Fitzgerald's attitude about aging reflected "a broader fetishization of youth that proved endemic to twentieth-century popular culture."[2] Before then, the years between twelve and twenty had not been accorded much significance. The Bard may have lamented that "Youth's a stuff will not endure," but no one really thought that "sweet and twenty" had much to offer society at large.

As Curnutt sees it, the concept of adolescence didn't even exist outside the upper class until the 1890s.[3] One moved from childhood to adulthood without benefit of an intermediary phase: girls married in their teens, and boys no older than ten or twelve were put to work in mines and factories. But with the advent of compulsory public schooling, new child-labor laws, and the emergence of the YMCA and the Boy Scouts around 1900, attitudes about the postchildhood years began to change.

This is what Fitzgerald picked up on: the idea that eighteen-year-olds could be viewed and valued as a distinct social entity. No longer malleable children and not yet inflexible adults, they could be smarter than grown-ups because they were old enough to understand the world while innocent enough to question its rules and conventions. *This Side of Paradise* also meant this side of thirty. "Time was when age meant dignity, authority, and power, while youth meant helpless slavery. Age stands as the rear-guard of an advancing society," the writer Charlotte Perkins Gilman observed in 1922, a statement she probably would not have made ten years earlier.[4] Fitzgerald had awakened readers to the fact that the generation coming of age between 1918 and 1922 wasn't content simply to parrot the words of its elders. Petting parties and drinking were the least of it. Rather it was disillusionment, a lack of faith in God and men.

With the book's success, Fitzgerald became "a kind of king of our American youth."[5] In a sense, he never got over his own youth. He may have stopped feeling young at thirty, but he could never forget that once he had *been* young, and for the first few years of their marriage he and Zelda worked awfully hard at being young and careless. It was parties and speakeasies and drinking until dawn. It was arriving at someone's house and staying up all night or finding a corner somewhere and going to sleep while everyone else drank and danced. Zelda once took a bath in the Cottage Club at Princeton, which resulted in a campus scandal and the suspension of Fitzgerald's privileges. But if Scott was peeved, he also took pride in Zelda's naked derring-do, bragging that she had once stopped a train outside Birmingham, Alabama, by standing on the railroad tracks wearing nothing but a lantern.[6]

Those encountering them in the 1920s found them wildly in love and perfectly in sync. They laughed at each other's stories, finished each other's sentences, and were fiercely protective of one another. But, in truth, it was a marriage of two high-powered egos. For a while, Zelda was content to travel along with Scott, but she was too independent, too intelligent, and too artistic in her own right to defer to him, and gradually she came to resent the attention he received and expected to receive.

As for Scott, somehow he knew (even before Zelda's alleged fling on the Riviera) that love was precarious. All of his best stories in one way or another are about loss. There was usually "a touch of disaster in them," he acknowledged; "the lovely young creatures in my novels went to ruin, the diamond mountains of my short stories blew up, my millionaires were as beautiful and damned as Thomas Hardy's peasants."[7] Somewhat of an overstatement, but it does remind us that happy endings were not his forte. Even as a young man, he found layers of sadness beneath events that were sad to begin with. A telling moment in the "The Rich Boy" occurs when the protagonist, Anson Hunter, realizes what the end of a love affair *truly* means: "the memory of him has lost poignancy to her."[8]

One has to be careful when taking real-life soundings of fiction, but it's difficult not to think of Scott and Zelda when reading "The Rich Boy," a more psychologically astute work than *Gatsby* and one that foreshadows the dissolution of the Fitzgeralds' marriage: "[Anson] dominated and attracted her, and at the same time filled her with anxiety," thinks a former girlfriend. "Confused by his mixture of solidity and self-indulgence, of sentiment and cynicism—incongruities which her gentle mind was unable to resolve—Paula grew to think of [Anson] as two alternating personalities"[9]—identified in the story as "the paternal, understanding stature of his mind" and the "gross, humorous, reckless of everything but pleasure side to him." Anson is both "sybarite" and "solid rock," and their relationship unraveled as "the secret weavings of their temperaments came between them, drying up their kisses and their tears, making their voices less loud to one another, muffling the intimate chatter of their hearts until the old communication was only possible by letters from far away."[10]

Anson was partially based on a wealthy classmate of Fitzgerald's at Princeton, Ludlow Fowler, but is often described in terms strongly suggestive of Fitzgerald himself: Anson has many friends, "scarcely one for whom he had not done some unusual kindness and scarcely one whom he did not embarrass by his bursts of rough conversation or his habit of getting drunk whenever and however he liked."[11] There is a hard analytical core in Fitzgerald's best work that adds depth to the softer, more romantic touches. In his own way, he was a tough customer, a realist who saw himself as others did: "I don't think [Anson] was ever happy," he wrote, "unless someone was in love with him, responding to him like filings to a magnet, helping him to explain himself, promising him something. What it was I do not know. Perhaps they promised that there would always be women in the world who would spend their brightest, freshest, rarest hours to nurse and protect that superiority he cherished in his heart."[12]

Fitzgerald needed women to love and admire him, but he also knew that love was complicated. He went back and forth about his relationship with Zelda, eventually coming to believe that a strain had been there from the first. He would even claim that the marriage had been a mistake. In a 1938 letter to Scottie, he wrote:

> When I was your age I lived with a great dream. The dream grew
> and I learned to speak of it and make people listen. Then the dream
> divided one day when I decided to marry your mother after all, even
> though I knew she was spoiled and meant no good to me. I was sorry
> immediately I had married your mother, but being patient in those
> days, made the best of it, and got to love her in another way. You
> came along and for a long time we made quite a lot of happiness out
> of our lives. But I was a man divided—she wanted me to work too
> much for her and not enough for my dreams.[13]

Setting aside the inappropriateness of writing this to his teenage daughter, it doesn't square with the facts: Scott had pursued Zelda ardently and desperately, and if he had felt any misgivings at the time of the marriage, why had he been so happy riding down Fifth Avenue that autumn day in 1920? Most likely, he meant what he told Scottie, just as he meant it when he told one of Zelda's doctors: "a part of me will always pity [Zelda] with a sort of deep ache that is never absent from my mind for more than a few hours: an ache for the beautiful child that I loved and with whom I was happy as I shall never be again."[14]

As for "the great dream," it didn't divide quite the way he describes it. Zelda had provided him with material (and not just from her journal). Without her wit and intelligence, the tone and substance of his novels and a few of his stories would have been very different. Contradictions simply did not deter the man. *This Side of Paradise* was written not in spite of Zelda but because of her. Whatever its flaws, it was the first step toward the realization of the dream. Nor is it possible to imagine *The Beautiful and Damned* without Gloria Gilbert, whose persona, not to mention diary, strongly resembled that of Zelda Sayre. And would there even have been *Tender Is the Night* without the tragedy of Zelda's illness?

In fact, it seems base to lay the blame for the dream's demise on Zelda or on the hectic and financially strapped lives they led. Fitzgerald was sufficient unto himself to splinter the dream, and while it's true that, after 1929, Zelda's condition made life more difficult for him, it was a combination of circumstances and Fitzgerald's reaction to them that took him down. One might also say that the first two novels, weak as they are, were the price he had to pay before he could write *Gatsby*. If so, then he owed her a debt that even he was unaware of.

THE GREAT GATSBY was the book Fitzgerald was meant to write, though no one, perhaps not even he himself, suspected it at the time. He knew it was better than anything he had written before, but it's so superior to his previous novels that one wonders if Scott hadn't taken a midnight stroll to the crossroads and made a pact with an editor even better than Perkins.[15] Today, neither the good nor the bad reviews matter. *Gatsby* has become a national fixture, a piece of Americana that has outstripped the use for which it had been designed.

At its most basic, *Gatsby* reflects the characteristic American belief in self-improvement and upward mobility. Like most children born around the turn of the twentieth century, young Scott was steeped in notions of "rugged individualism" and Emersonian "self-reliance." Greed wasn't good, but wealth honestly come by was. It is precisely from within and also against the spirit of American pragmatism that Fitzgerald drew inspiration. The desire to make oneself over, more easily arranged in large cities than in small towns, was already a motif in the American narrative. Horatio Alger's tales of transformation, for example, quickly became a staple of Hollywood movies. As Ronald Berman notes, "The enormous amount of success stories in the movies during the twenties was a mirror not only of national economic opportunity but of Hollywood's institutional frame of mind."[16] *Gatsby*, however, was more than a success story; it was a validation of success and cast American pragmatism in an idealistic light. Only Fitzgerald could have envisioned a tawdry get-rich-quick scheme as a means of attaining a paradisaical world where aspiration and happiness are one and the same.

So one may regard Gatsby as both an ambitious dreamer who takes the practical steps to recapture a happiness he once knew *and* as the exemplary American idealist whose self-transformation resonates with all of us. Berman put it well: "Gatsby is at his most American in his transcendentalist quality of imagination. . . . [I]n the essentials of his alteration of identity, in his subordination of fact to vision, he is the representative form of what we think of as national character."[17] That may be, but surely disappointment, as Fitzgerald knew, must then lie in store. One can go a long way on money and celebrity, but not as far as the highest echelons of society. Even if Gatsby had won Daisy, he would always remain to the Tom Buchanans of the world a nobody from nowhere. Alger notwithstanding, most poor boys remain poor, and if they do get lucky, their wealth does not serve as a pass into the subdued halls of old money. At some point, society shuts its doors, and interlopers slink away.

Fitzgerald felt this and seems to be of two minds about Gatsby. He implies that poor boys can draw solace from Baden-Powell's dictum that "A knight (or boy scout) is at all times a gentleman" and that a gentleman "is anyone who carries out the rules of chivalry of the knights."[18] But he's also suggesting that *only* a hapless romantic like James Gatz could believe this. The other, not so implicit, contradiction is that Gatsby's devotion cannot be divorced from his criminal enterprise. At the heart of Gatsby's love for Daisy is a diseased valve ("what foul dust floated in the wake of his dreams"?).[19]

Even from a strictly narrative point of view, there is a ripe paradox inhabiting *Gatsby*. The heightened awareness of life's possibilities is not in Gatsby's nature but in Nick Carraway's narration. Gatsby himself would never think to put his story down in the terms that Nick does. (This is, of course, a perfectly valid fictional device: a man like Philip Marlowe would never write about a man like Philip Marlowe.) So Nick, a supposedly down-to-earth type, is given the task of telling the story of the outrageously romantic bootlegger James Gatz, a seeker after paradise and lost time. And isn't it odd that such a staunchly conventional narrator, a midwestern stockbroker, should be so intensely aware of his surroundings? It's Nick, not Gatsby, who thrills to the sights and sounds of the universe and who's alert to every glance, every nuance of behavior, every shaft of light glinting off a blade of grass or chrome fender. For a stockbroker, Nick has an inordinate fondness for adjective-laden descriptions that make even inanimate objects throb with the pulse of life.

James Gatz may be emblematic of the American character in his quest for self-improvement, but the manner in which his dream is conveyed is hardly American. *The Great Gatsby* resembles in form a romance from across the pond; its sensibility is Oxbridge by way of St. Paul, Minnesota. The spareness of dramatic execution may be pure midwestern America, but the overripe language is straight out of Pater and Wilde. *The Great Gatsby,* stylistically speaking, is not in the American grain at all.

It's only by virtue of Fitzgerald's combination of sentimentality and edgy realism that *Gatsby* has become the quintessential American novel, whose imperfections, enfolded within the shimmering apparition of its language, is perhaps analogous to the nation itself, an imperfect entity rising from the magnificent language of another unique document created 145 years earlier. For like the novel, the nation is also, in some sense, a work of fiction, a testament to the ideal of equality, which, whatever one's politics, has never lived up to its billing.

HOW GOOD IS *The Great Gatsby*? To be honest, *Gatsby* is best read before the age of forty, not because it isn't a remarkable book or cannot be appreciated by older readers, but because the novel doesn't acquire new depths on rereading. Maybe it's a truth limited only to more seasoned readers, but *Gatsby* does not "live" in the sense that its characters "grow" in the way that people in less perfect books often do. The protagonists in *Gatsby* are wonderfully drawn but seem more like perfect illustrations of a type than real people with tics and contradictions who have been captured and transfixed on the page. Naturally, one may dispute this view. Clive James does. James feels that *Gatsby* has "depth at the surface, which is a wonderful quality, and there's more depth underneath. If you go back in later life, when you're much older than you are now, more and more truth will arise from that book."[20]

Whatever one's opinion, few would deny that it's Fitzgerald's voice that draws us in. In his worshipful essay on Fitzgerald, Lionel Trilling saw fit to remind us that "what underlies all success in poetry, what is even more important than the shape of the poem or its wit or its metaphor, is the poet's voice. It either gives us confidence in what is being said or it tells us that we do not need to listen; and it carries both the modulation and the living form of what is being said."[21] That these words appear in an essay about a novelist makes perfect sense when the novelist happens to be Fitzgerald. For though *Gatsby* is wildly romantic, the narration is a study in precision.

For this reader, at any rate, the elaborateness of the conceit, countered by the deliberateness of the execution, affords us a lushness of style rather than access to the rich inner lives of the book's characters. Fitzgerald's dialogue may be sharp, clipped, and suggestive, but the narration itself, precisely because of the heightened language—all those thrilling, throbbing, stirring, darkening, breathing, and shining nouns that Nick summons—only calls attention to the artifice of the tale. And yet we believe implicitly in Gatsby's love for Daisy, even though it's a love as impossible as the idea that one can go back in time. (*"Can't repeat the past?"* he cried incredulously. "Why of course you can!").[22] It's the love that the young boy from St. Paul had believed in and that the twenty-seven-year-old author understood was no longer possible—which, of course, made it all the better to write about.

What teenager or young adult can read the last three paragraphs of chapter 6 without feeling drawn to the author? Here was a writer who felt as young people felt, who put into words what words before had not expressed so well, who managed to make us believe in the naïve and absolute power of love itself, which, when reciprocated, so focuses the mind that it can "never romp again like the mind of God."[23]

How good is *Gatsby*? It depends, I suppose, on what you want a novel to do. For sheer beauty of language, though, this one is hard to beat:

> Gradually I became aware of the old island here that flowered once for Dutch sailors' eyes—a fresh, green breast of the new world. Its vanished trees, the trees that had made way for Gatsby's house, had once pandered in whispers to the last and greatest of all human dreams; for a transitory enchanted moment man must have held his breath in the presence of this continent, compelled into an aesthetic contemplation he neither understood nor desired, face to face for the last time in history with something commensurate to his capacity for wonder.[24]

What Trilling heard in Fitzgerald's voice was "at once the tenderness toward human desire that modifies a true firmness of moral judgment" and "a largeness, even a stateliness, which derives from his connection with tradition and with mind."[25] And when Trilling refers to "the habitual music of Fitzgerald's seriousness," it's as though a small burst of sensory awareness detonates in the brain. Obviously neither the music nor the seriousness can be sustained throughout. Even so, there are moments as tangibly familiar as being in a railway station when a sense of a more perfect existence—moments when the romance of life has not been sullied by time and experience—suddenly takes shape. No writer, I think, except for John Cheever, has ever captured so well the fleeting sense of beauty in the incidental and ordinary occurrences that compose daily life:

> When we pulled out into the winter night and the real snow, our
> snow, began to stretch out beside us and twinkle against the
> windows, and the dim lights of small Wisconsin stations moved
> by, a sharp wild brace came suddenly into the air. We drew in
> deep breaths of it as we walked back from dinner through the cold
> vestibules, unutterably aware of our identity with this country for
> one strange hour, before we melted indistinguishably into it again.[26]

Odd how Fitzgerald, without spelling it out, makes the romance of those journeys come alive with a poignancy we reserve for paradises lost or only briefly glimpsed. For Fitzgerald, romance is always predicated on its inevitable disappearance; and it is this sense of loss, of beauty that must die, that his descriptive language evokes, a nostalgia that no other prose writer of the English language has ever achieved, something that is both evocative and exquisite; redolently vatic, yet also vivid and specific:

> That's my Middle West—not the wheat or the prairies or the lost
> Swede towns, but the thrilling returning trains of my youth, and

the street lamps and sleigh bells in the frosty dark and the shadows of holly wreaths thrown by lighted windows on the snow. I am part of that, a little solemn with the feel of those long winters, a little complacent from growing up in the Carraway house in a city where dwellings are still called through decades by a family's name.[27]

You can forgive a writer a lot of things for having the skill and sensibility to write that.

IF FITZGERALD STRIKES us, at times, as a haunted soul, a melancholic dreamer attuned to the vibrations of each passing moment, he was also a most punctilious and status-conscious fellow. It was as if he required an equally developed practical side to keep his more poetic and rarefied nature in check. The man was great for organization. He loved to categorize and draw up schedules, compiling "lists, charts, and tables of people and events."[28] He kept meticulous records and made numerous lists of "cavalry leaders and football players and cities, and popular tunes and pitchers, and happy times, and hobbies and houses I lived in."[29] His *Ledger,* with its neatly scrawled headings— *"Date Written," "Magazines," "Book Published By," "Movie Made By," "Sources," "Remarks," "Disposal"*—recorded every penny earned, borrowed, and paid back. "Plans and lists were the spine of his life," Sheilah Graham recalled. "He was the most orderly man in a state of disorder I ever knew."[30]

For a man who led one of the messiest lives in literary history, he was on paper as organized as the minutes of a congressional hearing. He once made a chart, sad in its way, of all the occasions that he had been with Hemingway. And around the age of thirty, he made a list of all the people who at one time or another had snubbed him; among them Tallulah Bankhead, Ada MacLeish (the poet's wife), and Bijou O'Connor, with whom he may have had an affair.[31] In short, he could be an unappealing combination of know-it-all and control freak, and like many writers he was obsessed with his place in the literary pantheon.

This doesn't make him unique—writers from Victor Hugo to T. S. Eliot have lobbied on their own behalf—but how many took such pains to promote their works? Fitzgerald wanted to have a hand in *everything*, from the design of his books to the stores in which they were placed. Indeed, no author paid more attention to the minutiae of marketing than he did.

One reads about some of the things he did and wonders, "Who does that?" The answer is someone always watching himself, someone resolutely aware of his own self-awareness. Regarding oneself purely as an observer excuses a variety of indulgences. "Once a philosopher, twice a pervert," quipped Voltaire. So Fitzgerald's storied affection for the rich was never in his own mind equated with the desire to move among them as an aspirant. He had the airs, the tastes, the inclinations of someone born into the moneyed class, but not the sense of privilege that comes with old money. And it was *old* money he wanted, not just in terms of dollars but because he associated those who had it with a natural aristocracy. And it was why the rich disappointed him. Welcomed on their estates, he saw how the rich insulated themselves and supposedly accelerated the decline of the West. At the same time, however, he made little effort to understand the poor or the middle class. In truth, it wasn't the class *system* that engaged him but rather wealth's untapped potential to improve our lot on earth.

He may have theatrically stated that he felt "the smoldering hatred of a peasant," but that was nonsense. It simply comforted him to think that when he visited the palatial homes on Long Island, he stood aligned against their owners.[32] As early as 1922, he described himself as a socialist, but this, too, was an affectation. There is no inherent contradiction in possessing a strongly developed analytical bent and the ability to fool oneself. Fitzgerald knew he was a bundle of contradictions, which is one reason—perhaps the main reason—that he valued balance: "He was suddenly confused . . . and for a moment his usual grace, the tensile strength of his balance, was absent," he says of Dick Diver, the hero of *Tender Is the Night*.[33] Balance was necessary; without it, Fitzgerald tilted toward remorse and anger, especially when drunk. One day on the Riviera, passing alongside a middle-aged woman carrying a tray of nuts and candies, he kicked it out of her hands.

Knowing himself, he knew he was far from perfect—hence his striving after perfection. But life itself was far from perfect. The swings of fortune, the anxiety over his writing, the decline of his health and reputation, the guilt he felt over his drinking and bad behavior, his grief over Zelda's descent into madness all weighed on him. But he persevered. After Zelda's presumed affair in the summer of 1924, he wrote to Perkins: "I've been unhappy but my work hasn't suffered from it. I am grown at last."[34] He wasn't. When is anyone, for that matter, grown at last?

Fitzgerald's America II

IF POETS ARE BOTH barometers and part of the weather, as Lionel Trilling proposed, then F. Scott Fitzgerald, though he never published a book of verse, was the poet of the 1920s.[1] He not only coined the term "Jazz Age," he fixed it in our minds: "It was an age of miracles, it was an age of art, it was an age of excess, and it was an age of satire."[2] It was also a transitional age, a time when America began to shift from an agrarian to an urban society, when a mass communication system made possible by electrification began to emerge, when a consumer culture, with all the marketing paraphernalia that goes along with it, began to undergo exponential growth.

Although the Jazz Age is now practically synonymous with the 1920s, Fitzgerald first used the term in 1922, when he was thinking less about the new decade (or the new music for that matter) than about the "state of nervous stimulation" that overtook the nation after the armistice of 1918.[3] In addition to the race riots of 1919, political unrest led to violent confrontations across the nation. Socialists, trade unionists, and Bolsheviks all had legitimate grievances against the government. The May Day riots in Cleveland and other cities resulted in the arrest of some three thousand Americans. The next year saw numerous labor strikes break out across the country, and in September 1920 a bombing on Wall Street killed thirty-eight people. Before the year was out, four thousand alleged radicals were arrested nationwide. The first of the Red Scares now afflicted the nation, taking personal shape in the Sacco-Vanzetti trial of May 1921.[4]

Fitzgerald may have described the 1920s as "the most expensive orgy ... the greatest, gaudiest spree in history," but he knew as well as anyone that the decade was not just about flappers, speakeasies, and Prohibition. "A whole race" was not "going hedonistic," as he foolishly put it. Nor was "the general decision to be amused that began with the cocktail parties of 1921" as general as he made out.[5] Older people and rural people and people who subsisted near the poverty line were decidedly not amused.

Farms were stagnating, tenements were proliferating, immigration was soaring, and the migration of Black people northward from Alabama and Mississippi was changing the demographic complexion. By 1924, membership in the Ku Klux Klan had reached an all-time high. The ratification of the Eighteenth and Nineteenth Amendments in 1920, which established Prohibition and the right of women to vote, did not assuage the feelings of assorted radicals and suffragettes who continued campaigning against corruption, big business, unfair labor practices, and the political machines. There was too much money in circulation, and there were too few decent-paying jobs.

In short, the Jazz Age is a reductive misnomer for a period of rapid social and technological change that helped thrust the United States onto the world stage. In 1880, when Fitzgerald's mother, Mollie McQuillan, was twenty, America was still an agrarian society. By the time she was sixty, more than half of all Americans were living in cities or in towns of more than 2,500 people.[6] And people could get to these cities and towns fairly easily because there were more roads and more automobiles to travel on them. Cars were not the only commodity bringing Americans closer. Between 1910 and 1920 the single-sided gramophone or audio disc started a commercial boom in sound recordings, and if one didn't feel like buying a phonograph, one could tune into a growing number of radio stations that were now selling time to advertisers.[7] By 1926, radio broadcasting was a national pastime, and Fitzgerald could allude to the few hours after dinner as an "homage to the radio."[8] What this meant was that for the first time in history, large numbers of people in different time zones could simultaneously listen to the same program.

With the electronic media extending their reach across the nation, people from Maine to California began to feel themselves part of a recognizable entity. Not only were more Americans listening to what more Americans were saying; they were now seeing what the landscape outside their own backyards *looked* like. Seven years after the Edison Company began marketing the Vitascope, the first commercially successful projector in America, Edwin S. Porter's twelve-minute film *The Great Train Robbery* (1903) used a camera that moved with the action. So while Americans were snapping photographs of the country (the Brownie was introduced in 1900), the motion picture industry was gearing up in California. And in a nicely synchronous development, the reproduction of both sound and sight joined together in 1927 in the first "talkie," called—what else?—*The Jazz Singer*.

"American civilization grows more hieroglyphic every day," Vachel Lindsay asserted in 1915. "The cartoons of Darling, the advertisements in the back of the magazines and on the billboards and in the streetcars, the acres of photographs in the Sunday newspapers, make us into a hieroglyphic civilization far nearer to Egypt than to England."[9] It depends, of course, on what you're used to. The visual assault experienced by Lindsay was scarcely more than a skirmish, but something *was* happening. America was developing a visual language apart from paintings and caricature. Illustrative art, for example, now crowded magazines and the pulps and appeared on billboards. Charles Dana Gibson dreamed up the Gibson Girl, and John Held (who illustrated some of Fitzgerald's books) gave shape to the flapper, showing Americans what a smartly turned-out woman looks like.

As a one-time advertising man, Fitzgerald fully appreciated the power of marketing, which expanded alongside the development of rotogravure and the rise of newer and glossier magazines. The influence of magazines before radio and television is difficult to gauge but was real enough in 1915 for William James to note that *McClure's,* the *American Magazine,* and *Collier's Weekly* "constitute together a real popular university."[10] When Fitzgerald sat down to write his first novel, the *Saturday Evening Post* and *Vanity Fair* were flourishing, and five years later, after a bumpy start, so was the *New Yorker.*[11]

Magazines were now helping to shape America's sense of itself. *Vanity Fair* became "a mirror of the progress and promise of American life," and for Ronald Berman it represented "the main source for the creation of social identity through high style."[12] And manufacturers naturally vied for space in its pages. The best way to get Americans to spend money was to make them believe not only that their purchases made their lives better, but also that ownership made *them* better. "We grew up founding our dreams on the infinite promise of American advertising," Zelda recalled. "I still believe that one can learn to play the piano by mail and that mud will give you a perfect complexion."[13]

Zelda was being droll, but Scott took advertising seriously. He understood that magazines and the movies didn't just sell styles of dress; they sold a self-image, an identity you could put on when you tried on a blouse or a hat. When Nick Carraway described Jordan Baker as looking "like a good illustration," he was telling us something about how Jordan saw herself. Without making a fuss about it, he was informing readers that selfhood was shaped partly by the media. As Berman takes pains to show, the major characters in *Gatsby* have idealized self-images derived from books, movies, or magazines.[14]

Indeed, critics and teachers might have less to say about *Gatsby* if Myrtle Wilson and James Gatz didn't believe that identity could be acquired by acquiring the trappings of a better life. "Ah ... you look so cool," Daisy says to Gatsby, and a moment later adds, "You resemble the advertisement of the man. . . . You know the advertisement of the man—."[15] Gatsby *was* an advertisement: he was James Gatz made over into a better version of himself. And in one of those perfectly apt crossover cultural moments, Gatsby himself became an actual look, a commodity and brand name associated with clothes, beauty salons, jazz festivals, and boutique hotels. In 1960 the Eagle Shirt Company marketed a Great Gatsby shirt; and later there were Gatsby-style jackets. The message? One could look as good as Gatsby if one knew what to wear. Does Gatsby look good? Who knows? He's never actually described in the novel except as "an elegant young rough-neck, a year or two over thirty."

ONE OF THE more obvious ironies of Fitzgerald's literary reputation is that for many years his work suffered from its association with the age that produced it. Because the 1920s were supposedly frivolous and shallow, Fitzgerald's fiction could not, so it was said, rise above its material. To some degree, especially with regard to the articles and lesser stories, this is true. As the self-appointed chronicler of his times, he recorded what he saw and heard and, given his desire to be au courant, was familiar with the best clubs, hotels, and hot spots. He knew what was in and what was out. He knew the names of actors and actresses, songs and songwriters, and who played end for Princeton every year after he left.

Yet the substance of his work was not the paraphernalia of the 1920s. He may have reveled in, as Mencken said, "the florid show of modern American life—and especially the devil's dance that goes on at the top," but what he really wrote about was what was past, passing, and to come.[16] He was "haunted by time, as if he wrote in a room full of clocks and calendars," Malcolm Cowley observed.[17] Arguably, no American writer felt more intensely the quickening pace of life or desired more to capture the moment as it was happening. This is what Mizener meant when he said that Fitzgerald lived "far more intimately than Hemingway the life of his times."[18]

Fitzgerald's America II

Fitzgerald was not more *about* the 1920s than other writers; he was simply more obsessed with his own passage through time. Whatever happened also happened to *him,* and this was, ipso facto, interesting. And because he took himself and the world seriously, his best stories are, in a sense, historical. And yet, they were seen by some critics as superficial precisely because they dealt with the Jazz Age. Hence, the same decade that made him was later used to dismiss him. The sad irony here is that Fitzgerald left the 1920s behind as much as anyone else. As he got older, he stopped deploring social norms and began deploring their neglect. In a 1933 interview with the *New York Times,* Fitzgerald, according to Scott Donaldson, declared that the older generation had failed to pass along the "eternally necessary human values . . . necessary for the formation of religious and moral convictions."[19]

The richer irony here is that it was only when the New Critics, who kept history at bay, emerged in the 1940s and 1950s that Fitzgerald's reputation began to crest. A close reading now revealed a hitherto undetected aesthetic: suddenly themes, myths, symbols, and ambiguities abounded in his work. There are, of course, formal elements in the work, but the reason that Fitzgerald is seen as the quintessential American writer of his day is because of his heightened awareness of the day.[20] No matter that it was self-obsession that made him sensitive to the changing conditions of modern life, those conditions got under his skin and into his fiction. Mizener sensed this and pronounced, "The substance out of which Fitzgerald constructed his stories . . . was America, perhaps more completely American than that of any other writer of his time."[21]

This resounding statement, seemingly unmindful of Dreiser, Lewis, and Faulkner, strengthens Fitzgerald's claim on our collective imagination. But it's too categorical an edict. And, if credited, can become a drawback. Fitzgerald's "greatest weakness," writes Charles Weir, is that "he was so completely of his time and of his country. He became a symbol of American life, or one aspect of American life."[22] But the "weakness" was hardly that. Critics often wrap writers in mythic cocoons, the better to deposit their own theoretical musings. But sometimes the point of a writer's work is simply what's on the writer's mind. And Fitzgerald had America on his mind all along. In "The Swimmers," as the protagonist embarks for Europe, he looks back at the fading shoreline and feels

> a sense of overwhelming gratitude and of gladness that America was there, that under the ugly débris of industry the rich land still pushed up, incorrigibly lavish and fertile. . . . France was a land, England was a people, but America, having about it still that quality of the idea, was harder to utter—it was the graves at Shiloh and the tired, drawn, nervous faces of its great men, and the country boys dying in the Argonne for a phrase that was empty before their bodies withered. It was a willingness of the heart.[23]

Fitzgerald was well aware that he was related to the composer of "The Star-Spangled Banner," and his chauvinism, strengthened by his travels, was sincere: "The best of America was the best of the world," he wrote in "The Swimmers."[24] He loved its people, and when he wrote about them—small-town children, young men on the make, dewy-eyed women addicted to dreams, thwarted lovers, and failed adventurers—he depicted them, as John Updike notes, "without the braggadocio of Wolfe or Whitman but thoughtfully, in contemplation of a spiritual puzzle."[25]

So, yes, Fitzgerald became a symbol of America, but he came by his apotheosis honestly, not because he merely embodied his time and place. Updike put it well: Hemingway made danger abroad seem sexy to Americans with his bullfighting and African safaris, but it was Fitzgerald who "flattered our national consciousness with a sense of domestic danger, of the failure and rebuke that haunts every aspiration. Of youthful overreaching swiftly followed by adult collapse, of a naïve romanticism courting the vengeance of blind destiny."[26]

Such evaluations, of course, were not yet in place when Fitzgerald was stumbling across the American landscape—a landscape viewed dissimilarly by his contemporaries and by future historians. While scholars seem to agree that the social fabric of America was being rewoven during the third and fourth decades of the century, no consensus exists as to exactly when the 1920s began or what they meant for the nation at large. For Fitzgerald, the "crucial" year of the decade was 1922, the year the country's economy took a sharp upswing, the year coal miners in West Virginia killed nineteen strikebreakers, the year that Nick Carraway moved to New York to learn the bond business.

Nineteen twenty-two was also the year the *New Republic* ran a series of articles examining the problems experienced by Boston, problems that were "becoming increasingly conspicuous and prevalent in many different parts of the United States."[27] Apparently, American cities were losing a sense of community, and their inhabitants were divided by more than "the cleavage of class." The real culprit was something "subtler"—namely "differences of racial origin, cultural outlook and social tradition."[28] The article, "The Rise of the 'New' American," did not look kindly on this new American, who represented an "upstart half-breed . . . destined to rule the larger American cities for many years in spite of the discomfiture, the dismay and ineffectual protests of the former ruling class."[29]

No wonder that Tom Buchanan was rattled. For Buchanan, a battle was raging between the virtuous past and the immoral present. Modernity—that is, all things that smacked of amorality and freethinking—was undermining the work of our forefathers. Buchanan was right to worry. Smug intellectual types railed against standardization and repression and heaped scorn on provincial towns and cities where Babbitry flourished. ("Not for the old lady from Dubuque," strutted the *New Yorker*.) They despised Prohibition, censorship, and religious fundamentalism, all of which, of course, were identified with an older generation. "Some generations are close to those that succeed them;

between others the gap is infinite and unbridgeable," Fitzgerald pronounced in 1928.[30]

The unbridgeable gap Fitzgerald had in mind appears in his story "The Scandal Detectives" between a middle-aged woman (Mrs. Bruckner) and her son. Mrs. Bruckner's sense of the world, Fitzgerald claimed, would have been perfectly intelligible to *her* great-grandmother, but now seems outmoded and absurd to her son and his friend, who "were making the first tentative combinations of the ideas and materials they found ready at their hand—ideas destined to become, in future years, first articulate, then startling and finally commonplace."[31]

Virginia Woolf, in her 1924 essay "Mr. Bennett and Mrs. Brown," would not have disputed this but thought the gap had occurred somewhat earlier: "On or about December 1910, human character changed... and, since one must be arbitrary, let us date it about the year 1910."[32] Both Woolf and Fitzgerald were dutifully acknowledging the advent of modernism, but the author of *Mrs. Dalloway* was thinking about weightier matters than generational differences. Her date refers to Roger Fry's 1910 seminal exhibition *Manet and the Post-Impressionists*, which not only altered the course of painting but represented a shift in how artists represented a world where fragmentation, instability, and the permanent loss of absolutes now characterized existence.[33]

Indeed, something significant and permanent began to take root here after 1919 that modulated our aesthetic sensibility. It may not have matched the philosophical upheaval occurring in Europe, where the senseless carnage of the war had shattered presumptions of progress and upended the moral categories underpinning artistic production. Nonetheless, the American disillusionment, as represented by writers of the Lost Generation, certainly transformed the literary enterprise. Looking back in 1929, Walter Lippmann mused: "What most distinguishes the generation who have approached maturity since the *debacle* of idealism at the end of the war is not their rebellion against the religion and the moral code of their parents, but their disillusionment with their own rebellion. It is common for young men and women to rebel, but that they should rebel sadly and without faith in their rebellion, and that they should distrust the new freedom no less than the old certainties—that is something of a novelty."[34]

But culture, to say it again, has currents and cross-currents, and despite the existential crisis shadowing those who came back from the war, disillusionment in America was not debilitating, nor did it take the form of Dada or nihilism. Younger writers and poets believed they were participating in a new enlightenment, an age of aesthetic fermentation comparable to Greece in the fifth century BC, or Italy at the time of Casanova, or England during the Regency.[35] Exactly when writers began to feel this way is another cultural intangible. In 1915, Fitzgerald's friend Van Wyck Brooks believed that American literature was suffering from a case of literary torpor, that "something has been wanting" in American literature, "a certain density, weight and richness." Creativity, Brooks suggested, was being stifled by the "Puritan ethic, the drive to acquisition and complacency."[36]

Brooks wasn't alone in his condemnation. In 1922 thirty writers and scholars, including Brooks, contributed to *Civilization in the United States,* a compilation of essays under the editorship of Harold E. Stearns, who maintained that "the most amusing and pathetic fact in the social life of America today is its emotional and aesthetic starvation." Brooks, in particular, argued that the American writer yielded too easily to "the iron hand of convention" because he was "insufficiently equipped, stimulated, nourished by the society into which he has been born."[37] And, in a singular phrase, which Fitzgerald almost certainly came across, Brooks wondered about "the quality of American fiction—how much does it contain of that creative element the character of which consists in dominating life instead of being dominated by it?"[38]

Naturally, a counterargument shouted to be heard. Some years later Frederick Lewis Allen insisted that Theodore Dreiser, Willa Cather, Carl Sandburg, Edgar Lee Masters, Robert Frost, Vachel Lindsay, Amy Lowell, and the Imagist poets "had been breaking new ground since before the war." Allen, in fact, saw their work as a "revolt against the frock-coated respectability and decorous formality of American literature," and he singled out Sinclair Lewis's *Main Street* (1920) and *Babbitt* (1922) as books that "revealed the ugliness of the American small town, the cultural poverty of its life, the tyranny of its mass prejudices, and the blatant vulgarity and insularity of the booster."[39] By the end of 1922, sales of *Main Street* had reached 390,000 copies. American readers, it seemed, were ready to hear about their own benightedness.

Brooks was exaggerating to make a point. Bad and boring writing is endemic to every age, and highbrows like Brooks, who incidentally coined the terms "lowbrow" and "highbrow," are always going to find fault with their contemporaries. For the most part, Brooks saw American literature before 1920 as an enervated variation of European interests. "No literature, no novels, no museums," as Henry James had put it.[40] It's not that Brooks didn't appreciate Melville and Twain or that he didn't see the value of Lewis and Dreiser; he simply wanted to register an impatience with American writers for not risking more, for not plumbing Dostoevskian depths or engaging in a Tolstoyan sweep a more diverse and vibrant American society. Essentially—perhaps unjustifiably—he was bemoaning the period between 1910 and 1920 when the older generation of writers—Twain, William Dean Howells, Henry James, and Edith Wharton—had already done their best work, and the current crop of younger writers—Dreiser, Lewis, Cather et al.—were just coming into their own. Literature wasn't standing still, but in 1919 it hadn't quite caught up to the technological and social changes of the second decade. For Brooks, American literature remained on the verge, too timid to embrace a modernist aesthetic.[41]

Brooks's hope for American literature was, in its own temperate way, not unlike what Ezra "Make It New" Pound envisioned in 1912 when he looked homeward from London and imagined an "American Risorgimento that will make the Italian Renaissance look like a tempest in a teapot."[42] Of course, the literary tempest Pound had in mind for these shores never acquired the strength he desired. As for

Brooks's dour assessment, it's open to debate. Lulls in the sometimes stormy progress of literature are to be expected and do not indicate a falling off so much as a settling in. If some writers felt that America in 1912 or 1920 was in need of a literary transfusion, it was because the inclination for novelty is always latent, emerging whenever a change occurs in technology or politics or the philosophical temper. Sometimes an artist or group of artists comes forward to release the tension; sometimes not. Contrary to popular opinion, very few artists single-handedly revolutionize taste. People don't wake up one morning to discover that a new aesthetic has risen with the sun.

Culturally there is usually no distinct *before* or *after*. If the novelists of Fitzgerald's generation felt that a break with the past was obligatory, they nonetheless remained stuck between a commitment to an American outlook (bound by methods of social realism) and the desire to incorporate the transgressive lessons of the European avant-garde. Although many American poets felt they had to adopt modernist technique to be original, novelists—who actually depended on the sales of their books to earn a living—couldn't simply write their own Joycean manifestos. The ambivalence was never satisfactorily resolved, and works of social realism continued to exist uncomfortably alongside more radical examples of modernism.

IT IS THE PREROGATIVE of every generation to feel that it lives in interesting times, and Fitzgerald's generation had more reason than most to feel this. With the war over and the economy booming, a sense of optimism overtook the middle classes. It made sense to think that America's time had come: "America has suddenly been called upon to carry forward the work of civilization," Henrik Willem Van Loon wrote in *Vanity Fair* in 1922.[43] Americans weren't just dancing to a new beat; the tempo of life itself had quickened. The air was charged with a new kind of cultural energy.

Fitzgerald, of course, was the exemplary young writer who made good. He may not have been a modernist, but he certainly familiarized himself with the modernist aesthetic.[44] He read voraciously, discussed ideas with Mencken, Wilson, and Brooks, and was not as uneducated as Hemingway made him out to be. When Fitzgerald confessed that he had "done very little thinking save within the problems of my craft," his aptitude for solving those "problems" often boiled down to apprehending the elastic dimension between life and literature.[45]

Although hardly an intellectual in the Joycean or Eliotic mode, Fitzgerald came of age with modern America and took stock of its transformation. He wanted to know everything, and he wanted to get it into his books.[46] He did his best to get his facts straight but became famous for making many of them crooked. Bruccoli claimed that he "never developed the habit of accuracy. His sense of direction was unreliable, and his arithmetic was approximate, especially in calculating the ages of characters."[47] Nonetheless, the man wanted to convey "the profound essence of what happened at a prom or after it . . . and how it is possible to make even a forlorn Laplander feel the importance of a trip to Cartier's!"[48]

In typically zealous fashion, he wanted *Gatsby* to possess both a "hauntedness" distinct from "all the ordinary material for Long Island, big crooks, adultery theme" and a concreteness, starting "from the *small* focal point that impressed [him] . . . meeting with Arnold Rothstein, for instance."[49] There was nothing naïve about Fitzgerald the writer; he knew he wanted to say something about the national mood, and he knew that the staccato rhythms of modernist writers did not suit him. "Not for him an invented American style, brashly experimental like those of Hemingway and Faulkner," Updike noted. "[Fitzgerald's] style is hard to parody, blended as it is of poetry and aperçu, of external detail quickly transmuted to internal sensation."[50] To which one might add that whatever Fitzgerald's literary aspirations, he knew from where his work sprang. He had loved Booth Tarkington's *Penrod* stories, and he'd been a Shaw and Wells man in college. But by the time he began writing *Gatsby,* he also knew that he needed to put more narrative distance between himself and his themes, and so he gravitated toward Turgenev and Conrad.

As well as a nominal man of the world, he also fancied himself a critic. Looking around in 1926, he concluded that most American novels lacked a distinctive voice: they either arrived leaning on the "sensory impressions of Thomas Hardy" or were "festooned with wreaths from *Ulysses* and the later Gertrude Stein."[51] He worried that writers were reflexively running through their material, unaware "that material, however closely observed, is as elusive as the moment in which it has its existence unless it is purified by an incorruptible style and by the catharsis of a passionate emotion."[52] Not too shabby a standard for a writer supposedly without intellectual qualifications, though, to be blunt, not a standard that many of his own stories often met.

Fitzgerald may not have always followed his own dictates, but he knew that the world around him, boundless and varied, was only the beginning of the artist's work. He knew that an incorruptible style coupled with palpable emotion was required to adumbrate large historical forces. Consider what the observant list-making novelist saw happening around him: the shift from a rural to an urban society; the influx of Italians and European Jews; the migration of Black people northward; the emergence of a new, organized criminal class spurred by Prohibition; the rise of the big bands and Tin Pan Alley; the invention of the Victrola, telephone, and radio; the increasing influence of Broadway and the movies; and, finally, the advent of the "Golden Age of Sports," with baseball, boxing, college football, and tennis becoming national obsessions. And who better to write about all this than a man smarting from class distinctions, who read Shakespeare but loved show tunes, who grew up in the heartland but frolicked in cities, who felt markedly American but traveled extensively in Europe, who desired nothing more than to experience life and to recount that experience to anyone who would listen?

The Facts of the Matter:
1930–1940

IN JANUARY 1931, FITZGERALD was in Switzerland, looking after Zelda, when his father died.[1] He returned to attend the burial in Rockville, Maryland, and then flew to Montgomery to visit Mr. and Mrs. Sayre. The visit did not go well. The judge had never reconciled himself to his daughter's marriage, and Zelda's sister Rosalind blamed Fitzgerald for her breakdown. In July he sailed back to Europe. Zelda seemed to be on the mend, and they visited Lake Annecy in Southeast France, where they swam and danced and pretended that things were as before. To Zelda it recalled a time "when we still believed in summer hotels and the philosophies of popular songs."[2]

In September she was released from the sanitarium, and the Fitzgeralds returned to America. They rented a house in Montgomery, thinking to rest up, but in November Hollywood reached out again. Fitzgerald was offered a job adapting Katherine Bush's novel *Red-Headed Woman* for Jean Harlow. He didn't particularly want to go, but $1,200 a week for five weeks was too good to pass up. Moreover, he would be working for Irving Thalberg, whom he'd met in the MGM commissary during his first trip out West. Fitzgerald had been tremendously impressed by the twenty-six-year-old studio head who, according to Charles MacArthur, "didn't know how to rest, or play, or even breathe without a script in his hands."[3]

Most writers, including Fitzgerald, regarded studio executives as vulgarians who wanted to beat a story down to its most obvious elements, but Thalberg was famous for detecting quality in, and demanding quality from, the scripts that came across his desk. Determined to do a good job, Fitzgerald cut back on his drinking and hunkered down. But after working on the script for a few weeks, he discovered that a producer was rewriting him even before he'd finished a first draft. Insulted, he prepared to complain to Thalberg but was dissuaded by more experienced hands. Thalberg didn't see people until he wanted to see them. He'd once kept the Marx Brothers waiting so long that they started a fire in a pan and fanned smoke under Thalberg's door until he came rushing out.

Fitzgerald's status in Hollywood in 1931 was a curious one. He was a famous novelist but also a writer-for-hire, a member of a guild that Jack Warner graciously described as "schmucks with Underwoods." As an uncredited screenwriter, Fitzgerald was a nonentity. But as the author of *This Side of Paradise* and *The Great Gatsby,* he was invited to an exclusive Sunday-afternoon tea party at the home of Thalberg and his wife, the actress Norma Shearer. Many of Hollywood's elite were in attendance, and Fitzgerald, eager to make a good impression, decided that a drink or two wouldn't hurt. Then, surrounded by some of the highest-paid entertainers in the world, he announced that he'd like to perform a song. Ramon Navarro (the first Ben-Hur) was induced to accompany him on the piano. When he had everyone's attention, Fitzgerald launched into a ditty that he and Wilson had composed at Princeton; and if Aaron Latham's account of the event is accurate, someone put Norma Shearer's poodle in Fitzgerald's arms as he warbled:

> Dog, dog—I like a good dog—
> Towser or Bowser or Star—
> Clean sort of pleasure—

A four-footed treasure—
And faithful as few humans are!
Here, Pup: put your paw up—
Roll over dead like a log!
Larger than a rat!
more faithful than a cat!
Dog! Dog! Dog![4]

Fitzgerald's performance was greeted by polite applause, and he immediately felt ridiculous. It wasn't the booze that made him do it. Intimidated by the company and feeling inadequate in their presence, he'd decided to meet his discomfort head-on. Perhaps he thought he could win everyone over by appearing at ease. Then again, calling attention to oneself through acts of buffoonery is also a form of self-hatred. Whatever the motivation, he captured his own embarrassment in "Crazy Sunday," his much-anthologized short story, in which his fictional stand-in, "his blood throbbing with the scarlet corpuscles of exhibitionism," delivers a parody instead of a song.[5]

The next day Fitzgerald reportedly sneaked into the writers building and refused to talk to anyone. It was only after receiving a telegram from Norma Shearer that he cheered up. The note read, "I thought you were one of the most agreeable persons at our tea."[6] It didn't seem to occur to him that Shearer had sent the note because he *had* made a fool of himself and that she, as a good hostess, was trying to perk him up.

A month into the project, Fitzgerald was let go. Thalberg wasn't satisfied with his work and felt there was no point in having Fitzgerald serve out the remaining week of his contract. Fitzgerald left meekly but conceived the notion that Thalberg had become jealous of his relationship with Shearer. When Thalberg died in 1936, Fitzgerald confided that "Talbert's [*sic*] final collapse is the death of an enemy for me, though I liked the guy enormously. He had an idea that his wife and I were playing around, which was absolute nonsense, but I think even so that he killed the idea of either [Miriam] Hopkins or Fredric March doing *Tender Is the Night*."[7]

No such thing was true, but if Fitzgerald got Thalberg wrong, he managed to get Hollywood right in terms of a screenwriter's footing. Writers were part of the food chain, their work daubed or painted over by other writers until the matter of credits almost became a crap shoot. "I hate the place like poison with a sincere hatred," he wrote to Harold Ober some years later.[8] Such sincerity, however, didn't prevent him from writing on spec a treatment for Burns and Allen or trying to interest Clark Gable in doing a remake of *The Great Gatsby*.[9]

Fitzgerald never got over his first two forays out West and felt that he hadn't been given a chance to prove himself. Hollywood "simply fails to use what qualities I have," he wrote to Ober. "If I could form a partnership with some technical expert out there it might be done.... I'd need a man who knew the game, knew the people, but would help me to tell and sell my story—not *his*.... I'm afraid unless some such break occurs I'd be no good in the industry."[10] A realistic assessment, but since it was only a matter of time before Fitzgerald contradicted himself, one knew, if given the chance, he'd go back.

IN FEBRUARY 1932, Zelda suffered a second breakdown and was confined to a psychiatric ward at Johns Hopkins Hospital. Fitzgerald followed her to Baltimore and in May rented a fifteen-room Victorian "cottage," La Paix, on the estate of Bayard and Margaret Turnbull. The Turnbulls were a prominent Baltimore family, and Fitzgerald became especially close to one of their three children, the eleven-year-old Andrew. The two played tennis, practiced magic tricks, sparred, and had long talks in which Fitzgerald advised Andrew about life, football, and women. Andrew never forgot these talks and years later published a rather stiff but sympathetic biography of Fitzgerald.

Jackson R. Bryer, another shrewd Fitzgeraldean, believes that Baltimore gave the peripatetic family something it never had before: a home.[11] Scott, Zelda, and Scottie lived in Baltimore for nearly five years, and even though Zelda was a patient at the Henry Phipps Clinic and the Sheppard-Pratt Hospital for much of that time (with a short stint at Craig House outside New York City), the Turnbull estate offered them some stability.

It was at the main house that Fitzgerald met T. S. Eliot in February 1933. Eliot came to town to deliver a lecture on the Metaphysical poets at Johns Hopkins and had accepted a dinner invitation from the Turnbulls. Naturally in awe of the poet and perhaps feeling the same nervousness he had experienced in Thalberg's home, Fitzgerald brashly decided to read aloud a section of *The Waste Land.* Eliot's response, unfortunately, has not been recorded.

On those occasions when Zelda seemed on the mend, she visited La Paix. It couldn't have been easy for any of them. Her emotional equilibrium was fragile at best. "Don't ever fall into the hands of brain and nerve specialists unless you are feeling very Faustian," she wrote to John Peale Bishop. "Scott reads Marx—I read the Cosmological philosophers. The brightest moments of our day are when we get them mixed up."[12] The bright moments, however, were becoming fewer and fewer. A sharp rift had developed between Scott and Zelda, a mutual resentment that sometimes bordered on the pathological.

Fitzgerald had gotten it into his head that Zelda's writing was a symptom of her disease. He appreciated the therapeutic effects of working but felt she was poaching his material. Moreover, he worried that her work might affect how his own would be received. Specifically, he didn't want her writing fiction, and if she was contemplating a play, it couldn't be about psychiatry or take place on the Riviera or in Switzerland. Although he unapologetically cribbed from Zelda's diaries and letters, he would not grant her the same leeway.[13]

He was especially irked by *Save Me the Waltz,* which told the story of a married American girl's fling with a French aviator. Even so, because he couldn't help himself, he asked Perkins to hold off making a decision until he, Scott, had a chance to go over the manuscript. He then helped Zelda revise the book, which Scribner's published in October 1932. If he was going to be unhappy about her writing, at least it was going to read well. Afterward, he helped her polish her play

Scandalabra, which was staged in the summer of 1933 by an amateur theatrical troupe (the Vagabond Junior Players) in Baltimore.

Hoping to stop her from writing, he arranged a meeting in May 1933 at La Paix with Zelda's psychiatrist, Dr. Thomas Rennie, who brought along a stenographer. An excerpt of the 114-page transcript of the therapy session is reproduced in Bruccoli's biography, enough to make us shudder:

SCOTT: It is a perfectly lonely struggle that I am making against other writers who are finely gifted and talented. You are a third-rate writer and third-rate ballet dancer. . . . I am a professional writer with a huge following. I am the highest paid short-story writer in the world. I have at various times dominated—

ZELDA: It seems to me you are making a rather violent attack on a third-rate talent then. . . . Why in the hell you are so jealous, I don't know. If I thought that about anyone I would not care what they wrote.

SCOTT: Because you are broaching at all times on my material.

ZELDA: What do you want me to do?

SCOTT: I want you to do as I say. That is exactly what I want you to do and you know it.

At another point:

SCOTT: So you are taking my material, is that right?

ZELDA: Is that your material? The asylums? The madness? The terrors? Were they yours?

SCOTT: Everything we have done is mine. . . . I am the professional novelist and I am supporting you. That is all my material. None of it is your material.

Zelda lays the blame for their problems on Scott's drinking and "neurasthenic condition," stating that she'd rather live in an "insane asylum" than submit to his demands. At this, Fitzgerald infuriatingly assumes the role of therapist: "When did that first happen?" he asks. "What do you think causes those two things?"

A bit later:

ZELDA: Here is the truth of the matter: that I have always felt some necessity for us to be on a more equal footing than we are now because I cannot possibly—there is just something, one thing, that I simply cannot live in a world that is completely dependent on Scott when he does not care anything about me and reproaches me all the time.

SCOTT: Now we have found rock bottom.

ZELDA: What is our marriage, anyway? It has been nothing but a long battle ever since I can remember.

SCOTT: I don't know about that. We were about the most envied couple in about 1921 America.

ZELDA: I guess so. We were awfully good showmen.

When the session was concluded, Dr. Rennie turned to the stenographer and asked: "Now who do you think ought to be in a sanitarium?" "All three of you," she replied. A nice touch, but not quite credible. Would a psychiatrist put such a question to his stenographer? And would she have replied in this manner? The reference in Mizener's biography is to a Mrs. Allein Owens, but she remains unidentified elsewhere.[14]

THINGS HAD GOTTEN so bad between Scott and Zelda that she twice mentions divorce during the session, an option he considered. Writing in June to his lawyer and fellow Princeton alum, Edgar Allan Poe (a distant relation to the poet), he mentioned initiating proceedings,[15] but then seems to have dropped the matter. The contention between them, however, grew worse. Her illness and his resentment, coupled with the ever-present financial strain, ate away at him. Then, in June, while setting fire to some papers in an unused fireplace, Zelda almost burned down the house. Bayard Turnbull asked them to leave, but Fitzgerald begged to remain until he could finish *Tender Is the Night*. Two months later he and Scottie packed up and moved to a townhouse at 1307 Park Avenue.

Back in the hospital, Zelda took painting classes at the Maryland Institute College of Art and on weekends visited the Park Avenue house, bringing along a nurse.[16] But soon after the move, she suffered another relapse and was moved to Craig House, an expensive sanitarium near Beacon, New York. Despite the turmoil of their lives, Fitzgerald managed to finish *Tender Is the Night,* a novel that does not spare Zelda's feelings. A decade earlier she had noted without rancor that plagiarism begins at home. But in November 1933, she read the galleys of the first two serialized installments of the novel and collapsed. Scott had paraphrased lines from her letters, drawn heavily on reports from the clinics she visited, and later openly acknowledged that Nicole Diver was a "Portrait of Zelda—that is, a part of Zelda."[17] Cline believes she reentered the Phipps Clinic in February 1934 partly because of what she read.

Despite their mutual resentment, Fitzgerald did not consider abandoning her. He continued paying her bills and bombarding her doctors with questions and suggestions. Nonetheless, after 1934 their lives as husband and wife effectively ended. In May 1934, Zelda was moved back to the Sheppard-Pratt Clinic. That summer John O'Hara paid a visit. "It was one Sunday afternoon in Towson, in 1934, that I had Scott and Zelda in my car and I wanted to kill him. Kill," O'Hara wrote to William Maxwell in 1963. "We were taking her back to the Institution, and he kept making passes at her that could not possibly be consummated. We stopped at a drug store to get him some gin. The druggist would not give it to him. I had to persuade the druggist to relent, and he got the gin. But I wanted to kill him for what he was doing to that crazy woman, who kept telling me she had to be locked up before the moon came up."[18]

Not a pretty story. And maybe not a true one. Meyers thinks O'Hara met Fitzgerald only in 1935 and doesn't include this episode in his book, a curious omission from a tell-all biographer, especially since Bruccoli mentions it in *his* book. Bruccoli also gives the year of the visit as 1935. Meanwhile, Sally Cline surprisingly takes O'Hara at his word, as does John Updike when reviewing O'Hara's *Selected Letters* in 1978.[19] But the letter to Maxwell was written more than thirty years after the event, surely enough time for O'Hara to misremember more than just the year.

Fitzgerald himself never alluded to the incident, but he was drinking heavily again. On one occasion he took young Andrew Turnbull to a Princeton football game, got loaded, and let the boy find his way back to Baltimore by himself. Fitzgerald felt terrible, but not terrible enough to lay off the booze. In January 1933, he met Wilson and Hemingway for dinner in New York. He arrived drunk and got drunker. Afterward, Wilson recalled Fitzgerald's "self-abasement" before Hemingway and how Scott with "his head down on the table between us like the dormouse at the Mad Tea Party . . . alternately made us hold his hand and asked us whether we liked him and insulted us."[20] As always, Fitzgerald deeply regretted making a fool of himself and the next day called both men to apologize. It was at this point that he recorded his well-known *Notebook* entry: "I talk with the authority of failure—Ernest with the authority of success. We could never sit across the table again."[21]

Only Fitzgerald's work sustained him during this period. In the winter of 1933, he hired a young Baltimore playwright by the name of Charles Marquis Warren, known as "Bill," to help put the finishing touches on *Tender Is the Night*. After nine years of false starts and periods of feverish rewriting, the novel was finally published in April 1934. Perkins may not have given the manuscript the attention it deserved, but he had great hopes for it and predicted to Hemingway that it would reinstate Fitzgerald as an important American author. He was wrong. Once again a Fitzgerald novel did not recover the money he had borrowed against it. Nonetheless, it didn't do badly for a book published in the midst of a depression. The first printing sold out promptly, and all in all, twelve to thirteen thousand copies were moved before sales began to decline.

Critics and readers expecting another *Gatsby* were disappointed, and Fitzgerald was disappointed as well, as much by the reviews as the sales. Although friends wrote him admiring letters, it was Hemingway's opinion he cared about: "Did you like the book? For God's sake," he pleaded, "drop me a line and tell me one way or the other."[22]

Hemingway obliged: "I liked it and I didn't like it," he wrote. "Forget your personal tragedy. We are all bitched from the start and you especially have to be hurt like hell before you can write seriously." The letter is by turns scolding, complimentary, condescending, and affectionate: "Of all people on earth you needed discipline in your work and instead you marry someone who is jealous of your work, wants to compete with you and ruins you." After reminding Fitzgerald that he's "a rummy," Hemingway encourages him by pointing out that James Joyce is one, too, and that Fitzgerald is better now than ever: "[G]ood writers always come back. Always."[23]

Although Hemingway gradually came to admire the novel, most critics and journalists did not. They didn't want to hear about the problems of a few wealthy expatriates gallivanting around Europe while people at home stood on bread lines. Philip Rahv caught the tone of the book's reception with a devastating phrase in the *Daily Worker:* "Dear Mr. Fitzgerald. You can't hide from a hurricane under a beach umbrella."[24]

Tender Is the Night, however, is not beach reading, nor is it a bad read. Its sin was not addressing the problems of the proletariat or the middle classes. It didn't seem to matter that *Tender* is far superior to Fitzgerald's first two novels and that it's anything but an idle tale about frivolous people. The taint of the 1920s followed Scott and Zelda for the rest of their lives. They had become an entwined period piece, relics of a trivial age. They were like the charming drunken couple you meet one night with whom you spend a few uproarious hours, but who become irrelevant in the morning when life turns serious again.

Although the novel is about love, goodness, fallibility, and the fall of a man whose character is not strong enough to weather misfortune, critics seemed miffed that it was the wealthy who suffer in the book rather than the poor.

The 1930s were not kind to Fitzgerald, and he couldn't help comparing his decline with that of the nation's, a conceit not without foundation. Although the stock market crash didn't drive Zelda over the edge or affect Fitzgerald's ability to earn, his reputation began to suffer after 1934. The fact is, *Tender* might have been coolly received had there been no depression. Its hero, after all, is a psychiatrist—perhaps the first shrink protagonist to grace the pages of an American novel—and the novel itself is somewhat hampered by the scaffolding on which it hangs. Nor did it help that a new generation of readers thought of Fitzgerald, if they thought of him at all, as a writer of *Saturday Evening Post* stories. Although he earned almost seventeen thousand dollars in 1935, he was accruing more and more debt.[25]

He despaired but didn't give in to despair. Instead he asked Bill Warren to help him turn *Tender Is the Night* into a screenplay. He still loved the movies (when he didn't hate them), and unlike his contemporaries—Lewis, Dreiser, Hemingway—he felt a connection to the cinema, a romantic attachment that had been formed in boyhood. According to Warren, "Scott would rather have written a movie than the Bible, than a best-seller."[26] I mention this again because at times it almost seems true. Fitzgerald was certainly the first American novelist to take the movies seriously and to regard his own talent as a natural fit with Hollywood. He loved the largeness of the medium, its potential for greatness, its ability to create a semblance of reality. He may have hated the studios, but, as Budd Schulberg recalled, he "liked pictures and felt his talent was particularly well-suited to the medium."[27]

Of course, he also distrusted the medium because it "was a mechanical and communal art that, whether in the hands of Hollywood merchants or Russian idealists, was capable of reflecting only the tritest thought, the most obvious emotion."[28] Furthermore, Hollywood was a town "where personality was worn down to the inevitable low gear of collaboration."[29] Yet he "had a hunch that the talkies would make even the best selling novelist as archaic as silent pictures"—and Fitzgerald wanted to be where the action was.[30] He played down his interest but he was drawn to the glamour, and his literary friends chided him for it: "It would be awful to see you piss away your talent in Hollywood again," Arnold Gingrich told him in 1934. "Because, regarding the written word like a musical instrument, you are the supreme virtuoso . . . and what the hell has the written word to do with Hollywood?"[31]

Fitzgerald's efforts to adapt *Tender Is the Night* for the movies never amounted to much—unless, of course, we factor in the career of Clint Eastwood. Although not mentioned, as far as I know, in any history of the movies, it's just possible that if Fitzgerald had not hired Charles Marquis (Bill) Warren, Eastwood might have ended up an insurance agent or keyboard musician. After Fitzgerald and Warren completed their adaptation of the novel, Fitzgerald wrote a letter of introduction and staked the younger man on a trip to Hollywood. Warren dutifully went off to peddle the treatment but failed to sell either it or himself.

Discouraged, he returned to Baltimore and later moved to New York, where he began to write for the pulps. After publishing a few western novels, he went back to Hollywood and helped create and produce television's *Gunsmoke* (1955–75). The show, whose first episode he co-wrote and directed, ran for nearly twenty years and helped establish the career of the young Sam Peckinpah. Warren then went on to create *Rawhide* (1959–65), which, as movie buffs know, provided a job for an unknown twenty-nine-year-old actor named Clint Eastwood.[32] It was in *Rawhide* that Eastwood caught the eye of Sergio Leone, who cast him, beginning in 1964, as the "Man with No Name" in the three spaghetti westerns that made him a star. From this unlikely angle, Scott's cinematic shadow stretches longer than one might have thought.

THE TWO YEARS following the publication of *Tender Is the Night* were probably the worst of his life. After the Fitzgeralds left the Turnbull estate, they often changed residences (asked to leave either for drunkenness or unpaid bills), and his stories, when he managed to complete one, were routinely rejected by the magazines that once sustained him. In April 1934 he embarked on a novel set in ninth-century France, whose hero, Philippe, would be based on Hemingway. The novel, entitled "The Count of Darkness," would portray Philippe as "the real modern man." Just as Julian Sorel had embodied the Byronic hero in Stendhal's *The Red and the Black,* so Philippe would be imbued with a Hemingwayesque sensibility. Fitzgerald finished only four chapters, and they were, as Mizener put it, "as bad as anything [he] ever wrote."[33]

Fitzgerald was in the dumps. A note in his *Ledger* reads in full: "Me caring for no one and nothing."[34] Pithy, but hardly sufficient for a writer who needed to explore his emotions. So he wrote a short essay, ostensibly about insomnia, "Sleeping and Waking," but in reality a testament to depression:

> —What I might have been and done that is lost, spent and gone, dissipated, unrecapturable. I could have acted thus, refrained from this, been bold where I was timid, cautious where I was rash. I need not have hurt her like that. Nor said this to him. Nor broken myself trying to break what was unbreakable.[35]

Fitzgerald's state of mind around this time surfaces in a disturbing scene in Aaron Latham's *Crazy Sundays: F. Scott Fitzgerald in Hollywood,* which—let it be noted—is based solely on the word of Bill Warren. One afternoon in the summer of 1934, Fitzgerald and Warren visited the Sheppard-Pratt Hospital. According to Warren, Fitzgerald insisted that Warren and Zelda play a game of tennis. Neither was eager to play, but Fitzgerald mounted the referee's chair and waved them on. After a while, Zelda began to remove an article of clothing every time she lost a point. Fitzgerald made no move to stop her, and before long she stood stark naked except for her shoes. When the orderlies came to remove her, she was screaming hysterically as Fitzgerald and Warren looked on.[36]

Bruccoli alludes to this sad vignette in *Some Sort of Epic Grandeur*, but makes sure to stress that it cannot be verified. Latham, who seems to have nothing against Fitzgerald, narrates the incident without questioning its authenticity. Could it have happened as Warren recalls? Possibly. With Fitzgerald nothing is impossible, and if he had had a flask with him, nothing would have been out of bounds except the tennis ball. But how many readers of *Crazy Sundays* will take the time to verify the story?[37] How many will even turn to the back of the book to determine whether it's documented? It isn't.[38]

When not shuttling between apartments in Baltimore, Fitzgerald could be found in Tryon, North Carolina, being treated for tuberculosis (lesions had been discovered in June 1933 and again in April 1935). In February 1935, Fitzgerald took Scottie out of school and moved to Tryon, where he became involved with a married woman named Beatrice Dance. The affair was touched on in his secretary's journal and confirmed by letters that he and Beatrice exchanged.[39] It seems to have been a real romance, though this time he was the less emotional one. When Beatrice offered to leave her husband, Fitzgerald scaled back the affair and wrote her a letter that is both plaintive and patronizing.[40]

Anyway, he wasn't about to abandon Zelda. Despite their bitter quarrels, there remained a bond between them. They had been happy once, and this meant a great deal to them. But they also knew that something had been irretrievably lost, and what remained was mostly pain and sorrow. "What do you need?" he writes to her in 1935. She replies, "I don't need anything at all except hope, which I cannot find by looking either backwards or forwards, so I suppose the thing to do is to shut my eyes."[41]

How do we measure what the denial of her ambitions meant to her or what she suffered when she was prevented from seeing her daughter? How do we fathom the damage to her psyche when she hallucinated or succumbed to religious mania, as she did after 1931? What we can do is imagine the awful treatment she received at the hands of her doctors. To counteract her "homosexuality," they prescribed endocrine, ovarian extracts, and dried thyroid powder. She may also have been given a serum made from the brain of a "stable" person. Morphine, belladonna, and Luminal were routinely administered, and she underwent purges of Seidlitz water, not to mention the insulin injections that were supposed to realign her behavior.[42]

In time, Fitzgerald came to understood that Zelda's diminution diminished him as well. In 1935, he wrote one of his few halfway decent poems, which begins:

> Do you remember, before keys turned in the locks,
> When life was a close-up, and not an occasional letter,
> That I hated to swim naked from the rocks
> While you liked absolutely nothing better?[43]

There were letters to Zelda's various doctors over the years, attesting to his abiding concern, and though he could not "live in the ghost town which Zelda has become," he also couldn't leave, no matter how far away he actually moved.[44] Imagine how he felt reading this letter from her:

Dearest and always

Dearest Scott–

I am sorry too that there should be nothing to greet you but an empty shell. The thought of the effort you have made over me, the suffering this *nothing* has cost you. . . .

Now that there isn't any more happiness and home is gone and there isn't even any past and no emotions but those that were yours where there could be any comfort. . . .

I want you to be happy—if there were justice you would be happy—maybe you will be anyway—

Oh, Do-Do

Do-Do–

I love you anyway—even if there isn't any me or any love or even any life—I love you.[45]

Bruccoli speculates that Fitzgerald showed Beatrice Dance this very letter to explain why he couldn't leave Zelda, which, if true, is one more reason to both like and dislike him. Exhibiting the letter was another betrayal of Zelda's privacy—which, of course, is being betrayed again in these pages. My weak justification for including it here is that it has been reprinted many times over.[46]

The affair with Beatrice Dance eventually ended, but Fitzgerald was still having a rough go of it in the winter of 1936. He was ill much of the time and suffered from insomnia. He took Seconals to sleep and amphetamines to wake up and veered between nervous exhaustion and the debilitating effects of booze and stimulants. Between 1933 and 1937, he checked himself into Johns Hopkins eight or nine times "both for alcoholism and for chronic inactive fibroid tuberculosis."[47] Nonetheless, he carried on: He went over the page proofs of *Taps at Reveille* and sent them back to Perkins with his usual notes and revisions. But as soon as the proofs were done in November 1935, he dropped everything and fled to Hendersonville, North Carolina, a small resort town near Asheville. As he put it: "One harassed and despairing night I packed a brief case and went off a thousand miles to think it over."[48]

He took a small room in the Skyland Hotel and sat down to explain himself. He was, so he said, no longer the man who had married Zelda or written *The Great Gatsby*, the man who formerly had been in control of his destiny. Somewhere along the line he had lost belief in himself and his talent. Still, what was he if not a writer? So *that* became his material, and quickly he wrote three confessional articles that he sold to Arnold Gingrich at *Esquire*, who ran them in three successive issues of the magazine from February to April 1936.

These pieces, which Edmund Wilson reprinted after Fitzgerald's death (along with other writings) as *The Crack-Up*, are a curious and problematic testament to Fitzgerald's emotional state. Just how far gone was he if he could write such a cogent description of how far gone he was? In any event, the articles caused a stir. He was news again—only the news wasn't so good. "Christ, man," John Dos Passos wrote to him in October. "How do you find time in the middle of the general conflagration to worry about all that stuff? We're living in one of the damnedest tragic moments in history. If you want to go to pieces I think it's absolutely OK but I think you ought to write a first-rate novel about it (and you probably will) instead of spilling it in little pieces for Arnold Gingrich."[49]

Perkins, too, wasn't pleased from either a personal or a professional standpoint. Hemingway, of course, laced into Fitzgerald and told him that he "was stupid to write that gloomy personal stuff."[50] He used harsher words when writing to Perkins: "It was a terrible thing for him to love youth so much that he jumped straight from youth to senility."[51] He then openly mocked Fitzgerald in the first version of "The Snows of Kilimanjaro," which appeared in the August issue of *Esquire:* "[Harry] remembered poor Scott Fitzgerald and his romantic awe of [the rich] and how he had started a story once that began, 'The rich are different from you and me.' And how someone had said to Scott, Yes, they have more money. But that was not humorous to Scott. He thought they were a special glamorous race and when he found they weren't it wrecked him just as much as any other thing that wrecked him."[52]

This is unfair on three levels. First, Hemingway deliberately ignored the next sentence in Fitzgerald's story "The Rich Boy": "[The rich] possess and enjoy early, and it does something to them, makes them soft where we are hard, and cynical where we are trustful, in a way that, unless you were born rich, it is very difficult to understand." Second, the put-down about "having more money" had not been addressed to Fitzgerald, but to Hemingway himself during a lunch with Perkins and the critic Mary Colum. Hemingway had been boasting that he was "getting to know the rich" when Colum remarked, "The only difference between the rich and other people is that the rich have more money."[53] And third, what sort of person writes this about a friend?

To make matters worse, Fitzgerald's slight memoiristic piece "Afternoon of an Author" appeared in the same issue of *Esquire* as Hemingway's now famous story. Naturally, he was hurt by this use of his name and immediately wrote to Hemingway, though he carefully downplayed his anger:

> Dear Ernest:
>
> Please lay off me in print. If I choose to write *de profundis* sometimes it doesn't mean I want friends praying aloud over my corpse. No doubt you meant it kindly but it cost me a night's sleep. And when you incorporate it (the story) in a book would you mind cutting my name?
>
> It's a fine story—one of your best—even though the "Poor Scott Fitzgerald ect [*sic*]" rather spoiled it for me
>
> Ever Your Friend
>
> Scott

> Riches have *never* facinated [*sic*] me, unless combined with the greatest charm or distinction[54]

Kindly? Fitzgerald knew that Hemingway hadn't meant it kindly, but he chose to overlook it. Hemingway agreed to Fitzgerald's request but probably because Perkins also urged him to omit or change the name. In subsequent versions the awestruck writer's name is "Julian."

Fitzgerald remained in Hendersonville for less than a month and returned to Baltimore to find Zelda no better than before. Meanwhile his debts had piled up, and the lukewarm responses to *Taps at Reveille* were trickling in. By the summer of 1936, he owed Scribner's nine thousand dollars and Ober another eleven thousand. He had borrowed against his life insurance and had even asked his mother for money. Then, while visiting Asheville, he took Zelda swimming and dove off a fifteen-foot high board and broke his right shoulder. A couple of weeks later he fell in his house and developed arthritis in the damaged arm. And in September his mother died of a cerebral hemorrhage.[55]

Where was Scottie during all this? She was matriculating at the Ethel Walker School in Connecticut. She was now fourteen and living with the Obers. Perhaps because he had no control over his own life, he began trying to control hers, sending her lengthy, often inappropriate letters: "Our danger is imagining that we have resources—material and moral—which we haven't got. . . . Do you know what bankruptcy exactly means? It means drawing on resources which one does not possess."[56] Incredibly, he was approaching the horrific age of forty. Rubbing salt on the wound, he agreed to be interviewed on his birthday by the *New York Post*. The interview by staff writer Michel Mok ran on September 25 under the heading: "The Other Side of Paradise, Scott Fitzgerald, 40, Engulfed in Despair."

It was generally thought that Mok, a young reporter, hoped to make his reputation at the expense of Fitzgerald's, but as Jay McInerny reasonably points out, Mok was just doing his job, communicating what he found. What he found was a middle-aged man "suffering the aftermath of an accident eight weeks ago. . . . But whatever pain the fracture might still cause him, it did not account for his jittery jumping off and on to his bed, his restless pacing, his trembling hands, his twitching face with its pitiful expression of a cruelly beaten child."[57] Fitzgerald had obviously had a belt or two before Mok's arrival, and Mok saw no reason to hide this from his readers: "Each time he poured a drink into the measuring glass on his bedside table, he would look appealingly at the nurse and ask, 'Just one ounce?'"[58] It's not Mok who makes Fitzgerald look bad:

"My father had lost his grip and I lost my grip. But now I'm trying to get back. I started by writing those pieces for *Esquire*. Perhaps they were a mistake. Too much de profundis. My best friend, a great American writer—he's the man I call my artistic conscience in one of the Esquire articles—wrote me a furious letter. He said I was stupid to write that gloomy personal stuff."

The Facts of the Matter: 1930–1940

The interview went from bad to worse. When Mok asked him about the people he had chronicled during the Jazz Age, he replied:

"Why should I bother myself about them? . . . Haven't I enough worries of my own? You know as well as I do what has happened to them. Some became brokers and threw themselves out of windows. Others became bankers and shot themselves. Still others became newspaper reporters. And a few became successful authors."

His face twitched.

"Successful authors!" he cried. "Oh, my God, successful authors!"

When life stops being kind, the media often follow suit. A few days after the disastrous interview, Fitzgerald wrote to Ober and confessed that he had "swallowed four grains [of morphine] enough to kill a horse," but had quickly vomited it up.[59] Eight months later, he described his state of mind after speaking to Mok: "My life looked like a hopeless mess there for a while and the point was I didn't *want* it to be better. I had completely ceased to give a good Goddamn."[60]

THINGS ONLY BEGAN to improve when he received another offer from Hollywood. He was fortunate to get it since Hollywood was in no hurry to have him back. It was only through the intercession of an old friend, Edward Knopf, who headed the story department at MGM, that the studio hired him at one thousand dollars a week for a trial period of six months. Hollywood had tossed him a lifeline. Blocked and burdened by debt, he saw the movies as a way out. If he could establish himself in the film industry, then maybe his health, his confidence, and his talent would be magically restored.[61]

Although he was, as he later described to Zelda, "a pretty broken and prematurely old man who hasn't a penny except what he can bring out of a weary mind and sick body," Fitzgerald boarded the train to Los Angeles with an optimistic step.[62] He had a plan. Fitzgerald always had a plan. Despite his two previous experiences out West, he wasn't deterred. As he wrote to Scottie from the train, "I must be very tactful but keep my hand on the wheel. Find out the key man among the bosses + the most malleable among the collaborators. Given a break I can make them double this contract in less than two years."[63]

He arrived in Hollywood in July 1937 and moved into the Garden of Allah, a bungalow colony on Sunset Boulevard. Among his neighbors: Dorothy Parker, Robert Benchley, S. J. Perelman, Ogden Nash, and other writers in the screen trade. Novelists, playwrights, and even poets have always been lured to Hollywood by the prospect of easy money. Among those who made the trip were Nathanael West, Anthony Powell, Aldous Huxley, William Faulkner, Lillian Hellman, and P. G. Wodehouse. Hemingway didn't need the money, and George Bernard Shaw deflected the blandishments of MGM studio head Sam Goldwyn by purportedly asserting, "The trouble is, Mr. Goldwyn, that you think of nothing but art, and I think of nothing but money."[64] Fitzgerald, however, thought of both and could never rid himself of the notion that he could write, if given a free hand, a popular movie.

At the MGM studio in Culver City, he was given a small office on the third floor of the writers building where from ten in the morning until six at night he worked on scripts and drank bottles of Coca-Cola, whose empties he carefully arranged around the room.[65] For the next three and a half years—except for a trip back East and one to Cuba—he lived and worked in LA. Apart from residences in and around Baltimore, Fitzgerald spent more time in Los Angeles than anywhere else, and when people think of him, they tend to see these years as a sad coda to the life. It's an impression created almost by default, since every biographer since Mizener has assiduously tried to convince us otherwise.

Mizener, in fact, skimmed over the Hollywood years, though he maintained that Fitzgerald moved from a "genuine enthusiasm" to "the feeling that he was watching 'the disintegration of his own personality'"[66]—a misleading characterization since the phrase appears in the second of the *Crack-Up* pieces, written more than a year *before*

Fitzgerald moved to Hollywood.[67] While it's true that some of Fitzgerald's letters from Los Angeles are peevish, others are more sanguine. Seeing as how he was an emotional pinball machine, zinging from bumper to ramp to bumper again, it all depends on which letters you look at and which of the Karamazovs wrote them. Latham's book gives us a quiet, withdrawn, hardworking Fitzgerald, who, by Hollywood standards, acquitted himself pretty well. Latham's description seems to have irritated Tom Dardis, who credits Hollywood with "the complete resurrection of [Fitzgerald's] creative powers, seemingly either dead or dormant since 1935."[68] Dardis goes further, contending that Budd Schulberg's treatment of Scott in *The Disenchanted* was unfair because it denied him "the personal dignity that Fitzgerald never seemed to lose even in the worst of circumstances."[69]

What was Dardis thinking? The man who humbled himself before Hemingway, who got on his hands and knees and barked like a dog to get into a party he wasn't invited to, who mistreated a serving woman in Cap D'Antibes is not exactly a poster boy for dignified behavior. Schulberg's portrait, if not hagiography, is certainly sympathetic. While Fitzgerald possessed charm, humor, and courtliness when sober, a dignified bearing was not his strong suit. Indeed, his was the dignity of a man who buttons himself up for fear that the flaps of his personality might suddenly fly open.

Years later, Bruccoli added his voice to the chorus: "The popular image of Fitzgerald as a broken-down, forgotten failure in Hollywood is a distortion as well as a simplification. His life there had a quiet order when he was not drinking. He knew that the movie work was unworthy of his genius and resented the power exercised over him by lesser men; but he earned an excellent salary at M-G-M and was proud that he was discharging his obligations."[70] Proud at times perhaps, but the compromises he had to make and the knowledge that he was just a cog in the studio system left him feeling unsatisfied. But then Fitzgerald was never one person for very long. Alyosha looked around and sent himself a postcard:

Some Unfinished Chaos

Dear Scott—How are you? Have been meaning to come in and see you. I have [been] living at the Garden of Allah.

Yours[,] Scott Fitzgerald [71]

Ivan frowned and tried to figure out how to impress the studio heads. Dmitri scowled and went out to get drunk.

As for their bodily host, he took up with gossip columnist Sheilah Graham. She was twelve years younger than Fitzgerald and had arrived in Hollywood only a few months earlier. She had been born Lily Shiel in Leeds, England. Her father, a Ukrainian Jewish tailor, died while she was still an infant, and the family moved to a basement flat in London's East End. When Lily was six, her mother, who cleaned public lavatories for a living, was forced to place her in a Jewish orphanage. With no education to speak of, Lily managed at eighteen to snare a man of the middle class, who improved her speech and manners and conveniently overlooked her love affairs. With his help, she enrolled in the Royal Academy of Dramatic Arts, changed her name, and became a music hall dancer and later a Fleet Street journalist. She then wrote two unsuccessful novels, divorced her benefactor, and moved to the United States, where she kept her Jewish Cockney background under wraps. In June 1937 she became engaged to the Marquess of Donegall—a rather brief engagement since she became smitten with Fitzgerald a month later at a party thrown for her by Robert Benchley at the Garden of Allah.[72]

Graham is like a character out of some pre–Hays Code Barbara Stanwyck movie: a plucky, scheming woman whose sketchy background and lack of education only fuel her imagination. And when her audacious ambition (abetted by her physical charms) culminates in a proposal of marriage from a man belonging to one of the oldest peerages in Ireland, one would think she has it made. But just when her improbable story reaches its predictable Hollywood ending, the plot suddenly takes a surprising turn. She breaks off her engagement with the Marquess and throws away a title for a "schmuck with an Underwood"—and a married schmuck at that.

The Facts of the Matter: 1930–1940

She did it, she said, out of love, and it must have been true since no other explanation makes sense. Fitzgerald may have been a burnt-out case, but he was famous and could still muster a little swagger, and perhaps Graham, who reminded him of the young Zelda, resurrected the young lieutenant he once had been. Anyway, to a poor girl from the London slums, a gossip columnist with literary aspirations, Fitzgerald must have seemed like the real thing.

They discussed Kafka and T. S. Eliot and Cardinal Richelieu and the Thirty Years' War. They listened to music and read reviews and watched movies. Ever the pedagogue, he designed a "curriculum" for her and called it the "F. Scott Fitzgerald College of One."[73] Although they maintained separate residences, they often shared apartments and houses. Unable to shed the residue of a midwestern Puritanism, he didn't want people to know they lived together. On the whole it was a loving relationship, with Fitzgerald the more loved. But it was also fraught with resentment and recriminations. After his death, Graham found a photograph of herself with the following words on the back: "Portrait of a Prostitute."[74] A hateful and obnoxious thing to have scrawled and most likely the result of three drinks and an argument.

It was a rocky affair, but she toughed it out. According to Sally Cline, Ober and Perkins were not impressed by her, and Cline herself thinks Graham had a "shallow and ignorant nature."[75] Be that as it may, she behaved decently. Frances Kroll, perhaps not the most impartial witness, thought Graham fortunate because "Once exposed to the glimmer of Scott's mind, it was hard for [Sheilah] to consider a less luminous man." Kroll also gives Graham high marks for helping to steady him. Fitzgerald clearly depended on her, but Helen Hayes, who saw the couple fairly often, could not help noticing that Fitzgerald "wasn't nice enough to her—ever."[76] Yet Fitzgerald had no qualms about introducing Graham to Scottie, who immediately saw her value.[77]

Graham essentially functioned as a caretaker for the Karamazovs: the sad, hypochondriacal one; the angry, unfulfilled one; the hardworking, responsible one, as well as the occasional drunken monster. The days inevitably had their ups and downs. Fitzgerald could be a wonderful lover, reading poetry aloud, sending flowers and funny notes, and helping her with her career. But he could also vanish for a night and reappear as a disheveled, foul-mouthed interloper chanting, "Lily Shiel, Lily Shiel." At such moments, Graham disclosed, the usually fastidious Fitzgerald exhibited "the sly leer, the unshaved face, filthy clothes, and occasional four letter word[s]."[78] There were also ominous telephone calls, special delivery letters, and, on one occasion, a nasty telegram sent to Graham's employer. Nonetheless, she put up with his abuse—she knew something about alcoholism—and when he was dead, she profited from their relationship.

Graham's memoirs—she wrote eight—are not all about the two and a half years she spent with Fitzgerald, though the relationship clearly inspired half of those books. At times her resentment shows through—as it should. He had looked down on her for being both Jewish and a gossip columnist and, perhaps even without recognizing the irony, disliked her social climbing. She wasn't a female Gatsby, but she, too, was a nobody from nowhere who ended up hobnobbing with her "betters." Having taught herself to write, she became competent enough to compete with Hedda Hopper and Louella Parsons. And we owe to her the wryly poignant tale of the couple attending an opening of the stage production of "The Diamond as Big as the Ritz." Learning that the Pasadena Playhouse was going to "produce" the story, Scott and Sheilah dressed to the nines and ordered a limo. Upon arrival they discovered the play was only a college production, a reading no less. Nonetheless, they went backstage after the show, and one can only imagine the faces of the drama students when the author of "The Diamond" showed up in full evening dress.[79]

FITZGERALD BEGAN HIS third and longest stint in Hollywood by working on *A Yank at Oxford*, or, as Meyer Wolfsheim would say, "Oggsford." When his treatment was finished, two other writers took over and jettisoned much of his dialogue. He was then handed a screenplay in progress of Erich Maria Remarque's popular novel *Three Comrades*. After submitting a draft to producer Joseph Mankiewicz, he learned that he would be paired with E. E. Paramore, a more experienced screenwriter. Disappointed, Fitzgerald resigned himself to a collaboration, and for five months the two men worked together, not always collegially, until they had a finished script. Mankiewicz, however, remained unimpressed, and decided to intervene. His changes horrified Fitzgerald, who shot off a letter:

> To say I'm disillusioned is putting it mildly. For nineteen years, with two years out for sickness, I've written best-selling entertainment, and my dialogue is supposedly right up at the top. . . . I am utterly miserable at seeing months of work and thought negated in one hasty week. I hope you're big enough to take this letter as it's meant—a desperate plea to restore the dialogue to its former quality. . . . Oh, Joe, can't producers ever be wrong. I'm a good writer—honest.[80]

In 1938, *Three Comrades* was named one of the ten best films of the year, but Fitzgerald took no pleasure in this. He thought Mankiewicz had traduced the spirit of Remarque's novel and of his own screenplay. Mankiewicz shrugged off Fitzgerald's accusations. He even claimed to have never received the pitiful letter. It was only decades later that he felt compelled to defend his actions: "I personally have been attacked as if I had spat on the American flag because it happened once that I rewrote some dialogue by F. Scott Fitzgerald. But indeed it needed it! . . . It was very literary dialogue, novelistic dialogue that lacked all the qualities required for screen dialogue."[81]

Despite Mankiewicz's retouching of *Three Comrades*, Fitzgerald's contract was extended for a year, and his salary rose to $1,250 a week. "I am now considered a success in Hollywood," he observed wryly, "because something which I did not write is going on under my name, and something which I did write has been quietly buried without any fuss or row—not even a squeak from me. The change from regarding this as a potential art to looking at it as a cynical business has begun. But I still think that some time during my stay out here I will be able to get something of my own on the screen that I can ask my friends to see."[82]

He thought that opportunity arrived when he was asked to write a script about adultery for Joan Crawford. His screenplay *Infidelity* pleased neither his producer nor the censorship office, and the project was shelved (though someone briefly thought it might fly if it were renamed *Fidelity*). He then worked on *Marie Antoinette*, followed by an adaptation of Clare Boothe Luce's *The Women*, neither of which he saw through to the end. He spent three months on *Madame Curie* (from a treatment by Aldous Huxley) and then, in early January 1939, he was lent out to David O. Selznick for a polish on *Gone with the Wind*. A week later, he was gone. MGM, meanwhile, without explanation, allowed his contract to lapse.

If Fitzgerald felt frustrated, he hid it from his daughter: "Maybe they're not going to make me Czar of the Industry right away as I thought ten months ago," he confided. "It's all right, Baby—life has humbled me—Czar or not, we'll survive. I am even willing to compromise for Assistant Czar."[83] But he really wasn't very good at compromise. Given a script to revise, he would break it down, advise the producers of its potential, backstory it, and then start to add layers. *A Yank at Oxford* couldn't be just a breezy romance; it had to establish a connection between language and mores. *Madame Curie* couldn't be just the story of a woman overcoming the odds; it had to reveal the intricacies of a marriage between equals. Also, he became too invested in the work, and like the British colonel in *The Bridge on the River Kwai*, he forgot that what he was building didn't belong to him and consequently felt dismayed at its destruction.[84]

The problem with Fitzgerald was that he tackled a script as a critic or editor rather than as a mechanic. He wanted to elevate the material, to infuse it with grand ideas and heightened language and, of course, a moral point. He wanted to redesign the car instead of just making it run smoothly, and so he often resorted to dialogue freighted with significance and to exposition that called too much attention to itself. And the sad thing is, he tried at the same time to give the studios what they wanted. Although he has his defenders, the consensus is that his screenwriting lacked the requisite slickness and momentum demanded by Hollywood producers.[85] Billy Wilder, who seemed genuinely fond of Fitzgerald, likened him to "a great sculptor who is hired to do a plumbing job"—with no idea how to connect the pipes and make the water flow.[86] In effect, he couldn't make the shift from words on the page to images on the screen.

Nonetheless, one screen credit and a reputation as an expert on college life was enough to get him another job. Almost as soon as MGM let him go, an important producer paired him with the twenty-four-year-old Budd Schulberg to write a romance using Dartmouth's annual Winter Carnival as background. Unfortunately, Schulberg brought along two bottles of Mumm for the flight east, and by the time they were over Kansas, Fitzgerald was a mess. He drank practically the entire time they were in New York and Hanover, New Hampshire, and points in between. The two men gabbed all day long and accomplished nothing except to royally irritate the producer, who fired them before they could even rough out the story. Years later, Schulberg remembered Fitzgerald as "tired, sick, embattled, vain and proud and painfully conscious of his fall from fame and fortune and creative productivity."[87]

The Dartmouth debacle weighed on him. He brooded, drank heavily, and fought with Sheilah. On one occasion, he grabbed a gun and began waving it around. "Shoot yourself, you son-of-a-bitch!" Graham supposedly yelled. "I didn't pull myself out of the gutter to waste my life on a drunk like you!"[88] She managed to wrest the gun from him, and later he wrote her a check for two thousand dollars as though it was a payoff. The very next day he went to Asheville and took Zelda to Cuba. He stumbled around Havana while Zelda remained in their hotel room, praying. Coming upon a cockfight, he intervened and was severely beaten for his pains.

Zelda managed to get him back to New York, where he kept drinking. He ended up in Bellevue Hospital's alcoholic ward, and later a sputum test at Doctors Hospital again revealed the presence of TB. It was the last time Scott and Zelda were together. In May he wrote to her: "You are the finest, loveliest, tenderest, most beautiful person I have ever known, but even that is an understatement because the length that you went to there at the end would have tried anybody beyond endurance."[89]

BACK IN LOS ANGELES, Fitzgerald spent a day on a Sonja Henie picture and a week on *Raffles,* palling around with David Niven. With no steady movie work, he began writing short stories again. From July 1939 to December 1940, he wrote twenty-four stories, of which seventeen deal with a forty-nine-year-old hack named Pat Hobby. Hobby had started out as a "structure" man in silent films and is now hanging on by the skin of his teeth. Hobby reads neither books nor screenplays and hasn't had an original idea since the womb, yet he sees himself as a man down on his luck rather than a has-been. He's cagey, manipulative, opportunistic, and full of schemes that never work out. Basically, he's a sitcom sidekick who thinks he's the hero of a James Bond movie.

The Pat Hobby stories were a nice outlet for Fitzgerald. He could mock Hollywood while getting his prose-writing legs beneath him, and the stories have a lightness and a brio not found in earlier satirical efforts. The fact that Hobby is "a complete rat," though not "sinister," as Fitzgerald put it, freed him to express how he felt about Hollywood.[90] Not every Hobby story is a success, but all are professionally if not brilliantly executed, and it's telling of how far Fitzgerald had fallen when neither *Collier's* nor the *Saturday Evening Post* expressed interest. He was forced to sell them to *Esquire* at $250 a pop.

In the summer of 1939, he began to work on another novel into which he poured what he had learned about life and love and Hollywood. His conduit is a Nick Carraway narrator (Cecilia Brady) and his hero (Monroe Stahr), a thinly disguised version of Irving Thalberg. He thought of calling it "The Love of the Last Tycoon: A Western," but it was never finished and was published posthumously as *The Last Tycoon*.

Meanwhile, financial troubles continued to beset him. Although he had earned more than eighty thousand dollars in three years, he'd barely saved a sou. Scottie's education (she was now attending Vassar), Zelda's hospital bills, old debts, and his usual profligacy ate up his earnings. He borrowed from Maxwell Perkins, and for the first time he hit up Gerald Murphy. And in July 1939 he asked his literary agent Harold Ober to lend him money against a possible advance on the novel. Ober, however, refused. And the refusal hit Fitzgerald hard. Ober wasn't just his agent; he was banker, friend, and financial adviser who had represented Fitzgerald for nearly twenty years. Ober felt it would do Fitzgerald more harm than good to keep borrowing and gently tried to discourage him from getting deeper into debt. Fitzgerald's response was to sever their relationship. Although he confided to Perkins that he would not "say anything against [Ober] either personally or professionally,"[91] three months later he was calling him "a stupid hardheaded man."[92]

He went into a funk. He brooded over his failure as a screenwriter, berated himself for drinking, and questioned if he could even write another novel. But he had no choice. So acting on his own behalf, he arranged for the serialization of "The Love of the Last Tycoon" in *Collier's*, which would pay him thirty thousand dollars upon acceptance. Unfortunately, the *Collier's* editor didn't accept it, and Fitzgerald was again stuck.

One day in March 1940, an independent producer, Lester Cowan, called him. Cowan had bought the rights to "Babylon Revisited" and wanted Fitzgerald to turn it into a screenplay. He couldn't pay much, but Fitzgerald would be able to work at home with no studio hatchet men looking over his shoulder. Fitzgerald agreed to the terms and suddenly was having "rather more fun than any I've ever had in pictures."[93] There was even a chance that his screenplay, retitled "Cosmopolitan," would get made. Cowan had persuaded Shirley Temple's mother to look at it, which necessitated Fitzgerald's spending an afternoon at the Temple home pitching the idea.

For any other major writer, having to charm an eleven-year-old actress while truckling to her mother would have been an awful comedown, but who knows how Fitzgerald felt about it? Signing Temple would have guaranteed production, and Fitzgerald understood what he had to do. Although we don't know how the star's mother felt about Fitzgerald's visit, Shirley Temple Black remembered him as "a kindly, thin, and pale man, who was recovering from an illness."[94] She seemed most impressed by the fact that he drank at least a half dozen Cokes during his visit.

When word got out that Temple was considering "Cosmopolitan," Fitzgerald's stock rose. Daryl Zanuck at Twentieth Century-Fox hired him to revise a script of Emlyn Williams's play *The Light of Heart*. Bolstered by such interest, Fitzgerald began to refer to "Cosmopolitan" as his "great hope for attaining some real status [in Hollywood] as a movie man and not a novelist."[95] As usual, he was still looking to catch a break. "If I get a credit on either of these two last efforts," he wrote to Zelda in October 1940, "things will never again seem so black as they did a year ago, when I felt that Hollywood had me down in its books as a ruined man—a label which I had done nothing to deserve."[96] But Shirley Temple's mother dithered, "Cosmopolitan" died, and, in November, Zanuck passed on his draft of *The Light of Heart*.[97]

With no movie work in the offing, Fitzgerald returned to his novel, which he maintained perversely was not about Hollywood. He told people that it was going well, but according to Kroll, whom he had hired shortly after his ill-fated trip to Cuba, he had very little energy and spent much of the day in bed. The illness that Shirley Temple thought he was recovering from was not really curable. His body and spirit had taken a beating over the years, and to the preexisting ailments he could now add a diseased heart. Kroll is convinced that Fitzgerald also suffered from hypoglycemia, which led to chronic fatigue, insomnia, and depression. She noticed empty gin bottles around the house and no attempt at a routine. He wrote when he felt like it, which wasn't often. Then one day she met the other Fitzgerald, the professional Fitzgerald. Having gotten a push from Perkins, he buckled down to work on his novel. Out came the charts and notes and outlines, and suddenly he was "a methodical, meticulous craftsman . . . as orderly as an accountant whose facts and figures balance his vision."[98]

Still, he wasn't well. In April 1940, doctors found another lesion on one of his lungs; he suffered from dizzy spells, his strength was gone, and he felt and looked sick. In September 1940, Clifford Odets ran into him at Dorothy Parker's house and reported that he seemed "pale, unhealthy, as if the tension of life had been wrenched out of him."[99] Was Fitzgerald thinking of himself when he described Monroe Stahr's face as "aging from within . . . [with] a drawn asceticism as if from a silent self-set struggle—or a long illness"?[100] Because it's *that* face we see in a photograph of Fitzgerald sitting alongside the hale John O'Hara in the fall of 1939. Fitzgerald is perched on the edge of a chair leaning toward O'Hara, his left arm around the larger man's shoulders. He's practically unrecognizable: sallow, resigned, resembling nothing so much as a refugee from eastern Europe.[101]

In late November he suffered an attack of angina pectoris at Schwab's drugstore on Sunset Boulevard. To avoid climbing stairs, he moved into Graham's ground-floor apartment on North Hayworth Avenue, where he continued working on "The Love of the Last Tycoon." He spent much of the day lying in bed, surrounded by charts "telling the different movements of the characters and their histories."[102] Ever the dedicated organizer and planner, he constructed on December 14 another one of his patented schedules. By writing so many words a day he figured to have a working draft of the book ready by January 15. But on December 21, while he was reading the *Princeton Alumni Weekly* and listening to Beethoven's *Eroica,* the Great Unscheduled arrived. He rose up from his chair, fell against the mantelpiece, and collapsed. He was forty-four years old.

Third Impressions

GRANTED THAT THE PERSON who writes is different from the one who goes out in the world, there are some writers to whom the distinction applies with more force. William Hazlitt was one such writer, Fitzgerald another. To read Fitzgerald's best fiction is to encounter an author aware of life's unpredictability, the heart's intermittent flutters, and the mind's restless curiosity. To read *about* him is to wonder how he managed to survive with his sensibilities intact. He said he knew more in his books than he did in life, and he was right. At twenty-seven and still in good health, he allowed Nick Carraway to think "there was no difference between men, in intelligence or race, so profound as the difference between the sick and the well."[1]

What remains unknown—perhaps even to himself—is the conviction he placed in his own words. The question of Fitzgerald's sincerity is not easily resolved. He was equal parts bravado and humility. He could refer jokingly to his ambition, acknowledging that he wanted to "write a novel better than any novel ever written in America and become par excellence the best second-rater in the world,"[2] or he could sound confident and self-assured: "The happiest thought I have is of my new novel [*Tender Is the Night*]—it is something really NEW in form, idea, structure—the model for the age that Joyce and Stein are searching for, that Conrad didn't find."[3] Was he serious? Possibly. He knew himself and valued himself accordingly. His feeling that American fiction "slightly [bore his] stamp" and that he was "in a *small* way . . . an original" rings true because the overstatement at the beginning and the understatement at the end have a similar plaintiveness.

Much of what gets said about Fitzgerald's authenticity is based on his *Notebooks* and the essays in *The Crack-Up,* and, frankly, too much is taken at face value. In 1935 Fitzgerald was approaching forty. He smoked too much, drank too much, and popped too many pills. Five years earlier he could have knocked off a story and made a quick two or three thousand dollars, but his stories, when he could muster the energy to finish one, were now being rejected. This was not the way it was supposed to be. He began with a belief in his own destiny, but then life got in the way, and slowly it began to dawn on him that life was "a cheat," that it had promised one thing but had delivered another. And because this seemed irrefutable, he bolted to Hendersonville, North Carolina, to "think things over."

What he mainly thought about was failure. He had failed at becoming a serious *and* a commercial novelist. So the question for him became "one of finding why and where I had changed, where was the leak through which, unknown to myself, my enthusiasm and my vitality had been steadily and prematurely trickling away?"[4] In answering the question, he wrote the three essays that compose *The Crack-Up,* a singular document in American letters.

Regarded initially as tortured self-analysis, too honest for their own good, the essays seem terribly restrained compared to the no-holds-barred revelations that flourish today. In 1935, however, they were felt to be *too* revealing. After all, they were written by an American, not some hysterical Italian or Frenchman who wept to the heavens for his sins. But emotional openness, too, is subject to fashion, and in time *The Crack-Up* came to be seen as honest a statement as had ever been penned by an American writer. Trilling admired Fitzgerald's willingness "to utter his vision of his own fate publicly and aloud ... with no lessening of his dignity, even with an enhancement of it."[5]

Not everyone, however, felt this way. Alfred Kazin, in a somewhat conflicted essay, described himself unmoved by *The Crack-Up* because he sensed that something was being withheld, that Fitzgerald offered us some facts in order to distract us from others. For Kazin the confession is "as careful as it is mournful, as shrewd as it is despairing, and as mechanically well-written as the experience it purports to describe was lawless and afraid."[6] Kazin believed that "It was as urgent for Fitzgerald to report on his breakdown as it was for himself to withhold some essential portion of its meaning for himself and from us. . . . Fitzgerald's essay is not mediated autobiography, but belongs with those facile canny professions of guilt which are so rife in our personal conversation and our love affairs."[7]

Either this is one of the more penetrating remarks made about *The Crack-Up* or it's the deduction of a 1940s New York intellectual steeped in Freud and used to confessions of an intensely private nature. For Kazin, the essays "had no innerness" because Fitzgerald's "senses always opened outward to the world, and the world was full of Long Island Sundays. . . . He was innocent without living in innocence and delighted in the external forms and colors without being taken in by them."[8]

This is well said, but slightly off the mark. If Fitzgerald presented to the world a man who both desired and detested wealth, his letters and *Notebooks* present a writer fully aware of his ambivalence toward worldly things. Instead of lacking innerness, he confronted his compulsions and acted, knowing full well that his actions could shame or betray him. And if he was "innocent," it wasn't because he understood or forgave his desire for material things, but because he always hoped, no matter how he behaved, to emerge unscathed. "He lacked armor," E. L. Doctorow aptly noted. "He jumped into the foolish heart of everything, as he had jumped into the Plaza fountain."[9]

Third Impressions

OK, but he didn't jump into his literary endeavors. Friends may have clucked their tongues at the intimate details recounted in the *Esquire* pieces, but do the essays really possess the raw outpouring of emotion we usually associate with people at the end of their rope? Fitzgerald might have been dispirited, used-up, disgusted, but the prose—the measured tone, artful comparisons, and carefully weighed sentences—attests to a sober and disciplined craftsman. Fitzgerald didn't so much crack up as grow up—for a while anyway. He realized, or said he did, that he had been defeated, and this defeat, which may have reminded him of his father's, made him realize that he had been harboring illusions about himself, and such a realization must necessarily alter the future. He could no longer count on hope or love to sustain him, no longer take for granted his talent. He was played out, he had used up his emotional capital. None of this, of course, turned out to be the case, but it felt true at the time—or did it?

A poser is not a fakir, and Fitzgerald ought to be given the benefit of the doubt. Writers, after all, are in the pretend business whether they're writing fiction or nonfiction. Fitzgerald wasn't being sly, nor did he deliberately set out to deceive. But to overlook the possibility that he is posing in *The Crack-Up* is to seriously underestimate the level of awareness he brought to his work. Because he was a writer obsessed with his own progress in the world, Fitzgerald was necessarily fascinated by his own decline. He'd gone from being a healthy young man to a sick, middle-aged one, from a celebrated novelist to a literary nonentity, from a social creature to a lone, brooding failure (though, of course, it was not that cut-and-dried), and this was, well, interesting. His disenchantment was real enough, but it was also something he could get copy out of. As long as he could write about his troubles, he could never sink into absolute darkness. Gingrich described him in those days as "a blend of insouciance and despair."[10]

Something was gone, Fitzgerald claimed, something essential, and all that remained was the writer: "I must continue to be a writer because that was my only way of life, but I would cease any attempts to be a person. . . . It was strange to have no self—to be like a little boy left alone in a big house, who knew that he could do anything that he wanted to do, but found that there was nothing that he wanted to do."[11] This, I'm afraid, does not sound like a man who believes what he's saying. It's no simple matter knowing when a writer is being completely honest, but a confessional tone guarantees very little.

Kazin, of course, picks up on this and, like any good analyst, listens to what doesn't get said. Because Fitzgerald's prose is so obviously burnished, Kazin cannot imagine that it is entirely sincere: "Everything had to be faintly and deliciously supported on a lightly running river of little golden words . . . even *The Crack-Up* had to be subtly bent to sound good."[12] Kazin is probably right. When Fitzgerald sat down to write, life deferred to the sound and sense of sentences being formed on the page. Another way of saying this is that the confessional essays he wrote in Hendersonville read too well to be the whole truth.[13]

Kazin stumbles, in my view, only when he speculates that Fitzgerald "could create Gatsby only at the price of never admitting that he *was* Gatsby, just as he could develop as a writer by disguising the fact that he thirsted for immediate goals, for that impalpable social world where people derived their self-importance by battening on each other."[14] It seems to me that Fitzgerald never hid either proposition from himself. Nor should we lose sight of the fact that the three essays were written *after* he had supposedly cracked up. What we're reading is really a three-part memoir, and we know that memoirs are not necessarily instruments of truth telling. Fitzgerald claims that he has changed. Maybe so. Does that mean he's no longer "one of the most expert liars in the world" who expects everyone "to discount nine-tenths" of what he says? As a liar, however, he was a dud. But as a man who made up stories, he tended to tell the truth.

Kazin might have benefited from reading Fitzgerald's obituary of Ring Lardner, who, Fitzgerald said, had "agreed with himself to speak only a small portion of his mind."[15] That is precisely what I think Fitzgerald did in "The Crack-Up," "Pasting It Together," and "Handle with

Third Impressions

Care." In the very first piece, Fitzgerald identifies himself as "a cracked plate." Soon he becomes a plate that "can never again be warmed on the stove nor stuffed with the other plates in the dishpan; it will not be brought out for company, but it will do to hold crackers."[16] This isn't desperation speaking; this is a writer at work.

In one of the most quoted lines from *The Crack-Up* (to which I alluded earlier), Fitzgerald reflects that until the age of thirty he believed that "life was something you dominated if you were any good." He probably believed this, and it must have come as a shock to discover he wasn't really equipped to dominate. In the same vein, he acknowledges beliefs about love, friendship, and ambition that had once seemed important to him but now meant very little. None of this is particularly persuasive, and when we step back and compare what he's saying with what we know about him, we realize that he's not so much confessing as building another persona for himself:

> I have now at last become a writer only. The man I had persistently tried to be became such a burden that I have "cut him loose" with as little compunction as a Negro lady cuts loose a rival on Saturday night....
>
> The old dream of being an entire man in the Goethe-Byron-Shaw tradition, with an opulent American touch, a sort of combination of J. P. Morgan, Topham Beauclerk [son of Lord Sidney Beauclerk and a friend of Dr. Johnson], and St. Francis of Assisi, has been relegated to the junk heap of the shoulder pads worn for one day on the Princeton freshman football field and the overseas cap never worn overseas.[17]

Aside from the curious allusion to the Goethe-Byron-Shaw tradition, which to my mind calls up no tradition at all, it's interesting that Fitzgerald not only makes a distinction between the writer and the writer as "an entire man" but also suggests that a writer *could* be a whole person while at the same time acknowledging it as a foolish dream. For Kazin the emphasis lies elsewhere. He thinks that Fitzgerald wanted to stop being a person because it was too difficult; being a writer was easier. So here Kazin takes him at his word. But should he? Fitzgerald, after all, expostulates at the drop of an emotion; he has an initial response to events, then another, then still another, each time qualifying what he's said before. The man could make you believe almost anything because he himself seemed certain of its truth—but the truth is, Fitzgerald never became "a writer only" whose shoulder pads and overseas cap rested in the back of a closet.

No one can state with certainty what Fitzgerald was feeling when he wrote the *Esquire* articles or whether he would have written them at all if Arnold Gingrich had not expressed an interest. What if his stories had been selling, what if *Tender Is the Night* had been a bestseller, what if Zelda had miraculously recovered—would the Skyland Hotel have figured among Fitzgerald's many residences? Sadly, he did have an appointment in Hendersonville, and we're still asking ourselves whether the essays he wrote there constitute a heartfelt, spontaneous confession or the careful exposition of a wounded soul. I, for one, don't find them as restrained as Kazin does; then again, I don't think they're less sincere for being the product of a literary intelligence. The two—sincerity and artifice of expression—are not mutually exclusive.

What seems reasonable is that his physical deterioration brought on by booze, pills, and cigarettes, his disintegrating marriage, his anxiety over money, the emotional cost of churning out mediocre stories to pay the bills, and his exhaustion all worked to erode his self-confidence, which, because it was so necessary for him to function socially, eroded the self as well. So whatever we may think of *The Crack-Up*, it *does* seem to be the work of a man who feels that he's no longer the man he used to be. Fitzgerald may have boarded the train to Los Angeles in 1937 with a determination to succeed in Hollywood, but according to friends who ran into him, the bounce had gone out of his step.

Jeffrey Meyers, following Aaron Latham's lead in *Crazy Sundays*, says without hesitation, "All of Fitzgerald's friends noticed a radical alteration in his character, after his misfortunes and nervous breakdown."[18] He quotes from an interview with Ring Lardner Jr., who as a boy had often seen Fitzgerald in the company of his father: "such a change in personality; from a brash, cheerful, optimistic, ambitious, driving young man to this withdrawn, very quiet, shy man that he had become."[19]

Lois Moran, the ingénue he had been smitten with in 1927, also found him much changed, and John O'Hara noted that he seemed "completely alone, had lost confidence, was wounded, insecure and uncertain."[20] Well, he was older, his health was poor, and he wasn't drinking as much. Staying sober has its drawbacks. Anita Loos thought that he "had taken on the apologetic humility which is often characteristic of reformed drunks." She found him to be shyer and sweeter than when she knew him in New York and noted ruefully that "between being dangerous when drunk and eating humble pie when sober, I preferred Scott dangerous."[21] No doubt he did appear changed, but this quiet, withdrawn Fitzgerald was simply another of his personas. He hadn't so much changed as he was now leaning into a less boisterous part of himself.

"WRITERS AREN'T PEOPLE exactly," the narrator in *The Last Tycoon* remarks. "Or, if they're any good, they're a whole lot of people trying so hard to be one person."[22] The comment is oddly reminiscent of Nicole's response in *Tender Is the Night* when she is accused of being complicated: "No, I'm not really—I'm just a—I'm just a whole lot of different simple people."[23] One of the people Fitzgerald envisioned being was a professional screenwriter. "I was confident to the point of conceit," he wrote to Scottie when heading out to California the third time. "I honestly believed that *with no effort on my part* I was a sort of magician with words—an odd delusion on my part when I had worked so desperately hard to develop a hard, colorful prose style."[24]

Part of the problem is that Fitzgerald took the movies seriously. His ego simply couldn't accept his lack of ability. He could be a good screenwriter, he thought; he could even be, if given the same opportunity as

Preston Sturges, a good director. But the studios held him back. And for someone who wanted to lead an unfettered life, it must have been especially galling to suffer the messy dictates of having to earn a living and kowtowing to the whims of others. In short, he knew everything there was to know about writing for the movies except how to write a good screenplay.

In Hollywood, people "treated him like an invalid," Anita Loos recalled.[25] A "very grim, very dim, slightly plump" man, George Cukor said dismissively.[26] And what did this dim and plump man feel about what he was doing? That would depend on which day you asked him. On a Monday, screenwriting could be "a sort of tense crossword puzzle game . . . a surprisingly interesting intellectual exercise."[27] On a Tuesday, it might represent "a rankling indignity."[28] Unresolved feelings bubbled up in him to the very end: "Isn't Hollywood a dump," he wrote to a friend in 1940, "in the human sense of the word. A hideous town, pointed up by the insulting gardens of its rich, full of the human spirit at a new low of debasement."[29] Sure it was—but it was also, as he well knew, part of the American character. It was Hollywood that lay stretched out before him when he jotted down in his notes, "I look out at it—and I think it is the most beautiful history in the world. It is the history of me and of my people. . . . It is the history of all aspiration—not just the American dream but the human dream and if I came at the end of it that too is a place in the line of the pioneers."[30]

But Hollywood required accommodations he could not make. Collaboration is not a novelist's strong suit; and perhaps more than most writers, Fitzgerald resented having his work poked at. But his hatred of the studio system was not bolstered sufficiently by contempt. He sincerely wanted the respect of studio executives, not just because they held the purse strings but because his self-esteem required it. It galled him to think that "while the story of an official blacklist is a legend, there is a kind of cabal that goes on between producers around a backgammon table" that had put a "sinister finger" on him. "I only know that I have a strong intuition that all is not well with my reputation," he wrote to the producer Leland Hayward, "and I'd like to know what is being said or not said."[31] A fair indication of how Fitzgerald got along with the Hollywood brass can be gleaned from a résumé Hayward asked him to write:

> I worked with Sidney Franklin on "The Women" and on "Madame Curie." Whether he would be interested in working with me again I don't know. Anyhow his boss, Bernie Hyman, quite definitely does not like me.... Hunt [Stromberg] and I ... wore each other out. He liked the first part of a picture called "Infidelity" ... [and] when the whole thing flopped I think he held it against me that I had aroused his hope so much.... Wanger is out absolutely. Goldwyn I know nothing about. Sam Wood and I had always gotten along before, but during the week that I was there on "Raffles" everything got a little strained and I don't think he would welcome me as a collaborator.[32]

Setting aside the indignity of having to submit a résumé at this stage in his career, there remains something admirable in Fitzgerald's old habit of honest self-appraisal. He's going to tell the truth even at the cost of his self-esteem. For years, though, he resisted the idea that he was at fault for not having succeeded in Hollywood. His friend Helen Hayes told Aaron Latham that "Hollywood was so much more bizarre than even he could be.... Pictures took writers right back to the working climate of high school."[33]

Fitzgerald wasn't entirely miserable. Arriving in Hollywood in 1937, he gaily wrote to Anne Ober that he had "talked with [Robert] Taylor, dined with [Fredric] March, danced with Ginger Rogers (this will burn Scottie up but it's true), been in Rosalind Russell's dressing room, wisecracked with [Robert] Montgomery ... lunched alone with Maureen O'Sullivan." Then, as if suddenly recalling that it's his agent's wife he's writing to, he declares that he's through with star gazing. He has lots to do and needs to buckle down.[34] But a few months later, he writes to Scottie: "Norma Shearer invited me to dinner three times but I couldn't go. . . . Took Beatrice [Lillie], Charley MacArthur . . . and Sheilah to the Tennis Club the other night, and Errol Flynn joined us—he seemed very nice though rather silly and fatuous."[35]

When not pleading or arguing with producers, he worked on his Pat Hobby stories, spent time with Sheilah Graham, assigned her books to read, acted out parts that he'd written, and visited friends. He bought a used car from S. J. Perelman, and sometimes he and Graham visited Perelman's brother-in-law Nathanael West and his wife, Eileen, in North Hollywood. Looking back, Sheilah Graham marveled at "what a full active life [they] had." They went to restaurants and movie theaters, they went dancing, and saw such friends as Dorothy Parker, Ogden Nash, Nunnally Johnson, and Marc Connelly.[36]

Fitzgerald wasn't forgotten exactly; he had simply been demoted to the rank of jobber or pieceworker—that is to say, a screenwriter. When Budd Schulberg learned that he was going to work with Fitzgerald, he confessed that he didn't even know that Fitzgerald was still alive: "My generation thought of F. Scott Fitzgerald as an age rather than as a writer, and when the economic strike of 1929 began to change the sheikhs and flappers into unemployed boys and underpaid girls, we consciously and a little belligerently turned our backs on Fitzgerald."[37] How odd it must have felt, the loss of the respect he had once enjoyed. He had acquired a great reputation in his youth, but now, having lost it, he lost something of himself as well. To a man like Fitzgerald, whose self-worth depended so much on the opinion of others, a lack of recognition was the same as a lack of accomplishment; and nothing is quite so humiliating to the serious man as finding himself trivialized in the public mind. Better by far to be maligned or misunderstood than marginalized.

Nonetheless, Fitzgerald didn't quit trying to make it. There was still something feisty in him, a gallows humor that emerges in the Pat Hobby stories. And, of course, he continued to list and take stock of everything that happened, recording in the *Notebooks* and letters all his follies, disappointments, and unruly urges. (One has to wonder what he was keeping back, what foul dust floated in the wake of *his* dreams?)

Third Impressions

As for regrets, he had a few. In a letter to Scottie in July 1938, he wrote, "You don't realize that what I am doing here is the last tired effort of a man who once did something finer and better."[38] And a year or so later he wrote again: "I wish now I'd never relaxed or looked back—but said at the end of *The Great Gatsby:* I've found my line—from now on this comes first. This is my immediate duty—without this I am nothing."[39] Although the sentiment rings true, it was said by a man who felt himself a failure. One can't help wondering if he would have made these remarks if his screenplays were getting produced. He was being sincere, just as he was being sincere in September 1940 when he wrote that he still hoped to be known as a movie man and not a novelist. It was only toward the very end of his life that he acknowledged he "just couldn't make the grade as a hack—that, like everything else, requires a certain practiced excellence."[40] But it's a sure bet he would have taken another stab at it had a studio given him another chance.

In the end, Fitzgerald drew his faith not from camera angles or even plotlines but from sentences, and what draws us powerfully to his work is the sensitive handling of emotional yearning and regret. When he was revising *Gatsby,* he characterized the burden of the novel as "the loss of those illusions that give such color to the world so that you don't care whether things are true or false as long as they partake of the magical glory."[41] As Mizener pointed out, "It is precisely this loss which allows Gatsby to discover 'what a grotesque thing a rose is and how raw the sunlight was upon the scarcely created grass.'"[42] Perhaps Fitzgerald could have captured this heightened state of awareness in a script, but was this what the studios were looking for? Fitzgerald's vision of becoming a great screenwriter was no more realistic than the likelihood of returning a kickoff for a touchdown or writing a hit Broadway show. But, then, Fitzgerald was not one to give up on dreams; if he had, he could not have written so beautifully, so penetratingly, about their loss.[43]

Fitzgerald's America III

IF THE 1920S HAD been about America priding itself on success, the 1930s were about America coming to terms with failure. If jobs didn't exist for those willing to work, if our leaders were fallible, if America was not necessarily the land of opportunity, then what was the country about? At the very moment when James Truslow Adams's *The Epic of America* (1931) popularized the phrase "the American Dream," people began to wonder if the dream was nothing more than that. Without work, without even the prospect of work, how could a person survive, much less thrive?[1] Social mobility, once the bedrock of the American Dream, itself seemed an illusion.

Nonetheless, Americans for the most part did not give up on their country. Roughly fifteen million people may have been jobless (25 percent of the workforce) and two million homeless, and more than one hundred thousand were members of the Communist Party, yet the great majority never thought to question the democratic system. Jobless or not, it was still good to be an American.[2] In fact, the nation's difficulties caused people to reassess what being an American meant. It was during the Depression, as the historian Warren Susman argued, that American culture became "domesticated. . . . Americans began thinking in terms of patterns of behavior and belief, values and life-styles, symbols and meanings. It was now that references to an 'American Way of Life' became a rhetorical fixture in speeches and books."[3] To be an American wasn't just a phrase; it encapsulated a point of view that not only distinguished us from our European cousins but also signified our response to hard times.

Although the myth of America the bountiful lost some of its luster, and the benefits of ownership and hard work were put to the test, this was still God's country, even if God was short of pocket money. We knew this because Hollywood and Tin Pan Alley told us so. In the 1930s, popular culture came out swinging with musicals and feel-good movies about magical changes of fortune. Horatio Alger didn't live long enough to write for the movies, but his plots burbled beneath films in which poor boys triumph and jobless men and women meet with guardian angels. As if to soften the economic blow, the movies began to find untapped values in an *earlier* America, in the bluff honesty of the frontier and the homespun wisdom of regular folk.

In the midst of a great urban upheaval when people were pouring into cities to find work, the American ideal became identified with the small town, where American values and virtues continued to flourish. If you wanted to escape corruption, cynicism, defeatism, and despair, all you had to do was find your way to Grover's Corners, USA, where good people made for good citizens. Moreover, this was an America where every citizen, wherever he or she lived, could now share in a culture that stretched from one coast to the other. Radio and the phonographic disc connected Tin Pan Alley to Wilshire Boulevard. "Brother, Can You Spare a Dime?" "Easter Parade," "Forty-Second Street," "Cheek to Cheek," "On the Good Ship Lollipop," "You're the Top," "Night and Day," and the movies in which they appeared became part of the national parlance.[4]

It's odd to think that so much of what we associate with America did not exist earlier. True, there were common reference points—the

Constitution and the Founding Fathers, the Civil War, the frontier, the First World War, presidential elections—but the nation itself was characterized more by sectarianism than uniformity. It can be argued that the consumer culture of the 1920s, along with the ascendancy of sports, entertainment, and advertising, also helped engender nationalistic feelings, but it was the Great Depression that made Americans feel that we were all in the same boat.

Apart from the Civil War, the Depression probably affected the lives of more Americans than any one phenomenon in the nation's history. Nonetheless, it did not become a *national* trauma until the media made it one. In a sense, the 1930s were a call to arms, offering hope by selling comforting and inspiring images of the nation. Hollywood executives, for example, did not see an America that was inherently flawed. Vaguely Gatsby-like in their own rise, they liked to tell stories of men with names like John Doe, Jefferson Smith, George Bailey, and Longfellow Deeds, whose values both reflected and replenished Americans' respect for simplicity, common sense, and hard work. So at the same time that Americans were feeling the economic pinch, a wave of populism curbed widespread insurrectionist feelings.

For artists and intellectuals, the decade presented another dichotomy: how were they to register the effects of poverty while also deploying modernist methods that focused more on complex states of consciousness than on society's ills? "The tension in the 1930s between a resurgent naturalism and a subterranean modernism, between a desire to bear witness to the social fact and an insistence on the individual character of all witness, all perception," Morris Dickstein asserts, "was at the heart of the portrayal of poverty in the 1930s."[5] So much poverty and misery could not be ignored by artists who were often themselves strapped for cash. John Steinbeck, for one, could not afford postage in 1932, much less a dentist for his rotting teeth.

Fitzgerald, of course, was not such an artist. Although not unmindful of innovative techniques in fiction and poetry, he was savvy enough to know his own strengths. Nor did he, as his critics never tired of pointing out, concern himself with the plight of ordinary people, much less the wretched conditions of the poor. Fitzgerald wasn't exactly recruitment material for the WPA or the Federal Writers Project. Of course, this didn't stop him from delivering the occasional snippet of anticapitalist rhetoric. In fact, Fitzgerald positioned himself on the left years before the Communist Party in 1936 established a "Popular Front"; he even had the gall to describe himself as "essentially Marxian."[6]

How long did the essential Marxist in him last? Only until his more analytical side decided that progress and progressive politics are not necessarily the same thing. In a 1933 letter to Perkins, he stated: "A decision to adopt Communism definitely, no matter how good for the soul, must of necessity be a saddening process for anyone who has ever tasted the intellectual pleasures of the world we live in."[7] And a year later, he writes to a cousin: "It will interest you to know that I've given up politics. For two years I've gone haywire trying to reconcile my double allegiance to the class I am part of and the Great Change I believe in. . . . I have become disgusted with the party leadership . . . + their treatment of the negro question finished me. This is confidential, of course."[8]

But he never hid his political leanings; it's just that no one took them very seriously. Budd Schulberg remembers Fitzgerald showing up at his home in 1939 very excited after reading Spengler's *Decline of the West*. On another occasion, he found him absorbed in Marx's *The Eighteenth Brumaire*. According to Schulberg, who considered him "an eager sociology student bucking for an A in Bunny Wilson's class in social consciousness," Fitzgerald had looked up from the book and exclaimed, "I have to reexamine the economic relationships and the economic context of all my characters."[9] He was referring to *The Last Tycoon*, which at one point pits Monroe Stahr against a local official of the Communist Party. Here, as in *Tender Is the Night* and *The Beautiful and Damned*, Fitzgerald sought a wider historical context for his protagonists. He had previously linked Dick Diver with Ulysses S. Grant (someone else whose career had stalled), and now he linked Stahr with

Lincoln. Ultimately, however, he was less interested in the troubles of society than in the turbulence of individuals.

Fitzgerald was hardly a dedicated leftist, but his sympathies were, all things considered, decidedly left-of-center, and his feelings about social and economic inequities found their way into his fiction almost from the first. In *This Side of Paradise,* he briefly allows Amory Blaine to speak for the underclass: "I'm sick of a system where the richest man gets the most beautiful girl if he wants her, where the artist without an income has to sell his talents to a button manufacturer."[10] Two years later he writes to Perkins that he's "still a socialist," though he fears that "things will grow worse the more the people nominally rule. The strong are too strong for us and the weak too weak."[11]

Whatever Marxist pieties Fitzgerald espoused in private, however, had little to do with his comportment in public. Although he regarded America as a bastion of class differences, his work did not challenge societal norms as did the novels of James T. Farrell, Henry Roth, or the Southern Agrarians such as Allan Tate, John Crowe Ransom, and Robert Penn Warren. Social criticism seemed almost obligatory at the time, and fictional portrayals of ethnic groups were often a denunciation of America's obsession with money and power. On one level at least, the portrayals of the redneck residents of Yoknapatawpha County, the Catholic Chicagoans of the *Studs Lonigan* trilogy, the Jewish poor of New York in *Call It Sleep,* and the wandering Okies in *The Grapes of Wrath* all questioned the values of a capitalist society.

Still, it was a complicated and variegated society, since one consequence of the Great Depression—spurred by the New Deal's funding for the arts—was the emergence of authors from formerly neglected segments of the population. Few previous decades could claim the production of such a diverse literature, to say nothing of the various movies, songs, photographs, and plays that bookended the 1930s. No wonder America seemed an amalgam of contradictory attitudes and impulses: traditionalism vs. radicalism, sentimentality vs. hard-boiledness, individualism vs. communal idealism.

But despite the reproaches of various political and aesthetic factions, most Americans kept faith with the American Dream. Whatever one thought of government or the excesses of capitalism, relatively few artists or writers actually denied the uniqueness of, or the promise in, our national charter.

BECAUSE AMERICA HAD risen so spectacularly and then fallen so rapidly between 1922 and 1932, the correlation between quality of life and the material advancement of civilization became problematic. Industrial progress and technological achievement apparently did not guarantee success or self-fulfillment. One could work hard, behave well, and still fail—a realization that led people to wonder if a laissez-faire capitalist society was consistent with a meaningful way of life.

But America was supposed to be about fulfillment, the one nation where men were *supposed* to pursue happiness.[12] Indeed, many Americans took it as an article of faith, and when the economy collapsed, they filed lawsuits in state and federal courts accusing the powers that be (and fellow citizens alike) of preventing or impeding the plaintiff's right to happiness.[13] These suits were frivolous, of course, but symbolically they indicted America for having abrogated its responsibility. For surely it was this belief in the possibility of happiness that engendered the American Dream. And just as Jay Gatsby sprang from a Platonic conception of himself, so, too, did America. What is America but a romantic ideal issuing from the minds of Rousseau and Locke by way of Jefferson and Franklin? As Trilling noted in his essay on Fitzgerald, "Ours is the only nation that prides itself upon a dream and gives its name to one, 'the American Dream.'"[14]

For a good part of his life, Fitzgerald bought into this dream. He came of age when America seemed ready to fulfill the promise engraved in the Declaration of Independence. America was a place where people—middle-class white people anyway—could better themselves, where songs, plays, magazines, and silent films offered the hope that people could have what they wanted. Fitzgerald's dream and the American Dream, both silhouetted in *The Great Gatsby,* thus converged at a moment when the novelist and the nation seemed poised for bigger and better things.

Not to put too fine a point on it, the 1930s ended the dream for both the novelist and the nation. It wasn't easy to give up on happiness—not when you had deliberately set out after it, not when you thought it was within your grasp. With the exception of Arthur Mizener, most biographers skip over Fitzgerald's many allusions to happiness. Mizener, however, saw that he "believed very deeply not only in the ecstasy of happiness, which he knew by direct experience, but in the possibility of making it a habit and the object of one's mind."[15] Indeed, the young Fitzgerald seemed at times fixated on happiness, thinking that if he just stretched his hand out a little further, tried a little harder, it would be his. No writer before or since, I think, has been so obsessed with happiness.[16] Because when Fitzgerald was happy, he was self-consciously happy: "My own happiness," he wrote, "often approached such an ecstasy that I could not share it even with the person dearest to me but had to walk it away in quiet streets and lanes with only fragments of it to distill into little lines in books."[17]

There must have been a moment, perhaps a dozen moments, after the publication of his first novel when Fitzgerald felt as though everything he had dreamed of as a boy in St. Paul was coming to pass. He had the girl, the money, the book, the fame, and the possibility of a brilliant future—but what did Fitzgerald think about? He thought about loss, that he would never again be so happy. If the story of his bawling in a cab in 1920 is true, then the person in the cab is the one we admire, the one who didn't need to conquer the world or look to it for validation but who sensed the impermanence of love and the perishability of desire. This is the admirer of Keats rather than the toady of Hemingway, the author of *Gatsby* rather than the scenarist fuming away in Culver City. It is *this* Fitzgerald who ultimately matters to us, the one who makes his life worth writing about.

Most people—to offer a general observation—do not actively seek happiness. They may desire it, but what they pursue are the things they think produce happiness: friendship, love, material possessions, status, and so on. Happiness isn't a goal but a by-product or, in the case of spiritual longing, a sense of contentment embedded in belief. In any event, happiness doesn't make for drama; indeed, it's the opposite of drama, which is why Tolstoy moves quickly from happy to unhappy families, and why Fitzgerald did as well.

Yet in his letters and *Notebooks,* the concept tugs at him. Whereas other men wish to retire to a house by the ocean, Fitzgerald searched for "the eternal Carnival by the Sea."[18] He desired worldly success but sensed it wasn't enough. Perhaps this longing stemmed from his exposure to Father Fay's Catholicism or from his own peculiar brand of Platonism, this desire for perfection in love, in friendship, and in life itself.[19] "I go crazy when people aren't always at their best," he wrote to Hemingway in 1926, a remark so pregnant with irony it makes one wince.[20]

F. Scott Fitzgerald didn't want much: He wanted love, literary acclaim, athletic prowess, and Broadway and Hollywood success. Worse still, he wanted happiness. He wanted these things so fervently, thought about them so intensely, and pursued them so avidly that he never stood a chance. Even if Zelda hadn't suffered a mental breakdown, even if the critics had uniformly praised him, even if his novels had made potloads of money, no man so keenly aware of his own weaknesses could be happy.

After Scott's death, Zelda wrote: "Now that he won't be coming east again with his pockets full of promises and his notebooks full of schemes and new refurbished hope, life doesn't offer as happy a vista. . . . He was as spiritually generous a soul as ever was. In retrospect it seems as if he was always planning happiness for Scottie, and for me. Books to read—places to go. Life seemed so promissory always when he was around: and I always believed that he could take care of anything."[21]

In time he came to understand the impracticality of fervent desire, of asking what life could not grant. "This is what I think now," he wrote in 1936, "that the natural state of the sentient adult is a qualified unhappiness. I think also that in an adult the desire to be finer in grain than you are . . . only adds to this unhappiness in the end—that end that comes to our youth and hope."[22] The thought, slightly reworded, could have been the concluding sentence to one of his stories, and it makes us think that there *is* an essential Scott, a better Scott than the one who often behaves ignobly or foolishly.

IN LILLIAN ROSS'S 1950 *New Yorker* profile of Hemingway, the Los Angeles restaurateur Prince Michael Romanoff summed up Fitzgerald's career in a glib yet apt phrase: "He was a failure as a success—and a failure as a failure."[23] The first statement is, of course, a gloss on his profligacy, his drinking, and drug taking; the second suggests that even as a washed-up novelist he wasn't exactly destitute. Except for a brief period in the mid-1930s, Fitzgerald always managed to earn money; he simply didn't know how to keep it. But such ineptitude ultimately did not define or deter him.

Perhaps it was once in the American character: the belief that you could set the speed and course of your own life. And certainly Fitzgerald wanted to dominate life because happiness existed when people realized their potential, a potential made tangible by wealth. Hemingway accused him of sucking up to the rich, and Fitzgerald himself made no bones about it: "I was always trying to be one of them," he admitted. "That's worse than being nothing at all."[24] But there was more to him than that. In truth, he thought the American leisure class "probably the most shallow, most hollow, most pernicious leisure class in the world. It has frequently no consciousness that leisure is a privilege, not a right, and that a privilege always implies a responsibility."[25]

Although he could be "a suck" around the rich, he was never able to forgive them for being rich, and it "colored [his] entire life and works."[26] Still, one should grant him some leeway. He wasn't simply seeking wealth; wealth was a means to an end. Ronald Berman put it succinctly: Fitzgerald "associated wealth with the power to improve character."[27] And character consisted in the resolve to become and to remain the person one wished to be.

And wasn't America about the self-made man, the man who could make a self? For Fitzgerald, the idea of inventing oneself was not an abstraction; it was a fact in the burly shape of Theodore Roosevelt, who, according to Mencken, epitomized the American character, the very incarnation of possibility. As Berman notes: "[Mencken] was fascinated precisely with the quality in Roosevelt least associated with his privileged class, the desire for self-transformation."[28] Needless to say, Fitzgerald, too, was struck by Roosevelt's capacity to change. When we think of Fitzgerald's heroes, we don't recall their worldly accomplishments but the dreams that compel them.

Both Dick Diver and Monroe Stahr initially possess a boundless belief in themselves, and this conviction, when it disappears, becomes their downfall. "Show me a hero and I'll write you a tragedy," their creator said.[29] Less capable men, men with less empathy and imagination, make their way through life never suffering the knowledge that they are less than they once believed themselves to be. It's a Jamesian theme given a poignant Fitzgeraldian twist: the superior individual who gradually comes to realize that sensitivity and intelligence are not enough to gain love or happiness, and that perhaps it's one's own heightened awareness of life's possibilities that makes one vulnerable.

Such self-consciousness is the stuff of modernism, and in this sense, Fitzgerald is a modernist writer. Whereas Gatsby was safe from self-knowledge, Diver and Stahr were not. Fitzgerald grew wiser as a writer, coming to understand that a character's integrity, while linked to his grandness of vision, might also be his downfall. Stahr, in fact, is an Icarus-like figure, someone who dares greatly but is unable to fulfill the promises he made to himself: "He had flown up very high to see, on strong wings, when he was young. And while he was up there he looked on all the kingdoms, with the kind of eyes that can stare straight into the sun. Beating his wings tenaciously—finally frantically—and keeping on beating them, he had stayed up there longer than most of us, and then, remembering all he had seen from his great height of how things were, he had settled gradually to earth."[30]

There are people who keep tabs on just about everything that happens to them, including their own thoughts. We call such people "writers"—but even among this particular genus, Fitzgerald stands out. His narcissism didn't shut out the world but engaged it, and in that engagement, which he framed in terms of "winning" or "dominating," lay the hope of a more perfect existence. No wonder he began to bawl when he thought he had everything; he sensed it was an illusion, he knew that whatever is gained must one day be lost. Although he never came to regard life as a punishment for having been born, he deeply resented his hapless state, his inability to control his own destiny.

The Reputation

"FITZGERALD IS A SUBJECT no one has a right to mess up. If the poor guy was already an alcoholic in his college days, it's a marvel that he did as well as he did."[1] I come back to Raymond Chandler's remark because his subject didn't make things easy for himself or his biographers. Some authors manage—because of their books—to rise above their behavior; Fitzgerald is not among them. His curious mix of deference and overbearance, of sentimentality and hard-headedness, of aiming high but settling for low, did not serve him well; and for much of his life, his fiction, with the exception of *Gatsby* and a good dozen of the stories, was seen as not quite first-rate. Even when his fiction struck a favorable chord with reviewers, it was as though its success had been achieved by verbal legerdemain rather than by intellect or reason.

His intelligence was impugned from the start by, as it happens, his best friends. "It has been said by a celebrated person that to meet F. Scott Fitzgerald is to think of a stupid old woman with whom someone has left a diamond," Edmund Wilson wrote, quoting Edna St. Vincent Millay. "She is extremely proud of the diamond and shows it to everyone who comes by, and everyone is surprised that such an ignorant old woman should possess so valuable a jewel; for in nothing does she appear so inept as in the remarks she makes about the diamond."[2]

Then, as if to correct Millay's impressions, Wilson adds:

> Scott Fitzgerald is, in fact, no old woman, but a very good-looking young man, nor is he in the least stupid, but, on the contrary, exhilaratingly clever. Yet there *is* a symbolic truth in the description quoted above: it is true that Fitzgerald has been left with a jewel which he doesn't know quite what to do with. For he has been given imagination without intellectual control of it; he has been given the desire for beauty without an aesthetic ideal; and he has been given a gift for expression without very many ideas to express.[3]

The condescension of these words is breathtaking, and one may want to spring to Fitzgerald's defense, except that Wilson is speaking of the early work. Aside from decent passages here and there, *This Side of Paradise* and *The Beautiful and Damned* are just not very good. Reviewing the latter, John Peale Bishop suggested that Fitzgerald treated ideas like "paper crackers, things to make a gay and pretty noise with and then be cast aside; he is frequently at the mercy of words with which he has only a nodding acquaintance; his aesthetics are faulty; his literary taste is at times extremely bad." Nor does Bishop redeem himself upon concluding, "But these are flaws of vulgarity in one who is awkward with his own vigor."[4]

H. L. Mencken, also a friend, began his review of *The Great Gatsby* by calling it "a glorified anecdote, and not too probable at that.... This clown [Gatsby] Fitzgerald rushes to his death in nine short chapters.... The story is obviously unimportant."[5] Although Mencken eventually gets around to applauding the author's pellucid style and his interest in "the florid show of modern American life," the review doesn't exactly summon respect for Fitzgerald's brainpower.[6] Another critic, also friendly to Fitzgerald, Glenway Wescott, acknowledged his talent but speculated that he "must have been the worst educated man in the world."[7]

Even after his books won critical acclaim, readers continued to doubt his IQ. In a 1945 article in the *Partisan Review*, Andrew Wanning held that Fitzgerald "was not an original thinker . . . not, as I said before, a thinker."[8] In 1952, Tom Burnam ventured, "The more one thinks about *The Great Gatsby,* the more one comes to believe that F. Scott Fitzgerald may not have entirely realized what he was doing."[9] One really has to pause at this. It's ridiculous to suggest that Fitzgerald was naïve; he knew perfectly well what he was up to, as his letters to Bishop and Perkins attest.

It gets worse. Malcolm Cowley, for reasons of his own, decided that Fitzgerald, despite all the books he read, was "not a thinker. He counted on his friends to do much of his thinking."[10] In the 1960s, Leslie Fiedler suggested that Fitzgerald had "a second-rate sensitive mind . . . and a weak gift for construction."[11] And Kazin, who admired the work, thought him a writer "whose actual intelligence was never equal to his talent and whose talent was always greater than his experiences."[12] "Suffering," Kazin claimed unwisely, "is always proportionate to intelligence, and is often an escape from intelligence. Fitzgerald's is of this kind; and that is why it is not moving."[13] The insult is both simplistic and double-edged: If one buys into the premise that the intelligent suffer more acutely than the less intelligent, how does one actually go about escaping from intelligence? Moreover, how do we appraise evidence of emotional pain when a writer's cri de coeur is often a carefully worded one?

Fitzgerald, of course, didn't help his own cause. His public displays and his obsession with fame, fashion, football, popular music, movies, and screen actresses are not perhaps the qualities of a serious person. The truth is, he battened on celebrity and often appeared glib and conceited in articles and interviews. But then a great many writers have behaved foolishly—Hazlitt, Poe, Dostoevsky, Wilde, Frost, Pound, and Bellow spring to mind. Look hard enough and one finds unappealing facets to Tolstoy, Joyce, and Henry James, not to mention Edmund Wilson himself. But, then, writers are not bound to behave better than other people, and just as a boorish shoemaker can make an excellent pair of boots, or a socially awkward physicist can discover important laws of nature, so a bumptious writer can write a great book. Edmund Wilson may have regarded Fitzgerald as "a rather childlike fellow," but that wasn't the fellow who wrote *Gatsby,* and it's a shame that Wilson couldn't distinguish between them until it was too late.

Fitzgerald can certainly strike us as someone whose mind flowed toward too many worldly concerns, but he was also a man of taste, and what he loved, he loved wisely. In a letter to Scottie, he says what every teacher of literature should recite to her class every morning:

> Poetry is either something that lives like fire inside of you—like music to the musician or Marxism to the Communist—or else it is nothing, an empty, formalized bore, around which pedants can endlessly drone their notes and explanations. *The Grecian Urn* is unbearably beautiful with every syllable as inevitable as the notes in Beethoven's Ninth Symphony, or it's just something you don't understand. It is what it is because an extraordinary genius paused at that point in history and touched it. I suppose I've read it a hundred times. About the tenth time I began to know what it was about, and caught the chime in it and the exquisite inner mechanics. . . . For awhile after you quit Keats all other poetry seems to be only whistling or humming.[14]

This Side of Paradise may be filled with "bogus ideas and faked literary references," as Wilson acidly pointed out, but Fitzgerald also had a finely tuned ear for poetry and prose. He knew the real thing when he read it because he knew what made it real: "All fine prose is based on the verbs carrying the sentences," he said, referring to "The Eve of St. Agnes." "A line like 'The hare limped trembling through the frozen grass' is so alive that you race through it, scarcely noticing it, yet it has colored the whole poem with its movement—the limping, trembling and freezing is going on before your eyes."[15]

No one can mistake Fitzgerald for a systematic thinker, but he thought enough about literature to be capable of separating the wheat from the chaff. He simply lacked the true intellectual's capacity to embrace confidently his own opinions. Would Joyce and Shaw think less of themselves if people, even people they admired, didn't like their work? James L. W. West III believes it was the bluntness of his friends' opinions that helped spur Fitzgerald's efforts to educate himself. Perhaps so. He clearly wanted their respect, but he also wanted something more: the feeling that he measured up to writers both living and dead. As a critic, he understood what had to be done, but as a debt-ridden writer, he did what was necessary. The 'incorruptible style' he longed for was pushed aside in order to support himself and his family.[16]

Fitzgerald's literary intelligence should not be doubted. Indeed, David S. Brown puts that intelligence in "the service of a deeper and seemingly timeless historical vision."[17] For Brown, Fitzgerald's "penetrating descriptions of the Western world's leap from feudalism to capitalism, from faith to secularization, and from the tradition oriented to the flux oriented make him one of the important cultural commentators America has produced."[18] Where is the proof? Essentially, it's found in Fitzgerald's longing for a more idealistic, less materialistic America, where "chivalry and honor, deference and paternalism" influenced behavior. The idea of a paradise lost, imbued by his father's recollections of a more genteel, more virtuous preindustrial age (presumably before neurasthenia set in), drove Fitzgerald to write incisively about the historical changes he witnessed.[19]

While this is undoubtedly true, Brown's attempt to cast Fitzgerald as a thinker in the mold of the economist Thorstein Veblen or the historian Frederick Jackson Turner seems far-fetched. If, in his own way, Fitzgerald denounced the "soulless materialism" infiltrating American society in the twentieth century, Brown does himself no favors by acknowledging that "only the fact that Fitzgerald almost certainly never read Veblen prohibits us from seeing [*The Great Gatsby*] as a parody of Veblen's ideas."[20]

It's a question of degree, as most critical judgments are. Kazin also felt that Fitzgerald took America more seriously as a subject than did other writers of his generation but that he undermined his historical perspective by "feeling himself to be the center of the universe and so a marked man. He was the reason for everything in sight but, at the same time, its wallflower observer; he was Frank Merriwell on the mound but a half-Irish, ultimately dubious 'outsider' as well. He was the center of things and the everlasting margin."[21]

That said, Brown's book has much to recommend it. It is thoroughly researched and reliably informative about the intellectual currents of Fitzgerald's day. Moreover, its focus on Fitzgerald's intellect reminds us that his life wasn't all high living and steep decline. His interests encompassed more than movies and musical theater. In the *Notebooks*, Fitzgerald inserted a rather odd statement: "I am the last of the novelists for a long time now," which Bruccoli believes "may be understood in terms of his allegiances to older American values. . . . He saw himself as coming at the end of a complex American historical process and identified with it."[22] As Brown notes, he "wished to be understood on his own terms, principally as an artist immersed in his times, sensitive to change, and writing for the ages."[23]

Fair enough, but wishes do not make facts. By equating seriousness of intent with its enactment in prose, Brown ascribes more intellectual heft to the work than it can support. One might call this elevating Ivan above his brothers. Even *The Crack-Up* serves Brown's purpose: "What saves the Crack-Up articles from being mere exercises in self-pity," he states, "is their connection to a broader world of politics and ideas."[24] First, the essays do not need saving; second, if they did, that's not what saves them. *The Crack-Up* is a combination of sincerity and posturing, executed by a writer determined to write well. In it one finds the adolescent need for attention, as well as the hard-won wisdom of a life lived in public but filled with private despair. At forty, Fitzgerald recognized the conditions that threatened to destroy him but remained fully capable of clapping his hands at the prospect of a film being made from one of his screenplays.

The Reputation

IF ONE OF the Karamazov brothers had a pronounced intellectual streak, another could be quite funny (though it's hard to know which one). In a 1928 letter to Wilson, Fitzgerald writes: "We never receive people the 29th. It is the anniversary of the 2nd Council of Nicea."[25] In "Boil Some Water—Lots of It," Pat Hobby is outraged when an extra dressed as a Cossack sits down at the "Big Table" in the commissary reserved for the studio big shots: "It was as if someone had crayoned Donald Duck into 'The Last Supper.'" A sense of humor isn't necessarily a sign of intelligence, but it's a good bet that someone who can step back from himself isn't altogether dense. In *The Last Tycoon*, the narrator, upon learning that a man she's met is a writer, muses: "It was my first inkling that he was a writer. And while I like writers—because if you ask a writer anything you usually get an answer—still it belittled him in my eyes."[26]

Probably the silliest moment in the novel arrives when Monroe Stahr brings a woman back to his unfinished house in Santa Monica. The woman reminds him of his dead wife, and he hopes to impress her with his wealth and position. Shortly after they enter the house, the phone rings. Apparently, the president of the United States is on the line, which is not altogether a bad thing on a first date. Stahr is an important movie producer, so the prospect of the president's phoning is not unreasonable, but the call isn't from Roosevelt; it's from a friend who wants Stahr to talk to an orangutan. Stahr patiently complies while his date listens. The scene is handled with grace and wit, and it's a side to the older and beleaguered Fitzgerald that is often overlooked.

Another reason that readers may underestimate him is the lyric quality of the prose and the lushness of the descriptions, which belie the hard analytic quality of the work. Like any professional writer, he depended on the ability to plan and execute. His vaunted lyricism didn't issue from an overflow of spontaneous emotion but was the product of thoughtful labor. He may have valued style, but he prided himself (not always accurately) on his knowingness, and when necessary he could train a gimlet eye on America. He understood that while social class was fixed, social *boundaries* were expanding. Long before most sociologists, he recognized that celebrity emanating from art, sports, and entertainment was creating a new class in America. In 1931, he looked back on the preceding decade and identified a time when "Society and the native [possibly a euphemism for Jewish] arts had not mingled—Ellin Mackay [a society heiress] was not yet married to Irving Berlin."[27]

It wasn't just money and class that intrigued him; it was culture and everything that culture encompassed: "With Americans ordering suits by the gross in London, the Bond Street tailors perforce agreed to modify their cut to the American long-waisted figure and loose fitting taste, something subtle passed to America, the style of man."[28] This isn't the theory of relativity or Kantian ethics or even an instance of historical vision, but it does denote an empirical cast to his thinking, fortified by close observation of people and their tics. Not always a subtle thinker, he recognized the subtle differences between people's conceptions of themselves and how they really were. And though his mind flickered too much to create a Proustian or Jamesian tableau of the upper classes, his eye invariably lit on the telling detail. He knew the trappings of class, knew the objects and artifacts that people surrounded themselves with, and understood the hidden meaning of accoutrements. He could have been a set designer or even, as he liked to think, a movie director—at any rate, it would have made for an interesting experiment.

Although he fancied himself a realist capable of disinterested analysis, his greater power was associative, a sympathetic ability to hear beneath the words, to grasp what wasn't being said. In *Tender Is the Night,* he alludes to this gift when describing Rosemary half-listening to someone at the dinner table: "Intermittently she caught the gist of his sentences and supplied the rest from her subconscious, as one picks up the striking of a clock in the middle with only the rhythm of the first uncounted strikes lingering in the mind."[29] Perhaps this same tendency caused him to leap without thinking, embracing ideas and causes that his analytical side, once it became engaged, would later reject. Indeed, his analytical soul was never dormant for long, and as experiences accumulated, it became more and more pronounced as he tried to make sense of his life.

By the time he wrote *Tender Is the Night,* he had outgrown the artificiality of his early stories and set out to compose a meditative study of psychological damage. Although *Tender* is by no means a perfect book, it is in its own way a wise and melancholy one, a novel whose beginning and ending seem to get better and better on rereading.[30] Indeed, the banality or foolishness that Fitzgerald was capable of disappeared when he took his sabbaticals from the world. When he sat down to write, his better nature took over. It wasn't just his literary sensibility that came into play; it was the part of him that responded to order, certainty, and truth.

SOME BOOKS DEEPEN over time; others may become more superficial as their readers grow older. Fitzgerald's books, I think, remain themselves or what you thought of them on first reading. One learns to appreciate better his artistry and powers of observation, but much of his work does not grow wiser. No harsh criticism is meant by this. Fitzgerald wasn't in the profundity business, and when you consider that life itself (apart from the unimaginable idea of its opposite) is not necessarily profound, then Fitzgerald is everything you might want in a certain kind of writer. Kazin's jibe that he "was about as metaphysical in his tastes as Franklin D. Roosevelt"[31] is as pointless a remark as Mary McCarthy's contention that once Henry James had "etherealized the novel . . . it no longer had any need for ideas."[32]

The simple truth is that there are thoughtful writers for whom the idea of profundity is irrelevant. This isn't to suggest that life isn't complicated, but once you remove God or absolutes from the narrative, life is what you make of it, and perhaps the writer's role is to re-present the ordinary in ways that make us see and feel it afresh. And I can't think of too many writers who have better summed up the lessons life teaches those who commerce in matters of the intellect:

> Once one is caught up into the material world not one person in ten thousand finds the time to form literary taste, to examine the validity of the philosophic concepts for himself or to form what, for lack of a better phrase, I might call the wise and tragic sense. By this I mean the thing that lies behind all great careers, from Shakespeare to Abraham Lincoln's, and as far back as there are books to read—the sense that life is essentially a cheat and its conditions are those of defeat, and that the redeeming things are not happiness and pleasure but the deeper satisfactions that come out of struggle.[33]

A writer's business consists in dramatizing what he or she learns or imagines. Some writers do it without fanfare or fuss; others do it boldly, calling attention to their powers of description. Fitzgerald began as a "look-at-my-prose" writer who evolved over time into a purer, less exhibitionist stylist. The author of *This Side of Paradise* made way for the author of *Gatsby,* who, in turn, moved aside for the author of the Pat Hobby stories and *The Last Tycoon.*

For reasons that had more to do with the changing times than the waning of his skills, Fitzgerald was ousted from the literary pantheon after 1935. "[M]y God I am a forgotten man," he writes plaintively to Zelda in 1940.[34] He wasn't far wrong. The Modern Library had discontinued *The Great Gatsby* in 1939, and though his books were all in stock in Scribner's warehouse and listed in the catalogue, there were no orders.[35] The reviews for *Gatsby* had been generally favorable, and its first run of 20,870 copies sold out, requiring in August 1925 another lot of 3,000 copies. But this probably owed more to Fitzgerald's name than to any firm loyalty to the novel itself. At any rate, that last printing, according to James L. W. West III, "sufficed at Scribner for another sixteen years," and his last royalty statement during his lifetime, "dated

1 August 1940, reports the sale of seven copies of *The Great Gatsby* during the preceding twelve months."[36]

It was only after the obituaries appeared that his books began to move again, and over the last eighty years around thirty million copies of *Gatsby* have sold worldwide: it continues to sell a staggering five hundred thousand copies a year in the United States alone.[37] At present, at least sixty collections of his writings have been published, as well as some eighty biographical and critical books and pamphlets.

What turned his reputation around? Two things: his death and a repentant Edmund Wilson. As if to atone for a lifetime of patronizing remarks, Wilson became the first and most industrious of the resurrectors. After Scott died, he wrote to Zelda: "I feel myself as if I had been suddenly robbed of some part of my own personality—since there must have been some aspect of myself that had been developed in relation to him."[38] Determined to pay homage to a man who received very little praise from him while alive, Wilson, then an editor at the *New Republic*, immediately commissioned critical essays from, among others, Dos Passos, O'Hara, and Schulberg. He then edited and published *The Last Tycoon*, making claims for it that he probably would not have made had Fitzgerald been alive: "What a conscientious artist he had become," he wrote, as if *Gatsby*, "The Rich Boy," "Babylon Revisited," "Crazy Sunday," and many other fine stories had never existed.[39]

Ten months after Fitzgerald's death, Viking Press came out with *The Portable Fitzgerald*, edited by Dorothy Parker and containing a laudatory introduction by John O'Hara.[40] Reviewing the book in the *Saturday Review of Literature*, Stephen Vincent Benét exclaimed: "You can take off your hats now, gentlemen, and I think perhaps you had better. This is not a legend, this is a reputation—and, seen in perspective, it may well be one of the most secure reputations of our time."[41] A year later, New Directions published Edmund Wilson's edition of *The Crack-Up*, which included Fitzgerald's *Esquire* pieces, miscellaneous writings, letters, sections from his *Notebooks*, and four critical essays about him.

In 1945, the Council on Books in Wartime shipped 155,000 paperback editions of *The Great Gatsby,* among other books, to American soldiers, which certainly did no harm.[42] In 1951, Schulberg published *The Disenchanted;* Malcolm Cowley issued *The Short Stories,* as well as a new edition of *Tender Is the Night;* Alfred Kazin gathered together a set of critical pieces by well-known writers and critics; and Arthur Mizener finished his biography *The Far Side of Paradise.* The resurrection, to paraphrase *Gatsby,* was complete.

By the mid-1950s *The Great Gatsby,* with little dissent, entered the canon, perhaps the one American novel that teachers and critics think is indispensable for students to parse. Which is not to say that there is universal agreement about it. "I find *Gatsby* aesthetically overrated, psychologically vacant, and morally complacent," Kathryn Schulz disclosed in a 2013 article for *New York Magazine.*[43] She dislikes its "convoluted moral logic, simultaneously Romantic and Machiavellian, by which the most epically crooked character in the book is the one we are commanded to admire." She finds superficial its "blanket embrace of that great American delusion by which wealth, poverty, and class itself stem from private virtue and vice." As for its portrayal of women—an "unthinking commitment to a gender order so archaic as to be Premodern"—Schulz doesn't want to hear about the standards of Fitzgerald's time; after all, he was "a contemporary of Dorothy Parker, Gertrude Stein, and Virginia Woolf, not to mention the great groundswell of activists who achieved the passage of the Nineteenth Amendment. (Yet here he is in *A Short Autobiography:* 'Women learn best not from books or from their own dreams but from reality and from contact with first-class men.')"

I allot so much space to these uncharitable remarks because they are not so much off-key as playing a different tune from the one most readers hear. Fitzgerald was a boob in many respects, displaying the sexism, racism, and anti-Semitism of his day. So Schulz has a case, but to make it she discounts the work and its reception by two of the very people she enlists in her cause: both Stein and Parker sincerely liked Fitzgerald and admired *Gatsby*. One cannot simply overlook the authority, the redolence, the loveliness of Fitzgerald's prose. If not every insight is profound, one has to bear in mind that *Gatsby* is very much a young man's book, a book influenced by what its author was reading at the time. And with *Gatsby*, the twenty-seven-year-old Fitzgerald achieved an almost severe expression of form (albeit tenderly modulated) in which the various components of his personality were subjugated to the self who knew life better in books than in life. With *Gatsby* he demonstrated that it is art, not what we know of life, that gives life to fiction.

But, of course, time and viewpoints change. Some years ago, the novelist Jesmyn Ward, while extolling the virtues of the novel in the *New York Times Book Review*, also fastened on Gatsby's exclusionary status as though it were the novel's most important feature: "The very social class that embodied the dream Gatsby wanted for himself was predicated on exclusion. . . . He'd been born on the outside; he would die on the outside."[44] It's not that Ward is wrong; it's just that harping on James Gatz's displacement conveniently lines up with our culture's need to condemn privilege. *Gatsby* is great not because James Gatz is an interloper who exposes class prejudice, but because Fitzgerald learned from Conrad, Booth Tarkington, Sherwood Anderson, and Compton Mackenzie. Wanting to be a great writer, he had to be his own writer, and with *Gatsby* he managed to do just that.[45] *Gatsby*, he told Perkins, would be "something *new*—something extraordinary and beautiful and simple + intricately patterned."[46]

Jay Gatsby, like another assassinated American, "belongs to the ages," and every age views him differently. Case in point: the introductions to the most recent editions of *Gatsby* rely on aggressive postmodern tropes regarding sexism and capitalism. Min Jin Lee "cannot imagine a more persuasive and readable book about lost illusions, class, White Americans in the 1920s, and the perils and vanity of assimilation. It remains a modern novel by exploring the intersection of social hierarchy, White femininity, White male love, and unfettered capitalism."[47]

Wesley Morris's snappier and more fantastical appraisal meanwhile lets us know that "the tragedy here is the death of the heart, capitalism as an emotion." "No one cares about anyone else. Not really," he writes. "The tragedy is not that usual stuff about love not being enough or arriving too late to save the day. It's creepier and profoundly, inexorably true to the spirit of the nation. This is not a book about people, per se. Secretly, it's a novel of ideas."[48] (Ivan Fitzgerald would be pleased by this.)

This is criticism in the age of Twitter and Amazon reviews, readers flamboyantly weighing in without giving much thought to historical context. There is simply no modesty here, no hesitation about one's right to critique a novel written by a White, Sexist, anti-Capitalist Male. Fitzgerald may have been what Lee, Schulz, and Morris claim, but he was also much more and also perhaps much less than what they suggest. No consensus may ever attach to any writer if that writer aspires to greatness. Saul Bellow, John Cheever, Robert Stone, and John Gardner all admired Fitzgerald, each one for different reasons. Which goes to show that novelists are no better than other readers when it comes to defining what makes a book memorable.

In any event, in 1999 the Modern American Library surveyed a range of scholars and authors to determine the greatest novels of the past one hundred years. *Ulysses* received the most votes, and *The Great Gatsby* came in second, thus making it the best American novel ever written, just as Fitzgerald had predicted. *Tender Is the Night,* incidentally, finished twenty-eighth, while *The Sun Also Rises* and *A Farewell to Arms* ranked, respectively, forty-fifth and seventy-fourth. Subjective and unofficial as these lists go, one still feels like saying, "Atta boy, Scott."

No doubt these rankings would have gratified the erstwhile list-maker from St. Paul, but something else, I think, would have delighted him even more. Fitzgerald's assorted papers constitute the most popular archive in the Princeton University library. Not only are they ensconced in the institution that never granted him a degree, they receive more visitors than those of Aaron Burr, Woodrow Wilson,

John Foster Dulles, and the other luminaries.[49] One imagines his ghost riding the dinky over to the campus and heading toward the library, where, alighting on the Department of Rare Books and Special Collections, he hovers over the eighty-nine archival boxes and eleven oversized containers, as students and scholars file in to pore over the notes, correspondence, working drafts, photographs, and other materials. Poor Scott, happy at last.

Final Impressions

(FOR THE MOMENT)

"NO ONE NATURE CAN extend entirely inside another," Fitzgerald admonished. He was right. "Definitive" biographies notwithstanding, guesswork is a large part of the reconstructive process, especially with those writers who, whether they leave behind vast amounts of material or very little, present a frustrating mix of fact and fiction, each inevitably modulating and transforming the other. If some writers seem more accessible by virtue of having unburdened themselves, we still cannot assume we know them. "A shilling life will give you all the facts," Auden observed—but nothing at all of the nuances and quiet emotions which leave no trace of their passing.

And isn't it here in the small things that sometimes a larger truth resides? From Scottie's recollections we learn that her father loved reading *Bleak House* to her when she was around ten; he read it so often that it put her off Dickens forever. He also loved Jules Verne and the Oz books. While in Paris, he bought hundreds of toy soldiers (supposedly for Scottie) but kept them for himself and staged elaborate mock battles about which she cared not a whit. In Baltimore, he "came to life" when George Burns and Gracie Allen dropped by and sat happily with them discussing the anatomy of a joke. As for music, he didn't know much at all about jazz (the irony is silent). He liked popular tunes and walked around humming over and over "Tea for Two." According to Scottie, his favorite song was "Valencia."[1]

> Valencia, in my dreams it always seems
> I hear you softly call to me
> Valencia, where the orange trees forever
> Send the breeze beside the sea
>
> Valencia, in my arms I hold your charms
> Beneath the blossoms high above
> You love me, in Valencia long ago
> We found our paradise of love.

Over the years, critics and biographers have kneaded, pummeled, and shaped the facts in order to present the "compleat" Fitzgerald. In 1951, Arthur Mizener wanted us to see Fitzgerald as "one of the lonely men of conscience . . . with their deep concern for the moral imperatives of private, felt emotion."[2] An admirable goal except that not every action based on "private, felt emotion" rises to the level of a moral imperative. But we applaud the sentiment because Fitzgerald deserves to be taken seriously and because for many years—with assistance from himself—he wasn't. He was a moral writer—he'd be the first to insist on it—but the extent to which he was a lonely man of conscience needs clarifying.

Perhaps no novelist's values have been subjected to as much critical scrutiny as have Fitzgerald's. Fifty years ago, Midge Decter, in a smart but coldly worded piece, observed: "Virtually everything he wrote raises in the minds of his readers the question of his own relation to the moral and spiritual emptiness of the ethos he so poignantly chronicles. Does he stand inside or outside the terms by which his characters judge the world and on account of which they are doomed?"[3] Decter then offers the following hypothesis: "It would take only a small failure of imagination, only a minute but essential shutting off of sympathy, to find Fitzgerald's life as doomed as are the lives of his characters, and for something like the same reason: not because he seemed so much to dignify their illusions but because the illusions he dignified were so cheap."[4]

It's a startling thought, this short step that enables us to dismiss both Fitzgerald's fiction and life. Is Decter right? *Were* the illusions cheap; are we so impressionable as to fall for syrupy emotions simply because they come wrapped in elegant prose? To her credit, Decter also offers a way out: perhaps Fitzgerald's characters suffer proportionately to *their* imagination, and what matters to them also matters to us—that is, we're all in the same fix. Decter's larger point is valid, though: it's hard to gauge just how far Fitzgerald stands apart from "the terms by which his characters judge the world."[5]

Sad to say, the more we know about the life, the more difficult it becomes to square the morality professed in the fiction with the behavior of its author. Nick Carraway may have wanted the world to stand at moral attention, but Fitzgerald slumped, stumbled, and often fell on his face. By espousing a moral purpose in both his books and letters, he makes it impossible to overlook the contradictions between the life he lived and the books he wrote.

It's a dichotomy wrapped in alcoholism. As with Zelda's mental instability, Scott's drinking was physiological in nature; it *was* his nature. This doesn't excuse behavior but suggests that he was more than the sum of that behavior. Drink made him boorish, maudlin, combative. But then he wasn't always drunk; he had his moments of grace. In a 1938 letter to one of Zelda's doctors, he writes: "I have of course my eternal hope that a miracle will happen to Zelda. . . . With my shadow removed, perhaps she will find something in life to care for more than just formerly. Certainly the outworn pretense that we can ever come together again is better for being shed. . . . So long as she is helpless, I'd never leave her or ever let her have a sense that she was deserted."[6] It is at such moments that one wants to shake his hand and shout, as Nick Carraway does at Gatsby, "You're worth the whole damn bunch put together."

This is the Fitzgerald we'd like to think predominates. His sincerity seems real, and aside from words uttered in the heat of anger, his devotion to Zelda continued undiminished. But what are we to make of the other Fitzgeralds, including the one who insisted that he had put everything he had into his fiction so that we could read it like braille? Was he actually so faithful to his calling? "Sometimes I wish I had gone along with that gang [Cole Porter, Rogers, and Hart], but I guess I am too much a moralist at heart, and really want to preach at people in some acceptable form, rather than entertain them," he told Scottie in 1939.[7] It's pretty to think so, as Papa might say, but Fitzgerald was simply too protean (since in a single morning he might feel all "the emotions ascribable to Wellington at Waterloo").

More than most of us, he was an amalgam of quirks and attitudes, exhibiting different sides of himself as he moved from one stage of life to the next. James Gatz had it easy: he created a persona, and the mask he fashioned became inseparable from the face beneath it. By an extraordinary act of will, James Gatz *became* Jay Gatsby, but Scott Fitzgerald never became the man he wanted to be. Instead, he got sucked into life's machinery and was mangled. So when he writes at the age of forty-four that he wished he had stuck to writing novels like *The Great Gatsby,* he was lamenting a life that had failed to measure up to his expectations.

It was nostalgia for what might have been. Although the wish was no doubt heartfelt, Fitzgerald was too easily tempted by pleasure and the perks of reputation. Yes, he wanted to be a great novelist, but he was also drawn to the cheaper seats, to the glitter of fame. Few artists were more openly covetous of the garish trappings of success, and if writing in a popular vein would have garnered him more readers and riches, he wouldn't have hesitated. Of course, he regretted not having written another *Gatsby*, but that didn't stop him from desiring as late as September 1940, while working on *The Last Tycoon,* to write a comedy series that would catch the eye of the big magazines or land a movie deal that would grant him the status of "a movie man and not a novelist."[8]

The fact is, Fitzgerald could write for money and not feel bad about it. He wasn't an artist in the mold of Henry James or James Joyce. He didn't have the commitment to fiction that drove Conrad or Hemingway. He appreciated great writing, and he was an excellent critic, but he wasn't Mallarmé amusing himself by writing ad copy for perfume or Faulkner sweating over a silly screenplay about ancient Egypt. He was a man who had a knack for the superficial and an eye to the main chance. The gimmickiness and the sentimentality of the lesser stories didn't appear by magic; they're not incidental to his character. He was both willing and able to give the popular magazines what they wanted.

Indeed, it's not far-fetched to concoct an entirely different career path for him. What if *The Vegetable* had been a roaring success? What if he'd written a successful musical or a screenplay when he was thirty? What if his screen test in Hollywood in 1927 had panned out? Who knows what he would have gone on to create or not create? He was a fine writer when the subject suited him, but he could not commit himself fully to art. One can chalk this up to life's distractions, to ill luck, to unavoidable circumstance, but in the end, he just wasn't fierce enough or secure enough to achieve greatness. He would, indeed, write a novel perhaps "better than any novel ever written in America," and if it made him only "the best second-rater in the world," that's not such a terrible fate given the competition.

In fact, it is precisely because he believed in literature that he pondered his own qualifications for greatness. His idealism forgave very little. He wanted to live the life of a great writer, but how could he when he depended so much on the approval of a world that after 1934 withheld it? On the other hand, there was a part of him that preferred being at the top of a Broadway marquee rather than among the heap of middlebrow novelists. He really *liked* musical theater and would rather have written the words of Lorenz Hart or Cole Porter than those of John P. Marquand or Harold Bell Wright.

Final Impressions

Fitzgerald had the misfortune of being capable of both greatness and mediocrity. This is not uncommon, but certainly few writers have been given as many opportunities to sink to their lowest level. After publishing *Tender Is the Night,* he sustained himself as a freelancer and hack. It was a small, restrictive existence, light years away from the cavalier days of his early twenties. Forced to write stories to pay hospital bills, forced to borrow against advances, forced to endure slights and humiliations, he was always chasing money. And it hurt. Men with high self-esteem, sure of their worth, whether the world acknowledges it or not, may succumb to self-pity but not self-doubt. Hardship is the price they pay for doing their work, but they possess the dignity of knowing the work is good.

Fitzgerald was denied such dignity. His desperate need for money coupled with the willingness of the magazines to publish him and the movies to pay him resulted in a host of glib stories, pseudosmart articles, and uneven screenplays. Although the Pat Hobby stories are certainly worth reading, his screenplays by and large do not bear too much scrutiny. What elevated him above his occasional lapses into mediocrity, however, was his contradictory and multifaceted self, including the ever-present wish to rise to the level of Conrad and Joyce. Fitzgerald couldn't always tamp down his adolescent instincts, or his pedagogical urges, or the insecurities that plagued him, but he could subsume them to a belief in literature.

"FITZGERALD WAS PERHAPS the last notable writer to affirm the Romantic fantasy, descended from the Renaissance, of personal ambition and heroism, of life committed to or thrown away for, some ideal of self."[9] This is a sentence one may skip over in Trilling's essay, but the more one learns about Fitzgerald, the more one feels the truth in it, not only because of its identification with a certain nobility of purpose but also because there is something faintly ridiculous about that purpose. More than any other writer, perhaps more than any other person, Fitzgerald measured himself against a specific ideal, which, in his case, we might liken to Chaucer's *"verray, parfit, gentil knyght."* This, you recall, was a writer who dreamt of "being an entire man in the Goethe-Byron-Shaw tradition, with an opulent American touch, a sort of combination of J. P. Morgan, Topham Beauclerk, and St. Francis of Assisi."[10]

So why did he end up living such a messy and, at times, a stupid life? Why did he make a fool of himself so often? The short answer is that life and art do not overlap except in the process of creating art. Add to this the fact that he was an alcoholic who—except for his early success and the birth of Scottie—didn't have much luck, and you understand why happiness meant so much to him. After a few heady years of marriage, Zelda succumbed to mental illness, his popularity ebbed, his health deteriorated, and time, as time will, wore him down. Eventually, he learned his lesson, and like most sensible people—and part of him *was* sensible—he realized there is something redeemable in struggle and that pleasure and happiness are not ends in themselves.

Indeed, it was this struggle that created some of his most poignant and enduring stories, but it was that yearning for perfection that ultimately nullified any chance for happiness. If he couldn't be perfect, he didn't want to be anything, he said at eighteen—thus sealing his fate. His mind would not romp like the mind of God, and so a tinge of bitterness attended his earthly tethering. And yet, despite everything, he somehow believed he could, if left to his own devices, be the man he wanted to be. This odd sense of the Platonic suffuses his work and absolves some of the weaker stories of cheap sentimentality. Nobility of character and nobility of purpose were not abstractions to Fitzgerald; they reflected an unrealized potential, a world where men and women behaved properly and where happiness was as natural as one's own skin. "You and I have been happy," he wrote to Zelda in April 1934. "We haven't been happy just once, we've been happy a thousand times."[11] But happiness could not compete with or abide self-consciousness.

Final Impressions

Self-consciousness can be a disaster. Fitzgerald not only worried incessantly about what others thought of him, he suffered from the unattainable. He never became a *verray, parfit, gentil knyght* and understood that he had failed to utilize what was best in himself. But he persevered, sustained like Gatsby by that extraordinary gift for hope. "Hope meant a lot in the best part of our lives, the first eight years we lived together, as it does in the lives of most young couples," he wrote to one of Zelda's doctors, "but I think in our case it was even exaggerated, because as a restless and ambitious man, I was never disposed to accept the present but always striving to change it, better it, or sometimes destroy it."[12] The present was always a short step from a different and better future; and if at times he succumbed to despair—"I left my capacity for hoping on the little roads that led to Zelda's sanitarium"—it wasn't for very long.[13]

Indeed, his restlessness (he never owned a home) might be considered a function of hope: the next place always held out more promise. Or perhaps his different selves couldn't decide on a suitable place to pitch camp—although, to be fair, it was partially Zelda's continual shuttling between hospitals that produced "this casual existence of many rooms and many doors that are not mine."[14] In any case, the man had more addresses than any other writer of his generation. Fitzgerald lived in apartments, hotels, and houses in Paris and on the Riviera. He rented in Manhattan, Westport, and Great Neck, Long Island. He lived outside Wilmington, Delaware, and in Asheville and Tryon, North Carolina. He lived in Baltimore and in Hollywood, where he moved from the Garden of Allah to a bungalow in Malibu to a cottage on Edward Everett Horton's Encino estate to an apartment on North Laurel Avenue, and, finally, to the first floor of Sheilah Graham's house.

Despite the wanderings, the bouts of illness and depression; despite the sad, uprooted, discordant, and peripatetic existence, his resilience resurfaced when it had to. He never lost hope, never gave up on the idea that he could write himself out of both debt and misery, and he recharged himself by doing what he did best: write sentences that flowed with "the tenderness toward human desire." And when he finally came around to accepting who he was and the world for what it was, he offered a reasonable account of himself: "I don't drink. I am not a great man but sometimes I think the impersonal and objective quality of my talent and the sacrifices of it, in pieces, to preserve its essential value has some sort of epic grandeur. Anyhow after hours I nurse myself with delusions of that sort."[15] And there it is: three sentences that singly and collectively put his life into perspective.

THERE ARE MANY things I am grateful that he wrote, grateful because they redeem him: they make his lesser work and his bad behavior, if not palatable, then simply something we have to accept. This doesn't condone his nonsense or irresponsibility. After all, we shouldn't excuse people's failings because they have given us work of luminous beauty. But we do have to acknowledge that an artist's flaws and weaknesses may, in fact, contribute to the production and scale of that work. Neither Eliot nor Frost would win a humanitarian award, but had they been different people, their poetry would be different, too. Of course, it's much easier to forgive Fitzgerald for writing well than, say, Pound or Céline, not just because he wrote so beautifully about loss, but because, in addition to the richness of the prose and the struggles of his characters, there is something intangible and enduring in his best work—enduring because it *is* intangible—something that suggests he is tapping into the recesses of self-knowledge.

This, I think, is where his appeal lies—not in the lingering melodies of his prose but in his oblique glances at mortality. In his best work, a simple truth: whatever we gain, in the end is lost. Consolation comes in the form of art and beauty and in the small transcendences that gleam intermittently from railroad stations or snow-laden fields or from a dock across Long Island Sound—but ultimately everything disappears. If there is nothing profound in this, it is at least one of those small realizations that explains his enduring twilight. Perfection is captured only by its disappearance.

Final Impressions

For Fitzgerald, another, more material perfection could be realized in working. Zelda was off in a world of her own; Scottie was in school back East; his friends could get along without him; and he could barely function without a drink. So when he sat down to write, he exercised a control absent elsewhere in his life. Writing wasn't easy when he cared enough, but that was part of its appeal: the crafting of workmanlike sentences that expressed what he felt most deeply, and he treated the process with respect. One discerns in the best stories and essays an attention to the smallest details, to the sound and sense of almost every word. And the care that he lavished on the work was evidence that he was, if not master of the house, then at least a master of form.

He knew a windmill when he saw one but dreamed of conquering men and movie studios. If he could dominate life, he could also become "an entire man . . . with an opulent American touch." But that was not to be. The Depression made his work seem trivial, Zelda spiraled out of control, and so did his career. Yet he never quite broke down; his sense of responsibility never deserted him. He continued to provide for Zelda and Scottie, though he was an absentee husband and father for many years. And while suffering numerous setbacks, assorted indignities, and various health issues, he faithfully discharged his contractual obligations. The core to Fitzgerald is found not in what he professed, but in his professionalism, his resilience, his perseverance.

He failed because he was all the Karamazovs at once, and he survived because he was all the Karamazovs at once. He survived because he believed he could live life on his own terms despite all the evidence that prevented him from doing so. He survived because hope spurred him to write, and writing was his salvation. He was, you might say, a man of infinite hope and a man of infinite regret, both of whom helped to create the prose for which we remember him. He was, as Auden gently said of Yeats, "silly like us," yet his "gift survived it all." And for that there is nothing left to do but thank him.

ACKNOWLEDGMENTS

THE AUTHOR WANTS TO extend his gratitude to Eric Brandt and Ellen Satrom at the University of Virginia Press, who took it upon themselves to make the best of a bad lot and almost succeeded in convincing the author that they were successful.

Susan Murray copyedited the manuscript, and Danny Mintz, in fine Weequahic style, valiantly proofread it.

I should also note that I borrow, sometimes liberally, from articles that I wrote for the *New Yorker* about Fitzgerald and from *Harper's* that dealt with the 1930s.

NOTES

Some Prefatory Remarks

1. Raymond Chandler, *Selected Letters of Raymond Chandler*, ed. Frank MacShane (New York: Columbia University Press, 1981), 239.
2. Christian Gauss, "Edmund Wilson, the Campus and the 'Nassau Lit,'" *Princeton University Library Chronicle*, February 1944, 50.
3. Gingrich quoted in Jeffrey Meyers, *Scott Fitzgerald: A Biography* (New York: HarperCollins, 1994), 307.
4. Perhaps Fitzgerald's famous statement that "the test of a first-rate intelligence is the ability to hold two opposed ideas in the mind at the same time, and still retain the ability to function" is an acknowledgment of his contradictory nature.
5. Aaron Latham, *Crazy Sundays: F. Scott Fitzgerald in Hollywood* (New York: Viking, 1971), 180.
6. David S. Brown, *Paradise Lost: A Life of F. Scott Fitzgerald* (Cambridge, MA: Belknap Press of Harvard University Press, 2017), 2.
7. John O'Hara, "In Memory of F. Scott Fitzgerald," *New Republic*, March 3, 1941, 311.
8. Alice B. Toklas quoted in Meyers, *Scott Fitzgerald*, 344.
9. Malcolm Cowley, "The Romance of Money," in *F. Scott Fitzgerald: Modern Critical Views*, ed. Harold Bloom (New York: Chelsea House, 1985), 59.
10. Always insecure, he nonetheless did not lack for ego. In a letter to Perkins, he refers to *The Great Gatsby* as "about the best American novel ever written" (F. Scott Fitzgerald and Maxwell Perkins, *Dear Scott/ Dear Max: The Fitzgerald-Perkins Correspondence*, ed. John Kuehl

and Jackson R. Bryer [New York: Charles Scribner's Sons, 1971], 76). Another letter to Perkins contains his modest self-assessment as "one of the half dozen masters of English prose now working in America" (ibid., 113).

11. Fitzgerald to Maxwell Perkins, May 20, 1940, in F. Scott Fitzgerald, *A Life in Letters,* ed. Bruccoli (New York: Simon and Schuster, 1995), 445.

12. Even facts have a way of losing concreteness. One thing you'd think that biographers would get right is a person's height and weight. Fitzgerald stood five foot seven and weighed 160 pounds in middle school, writes James L. West III. Matthew Bruccoli, however, lists Fitzgerald at five foot eight and 138 pounds in his first year at Princeton. In *Babe in the Woods: F. Scott Fitzgerald's Unlikely Summer in Montana,* Landon Y. Jones also claims that he was five foot eight but gives his weight at 150 pounds. Jeffrey Meyers, by giving Hemingway six inches on Fitzgerald, makes him five foot six. And for some reason, John Updike views him as "slight of build, dainty of feature"—neither of which seems accurate to me.

13. Jay McInerney, "Fitzgerald Revisited," *New York Review of Books,* August 15, 1991.

14. John Updike, "This Side of Coherence," *New Yorker,* June 27, 1994.

15. Michiko Kakutani, "Troubled Life and Times on This Side of Paradise," *New York Times,* April 24, 1994.

16. George Jean Nathan, *A George Jean Nathan Reader,* ed. A. L. Lazarus (Cranbury, NJ: Fairleigh Dickinson University Press, 1990), 157.

17. Nathan cannot be trusted. Although he and Scott were friends, his all-too-obvious interest in Zelda may have colored his impressions (see Sally Cline, *Zelda Fitzgerald: Her Voice in Paradise* [New York: Arcade, 2003], 1, 120). In a review of André Le Vot's *Scott Fitzgerald,* James R. Mellow points out that Edmund Wilson called into question some of Nathan's statements regarding time spent with Fitzgerald (Mellow, "Fact into Fiction," *New Criterion,* March 1, 1983, 83).

18. Hemingway quoted in James D. Brasch, *The Other Hemingway: The Master Inventor* (Victoria, British Columbia: Trafford, 2009), 70.

19. One can probably safely discount 50 percent of what Hemingway had to say about Fitzgerald. Even when Hemingway was not deliberately telling lies, his memory played him false. In *A Moveable Feast,* which mercilessly jabs away at Fitzgerald's character, Hemingway writes that at their first meeting in the Dingo Bar, Fitzgerald was accompanied by a classmate, Duncan Chapin. But Chapin was not in Europe that year (Cline, *Zelda Fitzgerald,* 429n73).

20. Scottie Fitzgerald Lanahan quoted in Brown, *Paradise Lost,* 341.

21. According to Meyers, Fitzgerald was also a monster of morbidity. He apparently "owned a bloodcurdling collection of photograph albums of horribly mutilated soldiers, stereopticon slides of executions and roasted aviators, and lavishly illustrated French tomes of living men

whose faces had been chewed away by shrapnel" (Meyers, *Scott Fitzgerald*, 134).

22. Ibid., 29.
23. Dinitia Smith, "Love Notes Drenched in Moonlight; Hints of Future Novels in Letters to Fitzgerald," *New York Times,* September 8, 2003.
24. Kendall Taylor, *Sometimes Madness Is Wisdom: Zelda and F. Scott Fitzgerald, A Marriage* (New York: Random House, 2001), 29.
25. James L. W. West III, *The Perfect Hour: The Romance of F. Scott Fitzgerald and Ginevra King, His First Love* (New York: Random House, 2005), 106.
26. Eddy Dow (Philadelphia), "The Rich Are Different," *New York Times,* November 13, 1988. For further details, see page 117 of this book.
27. Richard Holmes, *This Long Pursuit: Reflections of a Romantic Biographer* (New York: Pantheon, 2016), 17.
28. Janet Malcolm, *The Silent Woman: Sylvia Plath and Ted Hughes* (New York: Vintage, 1993), 6.
29. F. Scott Fitzgerald, *Tender Is the Night,* paperback ed. (New York: Charles Scribner's Sons, 1962), 280.
30. F. Scott Fitzgerald, *The Great Gatsby,* paperback ed. (New York: Charles Scribner's Sons, 1953), 2.
31. F. Scott Fitzgerald, *The Crack-Up,* ed. Edmund Wilson (New York: New Directions, 1993), 89.
32. Ibid., 71.
33. Fitzgerald quoted in Arthur Mizener, *The Far Side of Paradise: A Biography of F. Scott Fitzgerald* (Boston: Houghton Mifflin, 1951), xix.
34. Joseph Conrad to the *New York Times,* August 2, 1901.
35. Andrew Turnbull, *Scott Fitzgerald* (New York: Charles Scribner's Sons, 1962), 320.
36. Again, these observations can be found in my essay "Some Remarks on the Pitfalls of Biography," in *Except When I Write* (New York: Oxford University Press, 2011).

The Facts of the Matter: 1896–1920

1. F. Scott Fitzgerald, *Correspondence of F. Scott Fitzgerald,* ed. Matthew J. Bruccoli and Margaret M. Duggan (New York: Random House, 1980), xv.
2. See ScreenSeven games site (http://www.screenseven.com/games /hidden-object/classic-adventures-the-great-gatsby/).
3. The curve was the brainchild of Alan Kreuger, former chairman of the Council of Economic Advisers, who introduced the term in the 2012 *Economic Report of the President.* (See David Vandivier, "What Is The Great Gatsby Curve?" Obama White House blog, June 11, 2013, https:// obamawhitehouse.archives.gov/blog/2013/06/11/what-great-gatsby -curve).

4. Alexandra Alter, "New Life for Old Classics, as Their Copyrights Run Out," *New York Times*, December 29, 2018.

5. "Head and Shoulders" and "Myra Meets His Family" were both adapted in 1920 as *The Chorus Girl's Romance* and *The Husband Hunter*. The following years saw "The Offshore Pirate" and *The Beautiful and Damned* made into movies. The 1924 Film Guild movie *Grit* was based on an original story by Fitzgerald. "The Camel's Back" was adapted as *Conductor 1492* in 1924. *The Great Gatsby* was brought to the screen in 1926 (silent), 1949, 1974, 2000, and 2013. "The Pusher-in-the-Face" became a movie short in 1929. "Babylon Revisited" became *The Last Time I Saw Paris* in 1954. *Tender Is the Night* became a film in 1962, and *The Last Tycoon* was transferred to the screen in 1976. And in 2008 "The Curious Case of Benjamin Button" received the full Hollywood treatment. Finally, according to the *Hollywood Reporter* (September 23, 2008), Keira Knightley was set to star in *The Beautiful and Damned*, about those "Jazz Age icons known for living large, soaring high, and crashing hard." One waits warily, despite a crush on Ms. Knightley.

6. Ben Brantley, "Borne Back Ceaselessly into the Past," *New York Times*, December 16, 2010. The entire show runs eight hours, with two intermissions and a dinner break.

7. Gore Vidal, "Scott's Case," *New York Review of Books*, May 1, 1980.

8. "For Gatsby, divided between power and dream, comes inevitably to stand for America itself. Ours is the only nation that prides itself upon a dream and gives its name to one, 'the American dream'" ("F. Scott Fitzgerald," in Lionel Trilling, *The Liberal Imagination* [New York: Doubleday Anchor, 1953], 244).

9. Mitchell Breitwieser, "The Great Gatsby: Grief, Jazz and the Eye-Witness," *Arizona Quarterly: A Journal of American Literature, Culture and Theory* 47, no. 3 (Autumn 1991): 39.

10. Marius Bewley, "Scott Fitzgerald's Criticism of America," *Sewanee Review* 62 (1954).

11. Thomas Flanagan, "Fitzgerald's Radiant World," *New York Review of Books*, December 21, 2000.

12. Arthur Mizener writes that the "substance out of which Fitzgerald constructed his stories, that is to say, was American, perhaps more completely American than that of any writer of his time" (Mizener, "F. Scott Fitzgerald 1896–1940—The Poet of Borrowed Time," in *F. Scott Fitzgerald: The Man and His Work*, ed. Alfred Kazin [New York: Collier, 1966], 23).

13. Matthew Bruccoli, *Some Sort of Epic Grandeur: The Life of F. Scott Fitzgerald*, 2nd rev. ed. (Columbia: University of South Carolina Press, 2002), 13.

14. Arthur Mizener, *The Far Side of Paradise: A Biography of F. Scott Fitzgerald* (Boston: Houghton Mifflin, 1951), 4.

15. Fitzgerald, interview by Michel Mok, "The Other Side of Paradise, Scott Fitzgerald, 40, Engulfed in Despair," *New York Post,* September 25, 1936.
16. F. Scott Fitzgerald, *A Life in Letters,* ed. Bruccoli (New York: Simon and Schuster, 1995), 33.
17. Scott Donaldson, *Fool for Love: F. Scott Fitzgerald* (New York: St. Martin's, 1983), 12.
18. Quoted in Kirk Curnutt, *The Cambridge Introduction to F. Scott Fitzgerald* (Cambridge: Cambridge University Press, 2007).
19. Bruccoli, *Some Sort of Epic Grandeur,* 23.
20. Bruccoli, *Some Sort of Epic Grandeur,* 27. Scott's "Thoughtbook" is described by Matthew Bruccoli as "Twelve disbound notebook leaves. Autobiographical observations made by Fitzgerald in 1906" (see *Scottie Fitzgerald: The Stewardship of Literary Memory,* exhibition catalogue, p. 34, Matthew J. and Arlyn Bruccoli Collection of F. Scott Fitzgerald, Thomas Cooper Library, University of South Carolina, 2007).
21. There were various scrapbooks over the years. In a communiqué about this book, James L. W. West III noted that he thinks there were seven, consisting of "a loose collection of scraps of paper and sheets of paper, etc., which he started putting together into some kind of order near the end of his life."
22. Fitzgerald, *A Life in Letters,* ed. Bruccoli, 7–10.
23. F. Scott Fitzgerald, "Who's Who—And Why," in *Afternoon of an Author,* ed. Arthur Mizener (New York: Collier Books, 1957), 83.
24. Jeffrey Meyers nastily describes Fay as a "huge, eunuch-like priest" with "a shrill, high-pitched, giggling voice," who loved Fitzgerald with the love that dared not speak its name. (See Meyers, *Scott Fitzgerald,* 19.) Yes, Fay *could* have been gay (Meyers winks that he read Huysmans, Swinburne, and Wilde), but there's no evidence that he ever made a pass at Fitzgerald. In fact, it seems highly unlikely that Fay did anything more than encourage and instruct his young student, who, in turn, memorialized him in *This Side of Paradise* as Monsignor Darcy, "a brilliant, enveloping personality" whose entrance in a room somehow "resembled a Turner sunset."
25. Fitzgerald, *Correspondence of F. Scott Fitzgerald,* ed. Bruccoli and Duggan, 53.
26. "A Conversation by Scottie Fitzgerald and Matthew Bruccoli," recorded in 1977 for *Some Sort of Epic Grandeur,* Montgomery, AL, included in *Scottie Fitzgerald: The Stewardship of Literary Memory,* Matthew J. and Arlyn Bruccoli Collection of F. Scott Fitzgerald, Thomas Cooper Library, University of South Carolina, 2007.
27. There are those who disagree with me. See, for example, Benita A. Moore, *Escape into a Labyrinth: F. Scott Fitzgerald, Catholic Sensibility, and the American Way* (Oxfordshire, UK: Routledge, 1988).

28. "A Conversation by Scottie Fitzgerald and Matthew Bruccoli."
29. F. Scott Fitzgerald, *The Crack-Up*, ed. Edmund Wilson (New York: New Directions, 1993), 76.
30. Mizener, *The Far Side of Paradise*, 53–54.
31. Fitzgerald, *A Life in Letters*, ed. Bruccoli, 338.
32. James L. W. West III, *The Perfect Hour: The Romance of F. Scott Fitzgerald and Ginevra King, His First Love* (New York: Random House, 2005), 60.
33. F. Scott Fitzgerald, *The Great Gatsby*, paperback ed. (New York: Charles Scribner's Sons, 1953), 120.
34. Curnutt, *The Cambridge Introduction to F. Scott Fitzgerald*, 16.
35. James W. Tuttleton takes a rather more drastic view of Fitzgerald's relations with women. Citing Amory Blaine's view that the "problem of evil had solidified . . . into the problem of sex," specifically where beautiful women are concerned, Tuttleton finds in Fitzgerald's fiction many examples of beautiful women destroying sensitive young men (Tuttleton, "F. Scott Fitzgerald and the Magical Glory," *New Criterion*, November 1994).
36. West, *The Perfect Hour*, 91.
37. F. Scott Fitzgerald, "The Last of the Belles," *Saturday Evening Post*, March 2, 1929.
38. Kendall Taylor, *Sometimes Madness Is Wisdom: Zelda and Scott Fitzgerald: A Marriage* (New York: Ballantine, 2003), 26.
39. Fitzgerald, *The Beautiful and Damned* (New York: A. L. Burt, 1922), 48.
40. Mizener, *The Far Side of Paradise*, 73.
41. Bruccoli, *Some Sort of Epic Grandeur*, 96.
42. Fitzgerald, "Who's Who—And Why," in *Afternoon of an Author*, 85.

First Impressions

1. F. Scott Fitzgerald, *The Crack-Up*, ed. Edmund Wilson (New York: New Directions, 1993), 197.
2. See Arthur Mizener, *The Far Side of Paradise: A Biography of F. Scott Fitzgerald* (Boston: Houghton Mifflin, 1951), 20–21.
3. Ibid., 5.
4. Ibid., 6.
5. Matthew Bruccoli, *Some Sort of Epic Grandeur: The Life of F. Scott Fitzgerald*, 2nd rev. ed. (Columbia: University of South Carolina Press, 2002), 261.
6. Mizener, *The Far Side of Paradise*, 133. See also Noel Riley Fitch, *Sylvia Beach and the Lost Generation: A History of Literary Paris in the Twenties and Thirties* (New York: Norton, 1985), 275.
7. Fitzgerald, *The Crack-Up*, 69.
8. Matthew J. Bruccoli, *Fitzgerald and Hemingway: A Dangerous Friendship* (New York: Carroll and Graf, 1994), 215.

9. Mizener, *The Far Side of Paradise,* 31. As a teenager, Fitzgerald had read Owen Johnson's *Stover at Yale* (1912), the story of a high school and college gridiron star, which he later called the "textbook of my generation."

10. F. Scott Fitzgerald, "Princeton," *College Humor,* December 1927, 38.

11. Quoted in Jeffrey Hart, "The WASP Gentleman as Cultural Ideal," *New Criterion,* January 1989, 29.

12. Fitzgerald, *The Crack-Up,* 76.

13. Fitzgerald to John O'Hara, July 18, 1933, in F. Scott Fitzgerald, *A Life in Letters,* ed. Bruccoli (New York: Simon and Schuster, 1995), 233.

14. Ibid.

15. Ibid.

16. F. Scott Fitzgerald, *F. Scott Fitzgerald's Ledger: A Facsimile* (Washington, DC: NCR/Microcard, 1972), "February 1915," 169.

17. George Jean Nathan, *A George Jean Nathan Reader,* ed. A. L. Lazarus (Cranbury, NJ: Fairleigh Dickinson University Press, 1990), 157.

18. Ibid. See page 184 note 17 regarding Nathan's reliability.

19. Amanda Vaill, *Everybody Was So Young: Gerald and Sara Murphy, a Lost Generation Love Story* (New York: Broadway, 1999), 246.

20. Edmund Wilson, "Letters: To and about F. Scott Fitzgerald," *New York Review of Books,* February 17, 1977.

21. Fitzgerald, *The Crack-Up,* 86.

22. Mizener, *The Far Side of Paradise,* xiv.

23. Malcolm Cowley, "F. Scott Fitzgerald: The Romance of Money," *Western Review* 17 (1953): 245–55.

24. Fitzgerald, *The Crack-Up,* 77.

25. This may be a minority opinion. David S. Brown, for one, believes that "May Day," "Bernice," and "The Diamond as Big as the Ritz" constitute "a powerful triumvirate, smart, absorbing, and true to the mood from which they were conceived . . . surprisingly effective meditations on cultural and economic change" (Brown, *Paradise Lost: A Life of F. Scott Fitzgerald* [Cambridge, MA: Belknap Press of Harvard University Press, 2017], 111).

26. Fitzgerald, "One Hundred False Starts," in *My Lost City,* ed. James L. W. West III (Cambridge: Cambridge University Press, 2005), 89.

27. Alfred Kazin quoted in *F. Scott Fitzgerald: The Man and His Work,* ed. Kazin (New York: Collier, 1951), 15.

28. Fitzgerald, *The Crack-Up,* 211.

29. James L. W. West III, *The Perfect Hour: The Romance of F. Scott Fitzgerald and Ginevra King, His First Love* (New York: Random House, 2005), 86.

30. Fitzgerald, *A Life in Letters,* ed. Bruccoli, 367.

31. F. Scott Fitzgerald, *On Authorship,* ed. Matthew Bruccoli (Columbia: University of South Carolina Press, 1996), 181.

32. Fitzgerald, "One Hundred False Starts," 87.

33. Fitzgerald, *The Great Gatsby,* 112.

Fitzgerald's America I

1. Not all Americans were comfortable with unionism. Some maintained it was un-American and attracted immigrants who were either radical or "foreign devils." Hatred of unions took a deadly turn on May Day 1886, when a bomb went off in Chicago's Haymarket Square, killing a police officer. Police then fired into the crowd, killing one and wounding dozens. As a result, four labor organizers were later hanged.

    The depression of the mid-1890s also triggered some nasty strikes. During the national boycott on railways carrying Pullman cars in 1894, some 125,000 workers on twenty-nine railroads quit their jobs, and battles with state and federal troops broke out in twenty-six states. The strike ultimately failed, with its leaders imprisoned and many strikers blacklisted.

2. It wasn't until the Great Depression of 1929 that great wealth became synonymous in the public mind with exploitation and unscrupulousness. The medieval designation "robber baron" became popular in the United States only in 1934, with the publication of Matthew Josephson's *The Robber Barons.*

3. William Winter, *The Life of David Belasco,* vol. 2 (New York: Moffat, Yard, 1918), 425.

4. Jackson Lears, *Rebirth of a Nation: The Making of Modern America, 1877–1920* (New York: HarperCollins, 2009), 7.

5. Ralph Waldo Emerson, *The Annotated Emerson,* ed. David Mikics (Cambridge, MA: Belknap Press of Harvard University Press, 2012), 406.

6. Theodore Roosevelt, "Citizenship in a Republic," speech delivered in Paris, April 23, 1910.

7. The first volume of *Decline of the West* was published in 1918 and the second in 1923, but the book was not translated until 1926. According to David S. Brown, it was "the object of numerous English-language reviews and essays at the same time that Fitzgerald was writing *Gatsby*" (Brown, *Paradise Lost: A Life of F. Scott Fitzgerald* [Cambridge, MA: Belknap Press of Harvard University Press, 2017], 174).

    Fitzgerald, however, misremembers when he first read Spengler. In his letter to Perkins of June 6, 1940, he says: "I read him the same summer I was writing 'The Great Gatsby' and I don't think I ever quite recovered from him. He and Marx are the only modern philosophers that still manage to make sense in this horrible mess—I mean make sense by themselves and not in the hand of distorters." See also F. Scott Fitzgerald and Maxwell Perkins, *Dear Scott/Dear Max: The Fitzgerald-Perkins Correspondence,* ed. John Kuehl and Jackson R. Bryer (New York: Charles Scribner's Sons, 1971), 263.

8. More than one critic has argued for Spengler's influence on Fitzgerald's work. Richard D. Lehan, a professor of English at UCLA, framed Dick

Diver's career in *Tender Is the Night* as a Spenglerian trope because it parallels the decline of the West.

9. In the summer of 1915, Fitzgerald spent a month at a cattle-and-sheep ranch outside of White Sulphur Springs, Montana. It was owned by the family of his wealthy prep school and college friend Charles W. Donahoe.

10. "The Crack-Up," originally published in *Esquire,* February 1936. Quoted from F. Scott Fitzgerald, *The Crack-Up,* ed. Edmund Wilson (New York: New Directions, 1993), 74.

11. Ibid., 67.

12. Van Wyck Brooks, *America's Coming of Age* (New York: Doubleday Anchor, 1958), 119.

13. John Jay Chapman, "Charles Elliot Norton," *Harper's Weekly* 57, no. 2928 (February 1, 1913): 6.

14. Brooks, *America's Coming of Age,* 121.

15. George Santayana, *Character and Opinion in the United States* (New York: Charles Scribner's Sons, 1921), vii.

16. Irving Babbitt, *Democracy and Leadership* (Boston: Houghton Mifflin, 1924), 245.

17. H. L. Mencken, *A Mencken Chrestomathy* (New York: Knopf, 1949), 171.

18. Mencken quoted in Ronald Berman, *The Great Gatsby and Modern Times* (Champaign: University of Illinois Press, 1994), 28.

19. Andrea Denhoed, "The Forgotten Lessons of the American Eugenics Movement," *New Yorker,* April 27, 2016.

20. Winter, *The Life of David Belasco,* vol. 2, 425.

21. Roberts's articles were collected and published in 1922 by Bobbs-Merrill as *Why Europe Leaves Home: A True Account of the Reasons Which Cause Central Europeans to Overrun America.* Also quoted in Lewis H. Carlson and George A. Colburn, *In Their Place: White America Defines Her Minorities, 1850–1950* (New York: John Wiley and Sons, 1972), 312.

22. Berman, *The Great Gatsby and Modern Times,* 20.

23. "Shut the Door," speech by Ellison DuRant Smith, April 9, 1924, *Congressional Record,* 68th Cong., 1st sess. (Washington, DC: Government Printing Office, 1924), vol. 65, 5961–62. See also "Shut the Door: A Senator Speaks for Immigration Restriction," *History Matters,* http://historymatters.gmu.edu/d/5080.

24. From a speech Harding delivered in Birmingham, Alabama, on October 26, 1921 (see Berman, *The Great Gatsby and Modern Times,* 25).

25. F. Scott Fitzgerald, *The Great Gatsby,* paperback ed. (New York: Charles Scribner's Sons, 1953), 130.

26. Fitzgerald to Edmund Wilson, July 1921, in F. Scott Fitzgerald, *A Life in Letters,* ed. Bruccoli (New York: Simon and Schuster, 1995), 46–47.

27. F. Scott Fitzgerald, *Tender Is the Night,* paperback ed. (New York: Charles Scribner's Sons, 1962), 110.

28. George Jean Nathan, *A George Jean Nathan Reader,* ed. A. L. Lazarus (Cranbury, NJ: Fairleigh Dickinson University Press, 1990), 157.
29. See "Dyer Anti-Lynching Bill," NAACP Resources, at https://naacp.org /find-resources/history-explained/legislative-milestones/dyer-anti -lynching-bill.
30. On July 27, 1919, a seventeen-year-old African American, Eugene Williams, went swimming with friends in Lake Michigan. When he crossed the unofficial barrier between the city's "white" and "Black" beaches, a group of white men hit him with stones, and he drowned. Although the men were later identified, no arrests were made. Riots ensued that lasted until August 3. Fifteen whites and twenty-three Blacks were killed, and more than five hundred people injured. Another one thousand Black families were left homeless when their houses were torched.
31. Although a 2001 Oklahoma state commission confirmed thirty-six people dead (twenty-six Black and ten white), historians now estimate the death toll may have been as high as three hundred, with most fatalities presumably African American.
32. I discount for the moment his relationship with the Hollywood gossip columnist Sheilah Graham, who was born Lily Shiel in Leeds, England, to Ukrainian Jewish parents. Fitzgerald and Graham became an item in Hollywood, but she kept both her religion and her upbringing under wraps.
33. See Alison Flood, "F. Scott Fitzgerald Stories Published Uncensored for the First Time," *The Guardian,* May 1, 2014, which quotes James L. W. West III: "Before these stories were bowdlerised, they contained antisemitic slurs, sexual innuendo, instances of drug use and drunkenness. They also contained profanity and mild blasphemy. The texts were scrubbed clean at the [*Saturday Evening*] *Post.*"
34. Raymond Chandler, *Selected Letters of Raymond Chandler* (New York: Columbia University Press, 1981), 66.
35. F. Scott Fitzgerald, *The Notebooks of F. Scott Fitzgerald,* ed. Matthew Bruccoli (New York: Harcourt Brace Jovanovich, 1978), 94.
36. Frances Kroll Ring, *Against the Current: As I Remember F. Scott Fitzgerald* (Berkeley, CA: Creative Arts Book Company, 1987), 49.
37. Ron Rosenbaum, "American Shylock: Arnold Rothstein (1882–1928)," *New Republic,* October 24, 2012.
38. Kroll's portrait is affectionate but not skewed. Her boss's flaws are on display, but so is a basic decency that compensated for the binge drinking and occasional foolishness. Kroll idolized him, forgave his weaknesses, attended to his needs, and when he made a half-hearted pass at her had the grace to ignore it.
39. F. Scott Fitzgerald, *The Last Tycoon* (London: Penguin, 1971), 52. Elsewhere, the narrator describes Stahr enigmatically as "a rationalist who did his own reasoning without benefit of books—and had just managed

to climb out of a thousand years of Jewry into the late eighteenth century" (142). What Fitzgerald meant by this is hard to fathom. Every once in a while, you have to wonder if Hemingway was right: Fitzgerald really "couldn't think."

40. Fitzgerald, *The Notebooks of F. Scott Fitzgerald,* ed. Bruccoli, 333. See also Brown, *Paradise Lost,* 302.

41. See Nancy Milford, *Zelda* (New York: Harper and Row, 1970): "We used to go to a delicatessen, a Jewish delicatessen, and he would ask the names of things. I think 'knish' just floored him. He would ask again and again for it just to hear it pronounced" (Sheilah Graham to Nancy Milford, interview, September 13, 1968).

42. The implications of the technological revolution would not be felt until electrification was in place. Although Thomas Edison's electric power plant began operating in 1882, and the motion picture camera came along in 1887 and the radio in 1895 or 1896 (depending on whether you think Nicolas Tesla or Guglielmo Marconi built it), the modern age did not, in my view, begin until grids and towers were built that could supply electricity to homes across the country.

43. Quoted in Mizener, *The Far Side of Paradise,* 114.

44. Henry James, *Literary Criticism: Essays on Literature, American Writers, English Writers,* ed. Leon Edel and Mark Wilson (New York: Library of America, 1984), 351–52.

45. Ralph Waldo Emerson, "The Poet," in *Essays and Lectures* (New York: Library of America, 1983), 465.

The Facts of the Matter: 1920–1930

1. F. Scott Fitzgerald, *The Crack-Up,* ed. Edmund Wilson (New York: New Directions, 1993), 29.

2. Alfred Kazin, *On Native Grounds* (New York: Harcourt Brace, 1942), 317.

3. Matthew Bruccoli, *Some Sort of Epic Grandeur: The Life of F. Scott Fitzgerald,* 2nd rev. ed. (Columbia: University of South Carolina Press, 2002), 117.

4. F. Scott Fitzgerald, *This Side of Paradise,* paperback ed. (New York: Charles Scribner's Sons, 1960), 58–59.

5. Ibid., 282.

6. American writers were not in short supply: Sinclair Lewis, Theodore Dreiser, Upton Sinclair, Frank Norris, Booth Tarkington, Hamlin Garland, Zane Grey, and Edgar Rice Burroughs all sold well. Jack London was still in vogue, as were Mary Roberts Rinehart, Harold Bell Wright, William Sydney Porter (O. Henry), Joel Chandler Harris, and Sarah Orne Jewett. And in 1919 readers had been gripped by Vicente Blasco Ibáñez's *The Four Horseman of the Apocalypse,* a resounding family saga about Argentina and the First World War.

7. William Rose Benét, "An Admirable Novel," *Saturday Review of Literature,* May 9, 1925, 739–40.

8. H. L. Mencken, *The Smart Set,* quoted in A. Scott Berg, *Max Perkins— Editor of Genius* (New York: Simon and Schuster, 1978), ii.

9. Edmund Wilson, "F. Scott Fitzgerald," *The Shores of Light: A Literary Chronicle of the Twenties and Thirties* (New York: Farrar, Straus and Young, 1952), 28. Wilson does go on to say that *"This Side of Paradise* commits almost every sin that a novel can possibly commit, but it does not commit the unpardonable sin: it does not fail to live." Hemingway, who admired both *Gatsby* and *Tender Is the Night,* regarded Fitzgerald's first novel as "a joke," and thought his second "so damned unbeautiful that [he] couldn't finish it" (see Jeffrey Meyers, *Scott Fitzgerald: A Biography* [New York: HarperCollins, 1994], 325).

10. Arthur Mizener, *The Far Side of Paradise: A Biography of F. Scott Fitzgerald* (Boston: Houghton Mifflin, 1951), 104.

11. Ibid.

12. F. Scott Fitzgerald, *Conversations with F. Scott Fitzgerald,* ed. Matthew J. Bruccoli and Judith S. Baughman (Jackson: University of Mississippi Press, 2004), 5.

13. Although Fitzgerald never repudiated his first novelistic effort, he did concede that "A lot of people thought it was a fake, and perhaps it was, and a lot of others thought it was a lie, which it was not" (Fitzgerald, *The Crack-Up,* 88).

14. Thomas Flanagan, "Fitzgerald's 'Radiant World,'" *New York Review of Books,* December 21, 2000.

15. Anthony Powell, "Reflection and Movement," "An edited review by Anthony Powell of *The Crack-up* and other works by F. Scott Fitzgerald, first published on January 20, 1950. The *TLS* historical archive, 1902–2014." The original review appeared in *TLS,* September 13, 2019, 38.

16. Wilson quoted in Sarah Churchwell, *Careless People: Murder, Mayhem, and the Invention of the Great Gatsby* (New York: Penguin, 2014), 27.

17. Gish quoted in Sally Cline, *Zelda Fitzgerald: Her Voice in Paradise* (London: John Murray, 2002), 99.

18. Ruth Prigozy, "Introduction: Scott, Zelda, and the Culture of Celebrity," in *The Cambridge Companion to F. Scott Fitzgerald,* ed. Prigozy (Cambridge: Cambridge University Press, 2001), 1–27.

19. See Underwood Archives/Getty Images, *Celebrity Beauty Contest Judge,* 1926, photograph, http://www.gettyimages.com/detail/news -photo/cornelius-vanderbilt-jr-and-novelist-f-scott-fitzgerald-are -news-photo/170995397#. The photograph's caption reads, "Cornelius Vanderbilt, Jr. (L) and novelist F. Scott Fitzgerald, (R) are judges in a contest for the most beautiful women in the American type categories of debutante, co-ed, wife, mother, and sportswoman, New York, New York, c. 1926."

20. Fitzgerald, *Conversations with F. Scott Fitzgerald,* ed. Bruccoli and Baughman, 105.

21. Fitzgerald to Charles A. Post, November 30, 1937, in *Correspondence of F. Scott Fitzgerald,* ed. Matthew Bruccoli and Margaret M. Duggan (New York: Random House, 1980), 484.

22. See James R. Mellow, "Fact into Fiction," *New Criterion,* 84.

23. Prigozy, *The Cambridge Companion to F. Scott Fitzgerald,* 6.

24. Ibid., 166.

25. Mizener, *The Far Side of Paradise,* 123.

26. The line appears in "The Lees of Happiness" from *Tales of the Jazz Age* (New York: Charles Scribner's Sons, 1922). Until 1930 Fitzgerald made four or five times the amount of money from his short stories as from his novels, whose royalties, incidentally, were not negligible. *This Side of Paradise* sold around forty-five thousand copies, a very respectable number; *The Beautiful and Damned* around fifty thousand.

27. Twenty years ago, Bryant Magnum estimated that he wrote 178 short stories, but since then others have turned up (Prigozy, *The Cambridge Companion to F. Scott Fitzgerald,* 57).

28. F. Scott Fitzgerald, *The Short Stories of F. Scott Fitzgerald: A New Collection,* ed. Matthew J. Bruccoli (New York: Scribner's, 1989), xiv.

29. Ibid.

30. Fitzgerald to John Peale Bishop, March 1925, in F. Scott Fitzgerald, *A Life in Letters,* ed. Bruccoli (New York: Simon and Schuster, 1995), 100.

31. F. Scott Fitzgerald, "Who's Who—and Why," in *Afternoon of an Author,* ed. Arthur Mizener (New York: Collier, 1957), 83.

32. Fitzgerald, *The Crack-Up,* 67.

33. Kirk Curnutt, *The Cambridge Introduction to F. Scott Fitzgerald* (Cambridge: Cambridge University Press, 2007), 12.

34. Although he earned at times a great amount of money, he also relied on advances from Scribner's and loans from Ober. During one three-month period in 1927, Ober received nine telegrams asking for money.

35. Andrew Turnbull, *Scott Fitzgerald* (New York: Charles Scribner's Sons, 1962), 127.

36. Robert Sklar, *F. Scott Fitzgerald: The Last Laocoön* (New York: Oxford University Press, 1967), 125.

37. "Friend Husband's Latest," *New York Tribune,* April 2, 1922, sec. 5, p. 11.

38. John Updike, "This Side of Coherence," *New Yorker,* June 27, 1994.

39. Cline, *Zelda Fitzgerald,* 148–52.

40. Ibid., 90.

41. Scott would later tell Sheilah Graham that he had challenged Jozan to a duel and that shots had been exchanged. Graham wisely chose to disbelieve it (see Graham, *The Real F. Scott Fitzgerald—Thirty-Five Years Later* [New York: Grosset and Dunlap, 1976], 61).

42. Quoted in David S. Brown, *Paradise Lost* (Cambridge, MA: Belknap Press of Harvard University Press, 2017), 183; Fitzgerald, *F. Scott*

Fitzgerald's Ledger: A Facsimile, ed. Matthew J. Bruccoli (Washington, DC: NCR/Microcard, 1972).

43. Sarah Churchwell, *Careless People: Murder, Mayhem, and the Invention of the Great Gatsby* (New York: Penguin, 2014), 307.

44. "Letter to Maxwell Perkins, March 31, 1925," in F. Scott Fitzgerald, *The Letters of F. Scott Fitzgerald,* ed. Andrew Turnbull (New York: Charles Scribner's Sons, 1963), 178.

45. *Ledger* for the month of April 1925.

46. Fitzgerald, *A Life in Letters,* ed. Bruccoli, 104.

47. L. P. Hartley, *Saturday Review,* February 20, 1926.

48. In a letter to Fitzgerald on October 6, 1925, Perkins cites a letter he received from William Collins. Collins was more ambivalent about the book than this might at first suggest. He found the manuscript to be "the best book Scott Fitzgerald has done" but also thought the British public would be unable to "make heads or tails of it. . . . [T]he atmosphere of the book is extraordinarily foreign to the English reader, and he simply would not believe in it" (in F. Scott Fitzgerald and Maxwell Perkins, *Dear Scott/Dear Max—The Fitzgerald-Perkins Correspondence,* ed. John Kuehl and Jackson R. Bryer [New York: Charles Scribner's Sons, 1971], 121).

49. *The Letters of T. S. Eliot,* vol. 2: *1923–1935,* ed. Valerie Eliot and Hugh Haughton (New Haven, CT: Yale University Press, 2011), 813. Fitzgerald had sent a copy of the book to Eliot with the following inscription: "For T. S. Eliott [*sic*] Greatest of living poets / From his enthusiastic / worshipper / F. Scott Fitzgerald / Paris / October / 1925."

50. Arthur Mizener, "F. Scott Fitzgerald's Tormented Paradise," *Life,* January 15, 1951, 94.

51. Mizener, *The Far Side of Paradise,* 337.

52. Jeffrey Meyers, *Scott Fitzgerald,* 156–57.

53. R. W. B. Lewis, *Edith Wharton: A Biography* (New York: HarperCollins, 1975), 467–68.

54. Ibid., 468.

55. "This is to tell you about a young man named Ernest Hemingway who lives in Paris (an American), writes for the *Transatlantic Review* & has a brilliant future," Fitzgerald wrote to Maxwell Perkins on October 10, 1924. "I'd look him up right away. He's the real thing" (Fitzgerald and Perkins, *Dear Scott/Dear Max,* ed. Kuehl and Bryer, 78).

56. Cline, *Zelda Fitzgerald,* 194.

57. Mary Jo Tate, *Critical Companion to F. Scott Fitzgerald: A Literary Reference to His Life and Work* (New York: Infobase, 2007), 7.

58. Fitzgerald to Maxwell Perkins, February 20, 1926, in Fitzgerald, *A Life in Letters,* ed. Bruccoli, 138.

59. Cline, *Zelda Fitzgerald,* 156, 187.

60. Ibid., 187.

61. Ibid.

62. For the names (and circumstances) of the women Fitzgerald reputedly slept with, see Cline, *Zelda Fitzgerald,* 174, 241–43, 247–53, 260–61, 264, 267, 269, and 285–87.

63. Ibid., 444n39.

64. Zelda to Scott, Summer/Early Fall 1930, in Fitzgerald, *A Life in Letters,* ed. Bruccoli, 193.

65. Fitzgerald to Maxwell Perkins, April 24, 1925, in Fitzgerald, *A Life in Letters,* ed. Bruccoli, 107.

66. F. Scott Fitzgerald, "Dice, Brassknuckles & Guitar," *International,* 1923. Interesting that he imagined the flunky screenwriter to be Jewish.

67. Ronald Berman, *The Great Gatsby and Modern Times* (Champaign: University of Illinois Press, 1996), 137.

68. Ibid., 139.

69. Fitzgerald made three trips to Hollywood: in winter 1927, spring 1932, and summer 1937.

70. Meyers believes they had an affair; Cline is convinced they didn't.

71. See F. Scott Fitzgerald and Zelda Fitzgerald, *Dearest Scott, Dearest Zelda,* ed. Jackson R. Bryer and Cathy W. Barks (New York: St. Martin's Griffin, 2002), 63. To be fair, he then added, "At the same time I knew it was nonsense."

72. This, as far as I've been able to determine, first appeared in Aaron Latham's *Crazy Sundays* (New York: Viking, 1971), 61, and has never been substantiated by another source.

73. James Thurber, *Credos and Curios* (New York: Harper and Row, 1962), 154.

74. Morley Callaghan, *That Summer in Paris* (New York: Dell, 1963), 133.

75. Jeffrey Meyers, *Hemingway: A Biography* (New York: Harper and Row, 1985), 164.

76. Fitzgerald to Richard Knight, September 29, 1932, in *F. Scott Fitzgerald: The Complete Works,* e-artnow, 2015, "formatted for your eReader with a functional and detailed table of contents."

77. Kenneth S. Lynn, *Hemingway* (Cambridge, MA: Harvard University Press, 1995), 277.

78. Callaghan, *That Summer in Paris,* 144.

79. Ibid., 145.

80. Ibid., 182.

81. Ibid.

82. Ernest Hemingway, *Selected Letters 1917–1961,* ed. Carlos Baker (New York: Scribner, 1981), 302.

83. Bruccoli, *Some Sort of Epic Grandeur,* 283–84. The imbroglio might have been forgotten had not a Paris journalist written a misleading version of the encounter that was picked up by the *Denver Post* and then reprinted in part by the *New York Herald Tribune* Sunday book section (November 24, 1929), whereupon Callaghan sent a correction to

the *Herald Tribune* (December 8, 1929). In the meantime, Hemingway, thinking the story had originated with Callaghan, pressured Fitzgerald to wire the Canadian and demand a retraction. To Hemingway's credit, he wrote to Callaghan, absolving Fitzgerald of all blame, although he couldn't resist challenging Callaghan to meet him at a place and time of his choosing. According to Bruccoli, Hemingway may not have intended to send the letter (his wife found and mailed it). In any event, Callaghan never again heard from either man.

84. Ernest Hemingway, *A Moveable Feast* (New York: Scribner's, 1964), 149.

85. Kendall Taylor, *Sometimes Madness Is Wisdom: Zelda and Scott Fitzgerald: A Marriage* (New York: Ballantine, 2003), 208.

86. Cline, *Zelda Fitzgerald*, 192, 237.

87. Cline also thinks that Zelda's health was no better than Scott's. Among Zelda's maladies, Cline lists severe eczema, colitis, and various stomach and gynecological disorders (Cline, *Zelda Fitzgerald*, 184).

88. Fitzgerald and Fitzgerald, *Dear Scott, Dearest Zelda*, ed. Bryer and Barks, 65–66.

89. See Therese Anne Fowler, *Z: A Novel of Zelda Fitzgerald* (New York: St. Martin's, 2013); Erika Robuck, *Call Me Zelda* (New York: New American Library, 2013); and Tiziana Lo Porto and Daniele Marotta, *Superzelda: The Graphic Life of Zelda Fitzgerald* (Long Island City: One Peace, 2013).

Second Impressions

1. Kurt Curnutt, "F. Scott Fitzgerald, Age Consciousness, and the Rise of American Youth Culture," in *The Cambridge Companion to F. Scott Fitzgerald,* ed. Ruth Prigozy (Cambridge: Cambridge University Press, 2001), 29.

2. Ibid.

3. Ibid.

4. Ibid.

5. Glenway Wescott, "The Moral of F. Scott Fitzgerald," in *F. Scott Fitzgerald: The Man and His Work,* ed. Alfred Kazin (New York: Collier, 1966), 115.

6. George Jean Nathan, "The Golden Boy of the Twenties," *Esquire,* October 1958, 148–53.

7. F. Scott Fitzgerald, *The Crack-Up,* ed. Edmund Wilson (New York: New Directions, 1993), 87.

8. F. Scott Fitzgerald, "The Rich Boy," in *Babylon Revisited and Other Stories* (New York: Charles Scribner's Sons, 1971), 183.

9. Ibid., 160.

10. Ibid.

11. Ibid., 165.

12. Ibid., 187.

13. Fitzgerald to Scottie, July 7, 1938, in F. Scott Fitzgerald, *A Life in Letters,* ed. Bruccoli (New York: Simon and Schuster, 1995), 363.

14. Andrew Turnbull, *Scott Fitzgerald* (New York: Charles Scribner's Sons, 1962), 291.

15. Legend has it that Robert Johnson made a pact with the devil in order to become the best blues guitarist on earth.

16. Ronald Berman, *The Great Gatsby and Modern Times* (Champaign: University of Illinois Press, 1994), 78.

17. Ibid., 178.

18. Robert Baden-Powell, *Scouting for Boys: A Handbook for Instruction in Good Citizenship* (New York: Oxford University Press, 2004), 214.

19. F. Scott Fitzgerald, *The Great Gatsby,* paperback ed. (New York: Charles Scribner's Sons, 1953), 2.

20. Clive James, "Talking about F. Scott Fitzgerald," interview by Nichola Deane, January 2009. See https://archive.clivejames.com/essays /fscottf.htm.

21. Lionel Trilling, "F. Scott Fitzgerald," in *The Liberal Imagination* (New York: Doubleday Anchor, 1953), 245.

22. Fitzgerald, *The Great Gatsby,* 11.

23. Ibid., 112.

24. Ibid., 182.

25. Trilling, *The Liberal Imagination,* 245.

26. Fitzgerald, *The Great Gatsby,* 177.

27. Ibid., 177.

28. Matthew Bruccoli, *Some Sort of Epic Grandeur: The Life of F. Scott Fitzgerald,* 2nd rev. ed. (Columbia: University of South Carolina Press, 2002), 29.

29. Fitzgerald, *The Crack-Up,* 71–72.

30. Sheilah Graham, *College of One* (New York: Viking Press, 1967), 59.

31. Sally Cline, *Zelda Fitzgerald: Her Voice in Paradise* (New York: Arcade, 2003), 440n37. Scott Donaldson, in *Fool for Love,* claims that during the fall and winter of 1930 and 1931, when Zelda was a patient at Prangins sanatorium in Switzerland, Fitzgerald had two affairs: one with Bijou O'Connor, the daughter of the English diplomat Sir Francis Elliott, and the other with an American psychiatry student by the name of Margaret Egloff.

32. In a 1938 letter to Anne Ober, he writes: "That was always my experience—a poor boy in a rich town; a poor boy in a rich boy's school; a poor boy in a rich man's club at Princeton. . . . However, I have never been able to forgive the rich for being rich, and it has colored my entire life and works" (in Fitzgerald, *A Life in Letters,* ed. Bruccoli, 352).

33. F. Scott Fitzgerald, *Tender Is the Night* (New York: Charles Scribner's Sons, 1962), 65.

34. Fitzgerald to Maxwell Perkins, August 27, 1924, in Fitzgerald, *A Life in Letters,* ed. Bruccoli, 80.

Fitzgerald's America II

1. A hyperbolic statement, but with a particle of truth in it.
2. F. Scott Fitzgerald, "Echoes of the Jazz Age," in Fitzgerald, *The Crack-Up*, ed. Edmund Wilson (New York: New Directions, 1993), 14.
3. Ibid., 16.
4. See the timeline in Kathleen Drowne and Patrick Huber, *The 1920's* (Westport, CT: Greenwood, 2004), xviii–xxii.
5. Ibid., 15.
6. *Historical Statistics of the United States.*
7. Thomas Edison had patented the phonograph cylinder as early as 1878, but it would be another thirty years before Americans began listening widely to phonograph records.
8. F. Scott Fitzgerald, "The Rich Boy," in *Babylon Revisited and Other Stories* (New York: Charles Scribner's Sons, 1971), 184.
9. Vachel Lindsay, *The Art of the Moving Picture* (New York: Macmillan, 1915), xxxvi.
10. William James, *Essays, Comments, and Reviews* (Cambridge, MA: Harvard University Press, 1987), 112.
11. Less than a year after starting up, the *New Yorker* ran a profile of the young author. Although the *New Yorker* was not the prominent magazine it would soon become, the article must have made him proud. He wasn't just a flash-in-the-pan, a shallow chronicler of undergraduate longing and angst; he was a novelist intent on showing America to itself.
12. Ronald Berman, *The Great Gatsby and Modern Times* (Champaign: University of Illinois Press, 1994), 17.
13. Zelda Fitzgerald, *Save Me the Waltz* (New York: Charles Scribner's Sons, 1932), chap. 4, sec. 3.
14. Berman, *The Great Gatsby and Modern Times*, 8.
15. F. Scott Fitzgerald, *The Great Gatsby*, paperback ed. (New York: Charles Scribner's Sons, 1953), 119.
16. H. L. Mencken, review of *The Great Gatsby*, *Chicago Sunday Tribune*, May 3, 1925.
17. Malcolm Cowley quoted in *The Bodley Head Scott Fitzgerald*, vol. 5: *Short Stories*, ed. Cowley (London: Bodley Head, 1963), 18.
18. Arthur Mizener, *Introduction to F. Scott Fitzgerald—A Collection of Critical Essays* (New York: Simon and Schuster, 1963), 4.
19. The statement appears in Scott Donaldson's "Fitzgerald's Nonfiction" (*The Cambridge Companion to F. Scott Fitzgerald*, ed. Prigozy [Cambridge: Cambridge University Press, 2001], 174), but it is not strictly accurate. Donaldson conflates two of Fitzgerald's utterances. The first—"but things were getting thinner and thinner as the eternal necessary human values tried to spread over all that expansion"—occurs

in "Echoes of the Jazz Age" (Fitzgerald, *The Crack-Up,* 22). Donaldson, perhaps unconsciously, slightly altered the phrase. The second statement is lifted from an interview that Fitzgerald and Scottie together gave to the *New York Times* (September 18, 1933), in which he notes that his generation, now parents themselves, found that "their own lack of religious and moral convictions makes them incompetent to train their children."

20. If, as a stylist, Fitzgerald did not discard the genteel tradition of British prose as much as did his contemporaries, or, for that matter, Mark Twain, he was in his subject matter more consciously American than any writer except for Twain, whom he admired (see Edward Gillin, "Fitzgerald's Twain," in *F. Scott Fitzgerald: New Perspectives,* ed. Jackson Bryer, Alan Margolies, and Ruth Prigozy [Athens: University of Georgia Press, 2000]).

21. Arthur Mizener, "The Poet of Borrowed Time," in *Lives of Eighteen from Princeton* (1946), reprinted in *F. Scott Fitzgerald: The Man and His Work,* ed. Alfred Kazin (New York: Collier, 1966), 23.

22. Charles Weir Jr., "An Invite with Gilded Edges," *Virginia Quarterly Review* 20, no. 1 (Winter 1944): 100–113.

23. F. Scott Fitzgerald, "The Swimmers," in *The Short Stories of F. Scott Fitzgerald* (New York: Simon and Schuster, 1998), 527.

24. Ibid.

25. John Updike, *Higher Gossip: Essays and Criticism,* ed. Christopher Carduff, paperback ed. (New York: Random House, 2011), 73.

26. John Updike, *More Matter: Essays and Criticism* (New York: Random House, 2009), 539.

27. Herbert David Croly, "The Rise of the 'New' American," *New Republic* 30 (May 10, 1922), 301.

28. Ibid.

29. Ibid., 302.

30. F. Scott Fitzgerald, "The Scandal Detectives," *Saturday Evening Post,* April 28, 1928.

31. Surprisingly, Malcolm Cowley initially took exception to the generation gap, arguing that it was "insufficiently grounded in fact and that Mrs. Bruckner was closer to her son and his friend than the youngsters realized." In Cowley's view, "Edith Wharton was of Mrs. Bruckner's age and she could understand Fitzgerald perhaps better than he could understand Mrs. Wharton" (Malcolm Cowley, *The Exile's Return: A Literary Odyssey of the 1920s* [New York: Norton, 1934], 8).

32. Virginia Woolf, "Mr. Bennett and Mrs. Brown," *Hogarth Essays,* no. 1 (1924). See https://www.gutenberg.org/cache/epub/63022/pg63022 -images.html.

33. Eventually Cowley came around to the idea that it wasn't so much an aesthetic sensibility that separated young and old writers as simply

the widening gulf between age and youth. In Cowley's reestimation, the younger set—not just writers—went out of their way to embrace self-gratification, intoxication, and genius. Very few of them, he now believed, kowtowed to their elders or even "visited their parents' homes and some of them hardly exchanged a social word with men or women over forty" (Malcolm Cowley, "FSF: The Romance of Money," *Western Review* 17 [Summer 1953]: 245–55).

34. Walter Lippmann, *A Preface to Morals* (New York: Macmillan, 1929).

35. See chapter 9, "The Revolt of the Highbrows," in Frederick Lewis Allen, *Only Yesterday: An Informal History of the 1920s* (New York: Harper and Row, 1931).

36. Van Wyck Brooks, *America's Coming-of-Age* (New York: Doubleday Anchor, 1958), 39–40.

37. Van Wyck Brooks, "The Literary Life," in *Civilization in the United States: An Inquiry by Thirty Americans,* ed. Harold E. Stearns (New York: Harcourt, Brace, 1922), 183.

38. Ibid.

39. Allen, *Only Yesterday,* 229.

40. Henry James, *Hawthorne* (Ithaca, NY: Cornell University Press, 1879), 34.

41. In 1922 another country was heard from. In *Studies in Classic American Literature,* D. H. Lawrence begins: "Listen to the States asserting: 'The hour has struck! Americans shall be Americans. The U.S.A is now grown up artistically.'" Oddly enough, the artists Lawrence uses to make his case are from the old guard: Hawthorne, Poe, Melville, Richard Henry Dana, and Whitman, all of whom he felt were not given enough credit in Europe. He had a point, but it was the generation of writers who came of age *after* the First World War who would reanimate what he called "the great book of life."

42. Pound's optimism was fueled by the 1910 and 1912 exhibitions of post-impressionist paintings in London and perhaps later by the founding of Harriet Monroe's *Poetry* (1912) in Chicago, but these were just modest stirrings that didn't really amount to much until the revamped *Dial* (1920) and the suggestively titled *Broom* (1921) started operations.

43. Henrik Willem Van Loon, "The American Naissance," *Vanity Fair* 18, no. 3 (May 1922): 41.

44. Interestingly, the writers of the "Lost Generation" achieved success at a younger age than had their predecessors. Lewis, Dreiser, and Sherwood Anderson were in their forties before they were able to subsist comfortably from their writing, whereas Fitzgerald, Hemingway, Thornton Wilder, and Dos Passos were all famous before they were thirty.

45. Fitzgerald, *The Crack-Up,* 79.

46. Glenway Westcott, "The Moral of Scott Fitzgerald," *New Republic,* February 17, 1941.

47. See Matthew J. Bruccoli, "Getting It Right: The Publishing Process and the Correction of Factual Errors—with Reference to *The Great Gatsby*," in *Essays in Honor of William B. Todd*, ed. Bruccoli, compiled by Warner Barnes and Larry Carver, 40–59 (Austin: Harry Ransom Humanities Research Center, University of Texas, 1991). Fitzgerald was not unaware of his failings and urged Maxwell Perkins to provide corrections for the London edition of *This Side of Paradise*. Years later he also proposed adding a "glossary of absurdities and inaccuracies." But Perkins himself, according to Charles Scribner Jr., "was totally useless when it came to copy editing or correcting a text. Such details meant very little to him. Consequently, the early editions of books such as Scott Fitzgerald's *The Great Gatsby* were textually corrupt to a nauseating degree" (see Charles Scribner Jr., *In the Company of Writers* [New York: Scribner's, 1991], 44).

   Malcolm Cowley also noted Perkins's "aristocratic disregard for details so long as a book was right in its feeling for life." Cowley even suggested that the errors in *Tender Is the Night* "had a cumulative effect on readers and ended by distracting their attention" (see Matthew Bruccoli, *The Composition of "Tender Is the Night"* [Pittsburgh, PA: University of Pittsburgh Press, 1963], 214). In editing the restructured edition, Cowley made some ninety corrections of spelling, usage, geography, and fact (*Tender Is the Night* [New York: Scribner's, 1951], vi).

48. "From Undated Letters," in *The Crack-Up*, 304.

49. Fitzgerald to Corey Ford, July 1937, in Fitzgerald, *The Letters of F. Scott Fitzgerald*, ed. Andrew Turnbull (New York: Bantam, 1971), 551.

50. John Updike, *Higher Gossip: Essays and Criticism*, ed. Christopher Carduff, paperback ed. (New York: Random House, 2011), 72.

51. F. Scott Fitzgerald, *On Authorship*, ed. Matthew Bruccoli (Columbia: University of South Carolina Press, 1996), 106.

52. F. Scott Fitzgerald, "How to Waste Material: A Note on My Generation," *Bookman*, May 1926, reprinted in F. Scott Fitzgerald, *Afternoon of an Author: A Selection of Uncollected Stories and Essays* (London: Bodley Head, 1958), 120.

The Facts of the Matter: 1930–1940

1. If Fitzgerald felt ashamed of his father's lack of position, he also regarded him with affection and esteem. Sheilah Graham told Harold Ober that Scott did not want to be buried in California but "would like to buried where his father is buried because he admired him" (Perry Deane Young, "This Side of Rockville," *Washington Post*, January 14, 1979).

2. The line appears in a piece coauthored by both Scott and Zelda but may, in fact, have been his since the original manuscript is written in

his hand (F. Scott Fitzgerald, *My Lost City: Personal Essays 1920–1940,* ed. James L. W. West III [Cambridge: Cambridge University Press, 2005], xxiv).

3. Charles MacArthur quoted in Christopher Sylvester, ed., *The Grove Book of Hollywood* (New York: Grove, 1998), 196.

4. Aaron Latham, *Crazy Sundays* (New York: Viking, 1971), 72.

5. Fitzgerald's "Crazy Sunday" was first published in *American Mercury,* October 1932, and reprinted in *Taps at Reveille.*

6. Andrew Turnbull, *Scott Fitzgerald* (New York: Charles Scribner's Sons, 1962), 203.

7. Fitzgerald to Oscar Kalman, September 1936, in F. Scott Fitzgerald, *Correspondence of F. Scott Fitzgerald,* ed. Matthew J. Bruccoli and Margaret M. Duggan (New York: Random House, 1980), 451.

8. Ian Hamilton, *Writers in Hollywood 1915–1951* (New York: Harper and Row, 1990), vi.

9. Matthew Bruccoli, *Some Sort of Epic Grandeur: The Life of F. Scott Fitzgerald,* 2nd rev. ed. (Columbia: University of South Carolina Press, 2002), 386.

10. F. Scott Fitzgerald, *A Life in Letters,* ed. Bruccoli (New York: Simon and Schuster, 1995), 294.

11. Bryer quoted in Deborah Rudacille, "F. Scott Fitzgerald in Baltimore," *Baltimore Style,* December 8, 2009.

12. Zelda Fitzgerald quoted in Sally Cline, *Zelda Fitzgerald: Her Voice in Paradise* (New York: Arcade, 2003), 36.

13. According to Cline, "Zelda's life he saw as his raw material. Zelda's writings as his literary property" (see Cline's *Zelda Fitzgerald,* 307). For specific examples of Scott using Zelda's words, see ibid., 89, 101.

14. Bruccoli, *Some Sort of Epic Grandeur,* chap. 43. Arthur Mizener, *The Far Side of Paradise: A Biography of F. Scott Fitzgerald* (Boston: Houghton Mifflin, 1951), 341.

15. See also ibid., 226; Cline, *Zelda Fitzgerald,* 334.

16. In April, Zelda had a show of her work in the city.

17. Cline, *Zelda Fitzgerald,* 337–38.

18. John O'Hara quoted in Bruccoli, *Some Sort of Epic Grandeur,* 391.

19. John Updike, "The Doctor's Son," *New Yorker,* November 6, 1978, 200–214.

20. Quoted in Lewis M. Dabney, *Edmund Wilson, A Life in Literature* (New York: Farrar, Straus and Giroux, 2005), 200.

21. F. Scott Fitzgerald, *The Notebooks of F. Scott Fitzgerald,* ed. Matthew J. Bruccoli (New York: Harcourt Brace Jovanovich, 1978). See also Matthew J. Bruccoli, *Fitzgerald and Hemingway: A Dangerous Friendship* (New York: Carroll and Graf, 1994), 165.

22. Fitzgerald to Hemingway, May 10, 1934, in Fitzgerald, *A Life in Letters,* ed. Bruccoli, 259.

23. Hemingway to Fitzgerald, May 28, 1934, in Ernest Hemingway, *Selected Letters 1917–1961*, ed. Carlos Baker (New York: Scribner, 1981), 407–8.

24. See Morris Dickstein, *A Mirror in the Roadway* (Princeton, NJ: Princeton University Press, 2005), 81.

25. Bruccoli, *Some Sort of Epic Grandeur*, 402.

26. Warren quoted in Latham, *Crazy Sundays*, 180.

27. Budd Schulberg, *Writers in America: The Four Seasons of Success* (New York: Stein and Day, 1983), 112.

28. F. Scott Fitzgerald, *The Crack-Up*, ed. Edmund Wilson (New York: New Directions, 1993), 78.

29. Ibid.

30. Ibid.

31. Fitzgerald, *Correspondence of F. Scott Fitzgerald*, ed. Bruccoli and Duggan, 397.

32. Anyone who sticks around for the credits of a rerun of *Rawhide* will notice the name of Charles Marquis Warren, who later went on to produce and direct movies.

33. Mizener, *The Far Side of Paradise*, 275.

34. Ibid., 261.

35. F. Scott Fitzgerald, "Sleeping and Waking," in *The Crack-Up*, 67.

36. Latham, *Crazy Sundays*, 83.

37. Cline, somewhat surprisingly, embellishes without questioning the story (Cline, *Zelda Fitzgerald*, 353).

38. Mizener, too, could not resist a colorful but dubious anecdote. He relates an incident that supposedly occurred in 1936, when Fitzgerald was living in a hotel in Asheville. One afternoon Zelda came to visit; they got into one of their patented fights, and Zelda stormed out. Scott then emptied her suitcase and began "tearing up her clothes, slowly, piece by piece." We know this because, according to Mizener, Fitzgerald called a friend and asked him to find Zelda. The unnamed friend, who must have entered the room when Fitzgerald was rending the garments, eventually discovered Zelda at the train station, sitting on a bench wearing a child's bonnet. Unfortunately, we have only the mysterious friend's word for this (Mizener, *The Far Side of Paradise*, 263).

39. See Bruccoli, *Some Sort of Epic Grandeur*, 394–95.

40. Fitzgerald to Beatrice Dance, August 1935, in Fitzgerald, *Correspondence of F. Scott Fitzgerald*, ed. Bruccoli and Duggan, 419–20.

41. See Cline, *Zelda Fitzgerald*, chap. 23.

42. Ibid., 283, 286.

43. F. Scott Fitzgerald, "Lamp in a Window," *New Yorker*, March 23, 1935.

44. Sarah Churchwell, *Careless People: Murder, Mayhem, and the Invention of The Great Gatsby* (New York: Penguin, 2014), 323.

45. Zelda Fitzgerald to F. Scott Fitzgerald, June 19, 1935, in Fitzgerald, *A Life in Letters*, ed. Bruccoli, 285.

46. Had I discovered the letter on my own, hidden away in some dusty drawer, I hope I would have had the decency to let it lie. Why shouldn't the dead be accorded the same privileges as the living?

47. Bruccoli, *Some Sort of Epic Grandeur*, 327.

48. Fitzgerald, *The Crack-Up*, 80. Depending on whether he left from Asheville or Baltimore, the mileage is, respectively, 26 or 530.

49. "A Letter from John Dos Passos (October 1936)," in Fitzgerald, *The Crack-Up*, 311.

50. Michel Mok, "The Other Side of Paradise, Scott Fitzgerald, 40, Engulfed in Despair," *New York Post*, September 25, 1936.

51. Hemingway to Maxwell Perkins, February 7, 1936, in *Ernest Hemingway, Selected Letters 1917–1961*, ed. Baker, 438.

52. *Esquire*, August 1936.

53. A. Scott Berg, *Maxwell Perkins: Editor of Genius* (New York: Dutton, 1978).

54. Fitzgerald to Hemingway, July 16, 1936, in Fitzgerald, *A Life in Letters*, ed. Bruccoli, 302.

55. Fitzgerald did not attend her funeral, though he had visited her earlier that summer, as she lay dying.

56. Quoted in Mizener, *The Far Side of Paradise*, 261.

57. Jay McInerney, "The Butterfly Crusher," *The Guardian*, September 18, 2007.

58. Mok, "The Other Side of Paradise, Scott Fitzgerald, 40, Engulfed in Despair."

59. Fitzgerald to Harold Ober, October 5, 1936, in Fitzgerald, *A Life in Letters*, ed. Bruccoli, 308–9.

60. Fitzgerald to C. O. Kalman, June 1937, in Fitzgerald, *A Life in Letters*, ed. Bruccoli, 324.

61. See my essay "Slow Fade: F. Scott Fitzgerald in Hollywood," *New Yorker*, November 16, 2009.

62. Fitzgerald to Zelda, April 1938, in Fitzgerald, *A Life in Letters*, ed. Bruccoli, 354.

63. Fitzgerald to Scottie, July 1937, in Fitzgerald, *A Life in Letters*, ed Bruccoli, 331.

64. Alva Johnson, *The Great Goldwyn* (New York: Random House, 1937), chap. 3.

65. Latham, *Crazy Sundays*, 6.

66. Mizener, *The Far Side of Paradise*, 274.

67. Fitzgerald, *The Crack-Up*, 76.

68. Tom Dardis, *Some Time in the Sun* (New York: Scribner, 1976), 19.

69. Ibid., 61.

70. Bruccoli, *Some Sort of Epic Grandeur*, 451.

71. Arthur Mizener, "F. Scott Fitzgerald's Tormented Paradise," *Life*, January 15, 1951, 97–98.

72. In reviewing this manuscript, James West expressed doubt about Graham's engagement to a British peer.

73. See Sheilah Graham, *College of One* (New York: Viking, 1967).

74. Graham believed that "Portrait of a Prostitute" was the work of a drunk: "He must have written it on the photograph after the first of our two bad quarrels in 1939 when he was drinking so heavily. We had struggled for his gun, I had slapped him—the first person in his life ever to do so—and as I walked out, I had delivered a harsh exit line, 'Shoot yourself, you son of a bitch. I didn't raise myself from the gutter to waste my life on a drunk like you'" (Sheilah Graham, *The Real F. Scott Fitzgerald—Thirty-Five Years Later* [New York: Grosset and Dunlap, 1976], 19).

75. Cline, *Zelda Fitzgerald*, 365–66.

76. Latham, *Crazy Sundays*, 181.

77. A different view has been set forth by Kroll's granddaughter, who claims that Kroll and Scottie "bonded over their mutual dislike of Graham" (see Frances Kroll Ring, *Jewish Women's Archive*, https://jwa.org /weremember/ring-frances).

78. John Kuehl, "Sheilah and Scottie," *Virginia Quarterly Review*, Spring 1996.

79. Sheilah Graham and Gerold Frank, *Beloved Infidel: The Education of a Woman* (New York: Henry Holt, 1958), 162–63.

80. Fitzgerald to Joseph Mankiewicz, January 20, 1938, in Fitzgerald, *A Life in Letters*, ed. Bruccoli, 345.

81. Joseph Mankiewicz quoted in Hamilton, *Writers in Hollywood*, xi.

82. Fitzgerald to Beatrice Dance, March 4, 1938, in *Correspondence of F. Scott Fitzgerald*, ed. Bruccoli and Duggan, 489.

83. Fitzgerald to Scottie, Winter 1939, in Fitzgerald, *The Letters of F. Scott Fitzgerald*, ed. Andrew Turnbull (New York: Charles Scribner's Sons, 1963), 48.

84. I am cribbing here from my essay "Slow Fade: F. Scott Fitzgerald in Hollywood," *New Yorker*, November 16, 2009.

85. In *The Cinematic Vision of F. Scott Fitzgerald*, Wheeler Winston Dixon, a professor of film at the University of Nebraska, contends that Fitzgerald developed "an adroit and engagingly complex visual sensibility" based on fluid camera movement and astute intercutting. Dixon's case, however, rests entirely on *Infidelity*, which, admittedly, does emphasize the visual over the verbal. In fact, Fitzgerald went a little camera crazy with *Infidelity*. In his desire to register states of mind and the changing moods of a relationship, he has the camera constantly picking up and dropping off, trucking, panning, and shifting from a conventional two-shot to a POV shot. These excessive instructions do not, however, compensate for the script's overall weaknesses.

86. Charles McGrath, "Fitzgerald as Screenwriter: No Hollywood Ending," *New York Times*, April 22, 2004.

87. Schulberg, *Writers in America*, 111.

88. Robert Westbrook, *Intimate Lies: F. Scott Fitzgerald and Sheilah Graham: Her Son's Story* (New York: HarperCollins, 1995), 482.

89. Fitzgerald to Zelda Fitzgerald, May 6, 1939, in Fitzgerald, *A Life in Letters,* ed. Bruccoli, 391.

90. See Tate, *A Critical Companion,* 174: "Fitzgerald described Pat as 'a complete rat' (to Arnold Gingrich, December 19, 1939; Fitzgerald, *A Life in Letters,* ed. Bruccoli, 426)."

91. Fitzgerald to Maxwell Perkins, July 19, 1939, in Fitzgerald, *A Life in Letters,* ed. Bruccoli, 400.

92. Fitzgerald to Maxwell Perkins, October 20, 1939, in Fitzgerald, *A Life in Letters,* ed. Bruccoli, 416.

93. In a letter to agent Bill Dozier, Fitzgerald writes about working on *Babylon Revisited,* "Though I've sweated over it, it's been pleasant sweat, so to speak, and rather more fun than I've ever had in pictures" (May 15, 1940, in Fitzgerald, *Correspondence of F. Scott Fitzgerald,* ed. Bruccoli and Duggan, 596).

94. Latham, *Crazy Sundays,* 253.

95. Fitzgerald to Zelda, September 21, 1940, in Fitzgerald, *The Letters of F. Scott Fitzgerald,* ed. Turnbull, 124–25.

96. Fitzgerald to Zelda, October 11, 1940, in Fitzgerald, *A Life in Letters,* ed. Bruccoli, 466.

97. A sad footnote to the story: Cowan later sold the rights to "Babylon Revisited" to MGM for a reported forty thousand dollars. Fitzgerald's screenplay was chucked and the story rewritten by Philip G. Epstein and Julius J. Epstein of *Casablanca* fame. Also credited as a writer was the director Richard Brooks. The film, *The Last Time I Saw Paris,* was released in 1954. Fitzgerald's original screenplay was eventually published in 1983 by Carroll and Graf as *Babylon Revisited: The Screenplay,* with an introduction by Budd Schulberg.

98. Frances Kroll Ring, *Against the Current: As I Remember F. Scott Fitzgerald* (Berkeley, CA: Creative Arts Book Company, 1987), 48.

99. Cline, *Zelda Fitzgerald,* 378.

100. F. Scott Fitzgerald, *The Last Tycoon* (London: Penguin, 1971), 87.

101. Anne Margaret Daniel, "John O'Hara and F. Scott Fitzgerald," *Huffington Post,* September 16, 2013, http://www.huffingtonpost.com/anne -margaret-daniel/john-ohara-and-f-scott-fi_b_3934589.html. F. Scott Fitzgerald and John O'Hara, California, 1939, photo © Bell O'Hara, in Bruccoli, *Some Sort of Epic Grandeur,* 476.

102. Fitzgerald to Zelda, October 19, 1940, in Fitzgerald, *A Life in Letters,* ed. Bruccoli.

Third Impressions

1. F. Scott Fitzgerald, *The Great Gatsby,* paperback ed. (New York: Charles Scribner's Sons, 1953), 124.

2. Fitzgerald to Thomas Boyd, May 1924, in F. Scott Fitzgerald, *A Life in Letters,* ed. Bruccoli (New York: Simon and Schuster, 1995), 69.

3. Fitzgerald to Maxwell Perkins, May 1, 1925, in F. Scott Fitzgerald and Maxwell Perkins, *Dear Scott/Dear Max, The Fitzgerald-Perkins Correspondence,* ed. John Kuehl and Jackson R. Bryer (New York: Charles Scribner's Sons, 1971), 104.

4. F. Scott Fitzgerald, *The Crack-Up,* ed. Edmund Wilson (New York: New Directions, 1993), 80.

5. Lionel Trilling, *The Liberal Imagination* (New York: Doubleday Anchor, 1953), 236.

6. Alfred Kazin, "An American Confession," *Quarterly Review of Literature* (1946), reprinted in *F. Scott Fitzgerald: The Man and His Work,* ed. Alfred Kazin (New York: Collier, 1951), 174.

7. Ibid.

8. *Alfred Kazin's America: Critical and Personal Writings,* ed. Ted Solotaroff (New York: HarperCollins, 2002), 119–20.

9. E. L. Doctorow, introduction to *The Jazz Age,* by F. Scott Fitzgerald (New York: New Directions Bibelot, 1996), ix.

10. Arnold Gingrich, "Scott, Ernest, and Whoever," *Esquire,* December 1966.

11. Fitzgerald, *The Crack-Up,* 79.

12. Kazin, *Fitzgerald: The Man and His Work,* 176.

13. Fitzgerald can't win even when people believe he's telling the truth. E. M. Ciorin dismisses *The Crack-Up,* contending that Fitzgerald "went through a Pascalian experience without a Pascalian mind" (see James R. Mellow, "Fact into Fiction," *New Criterion,* March 1983, 86).

14. Kazin, "An American Confession," 178.

15. F. Scott Fitzgerald, "Ring," in Fitzgerald, *My Lost City: Personal Essays 1920–1940,* ed. James L. W. West III (Cambridge: Cambridge University Press, 2005), 94.

16. Fitzgerald, *The Crack-Up,* 75.

17. Ibid., 84.

18. Jeffrey Meyers, *Scott Fitzgerald: A Biography* (New York: HarperCollins, 1994), 289.

19. Ibid.

20. Ibid.

21. Ibid. See also Anita Loos, *Cast of Thousands* (New York: Grosset and Dunlop, 1976), 129.

22. F. Scott Fitzgerald, *The Last Tycoon* (London: Penguin, 1971), 16.

23. F. Scott Fitzgerald, *Tender Is the Night,* paperback ed. (New York: Charles Scribner's Sons, 1962), 292.

24. Fitzgerald, *A Life in Letters,* ed. Bruccoli, 330.

25. Anita Loos quoted in Aaron Latham, *Crazy Sundays* (New York: Viking, 1971), 9.

26. George Cukor quoted in ibid., 10.

27. See my piece "Slow Fade: F. Scott Fitzgerald in Hollywood," *New Yorker*, November 16, 2009.

28. Fitzgerald, *The Crack-Up*, 78.

29. Fitzgerald to Alice Wooten Richardson, July 29, 1940, *F. Scott Fitzgerald Centenary Exhibition*, Matthew J. and Arlyn Bruccoli Collection (Columbia: University of South Carolina Press, 1996), 82.

30. Ibid., 140.

31. The notion of a cabal was suggested to him by Budd Schulberg (see Fitzgerald, *A Life in Letters*, ed. Bruccoli, 429).

32. Fitzgerald to Leland Hayward, December 6, 1939, in Fitzgerald, *A Life in Letters*, ed. Bruccoli, 424.

33. Latham, *Crazy Sundays*, 127.

34. Fitzgerald to Ann Ober, July 26, 1937, in Fitzgerald, *A Life in Letters*, ed. Bruccoli, 334.

35. Fitzgerald to Scottie, October 8, 1947, in Fitzgerald, *A Life in Letters*, ed. Bruccoli, 337.

36. Sheilah Graham, *The Real F. Scott Fitzgerald—Thirty-Five Years Later* (New York: Grosset and Dunlap, 1976).

37. Budd Schulberg quoted in Ruth Prigozy, ed., *The Cambridge Companion to F. Scott Fitzgerald* (Cambridge: Cambridge University Press, 2001), 15.

38. Fitzgerald to Scottie, July 7, 1938, in Fitzgerald, *A Life in Letters*, ed. Bruccoli, 363.

39. Fitzgerald to Scottie, June 12, 1940, in Fitzgerald, *A Life in Letters*, ed. Bruccoli, 451.

40. Fitzgerald to Maxwell Perkins, May 20, 1940, in Fitzgerald, *A Life in Letters*, ed. Bruccoli, 445.

41. Fitzgerald to Ludlow Fowler, August 1924, in Fitzgerald, *A Life in Letters*, ed. Bruccoli, 78.

42. Mizener's observation refers to Nick Carraway's musings in *The Great Gatsby*, 182.

43. Here, as elsewhere, I draw on my essay "Slow Fade: F. Scott Fitzgerald in Hollywood," *New Yorker*, November 16, 2009.

Fitzgerald's America III

1. The American Dream, Adams wrote, is "that dream of a land in which life should be better and richer and fuller for everyone, with opportunity for each according to ability or achievement. . . . It is not a dream of motor cars and high wages merely, but a dream of social order in which each man and each woman shall be able to attain to the fullest stature of which they are innately capable, and be recognized by others for what they are, regardless of the fortuitous circumstances of birth or

position" (James Truslow Adams, *The Epic of America* [New York: Little, Brown, 1931], 404).

2. Some of the thoughts and figures mentioned here can be found in my essay "The Worst of Times: Revisiting the Great Depression," *Harper's Magazine,* November 2009.

3. Warren L. Susman, "The Culture of the Thirties," in *Culture as History: The Transformation of American Society in the Twentieth Century* (New York: Pantheon, 1984), 154.

4. This was also a time, not incidentally, when folk culture, under the auspices of the Library of Congress and under the guidance of social historian Alan Lomax, began to be documented.

5. Morris Dickstein, *A Mirror in the Roadway* (Princeton, NJ: Princeton University Press, 2005), 41.

6. In a letter to Scottie, he writes: "You must have some politeness toward ideas. You can neither cut through, nor challenge nor beat the fact that there is an organized movement over the world before which you and I as individuals are less than the dust. Some time when you feel very brave and defiant and haven't been invited to one particular college function, read the terrible chapter in *Das Kapital* on *The Working Day,* and see if you are ever quite the same" (Fitzgerald to Scottie, February 26, 1940, in F. Scott Fitzgerald, *A Life in Letters,* ed. Bruccoli [New York: Simon and Schuster, 1995], 436).

7. January 19, 1933, in F. Scott Fitzgerald and Maxwell Perkins, *Dear Scott/ Dear Max, The Fitzgerald-Perkins Correspondence,* ed. John Kuehl and Jackson R. Bryer (New York: Charles Scribner's Sons, 1971), 177.

8. Fitzgerald to Cecilia Delihant Taylor, August 1934, in Fitzgerald, *A Life in Letters,* ed. Bruccoli, 265. The allusion is to the Communist Party's support of African Americans in the South, which Fitzgerald believed was intended to stir up trouble.

9. Budd Schulberg, *Writers in America: The Four Seasons of Success* (New York: Stein and Day, 1983). Again, there is something off-kilter about Schulberg's account of Fitzgerald's enthusiastic response to Spengler, since Fitzgerald had at least heard of Spengler as early as 1924. See Fitzgerald and Perkins, *Dear Scott/Dear Max,* ed. Kuehl and Bryer, 263.

10. F. Scott Fitzgerald, *This Side of Paradise,* paperback ed. (New York: Charles Scribner's Sons, 1960), 277.

11. March 5, 1922, in Fitzgerald and Perkins, *Dear Scott /Dear Max,* ed. Kuehl and Bryer, 57.

12. The pursuit of happiness may seem a perfectly natural sentiment today, but in 1776 it was a rather audacious notion, even containing a touch of heresy. When Jefferson deemed happiness a natural right, the Church could have taken issue with him. Happiness wasn't intended as an earthly goal; it was what Heaven was for; and the pursuit of happiness on earth was unseemly, if not actually theologically improper.

13. Darrin M. McMahon, *Happiness: A History* (New York: Atlantic Monthly Press, 2005), 332.

14. Lionel Trilling, *The Liberal Imagination* (New York: Doubleday Anchor, 1953), 244.

15. Arthur Mizener, introduction to F. Scott Fitzgerald, *Afternoon of An Author: A Selection of Uncollected Stories and Essays* (London: Bodley Head, 1958), 8.

16. See Dickstein, *A Mirror in the Roadway*, 259–60: For a long time he believed that he had a gift for happiness, though, being Fitzgerald, he also attributed this gift to a "talent for self-delusion."

17. F. Scott Fitzgerald, *The Crack-Up*, ed. Edmund Wilson (New York: New Directions, 1993), 84.

18. Ibid., 90.

19. The role or extent of Catholicism in Fitzgerald's work is problematic. Although there is relatively little that is outright Catholic in his writings, a case can be made that the rejection of his religious upbringing infuses his work. "I am ashamed to say that my Catholicism is scarcely more than a memory—no that's wrong it's more than that; at any rate I go not to the church nor mumble stray nothings over chrystaline beads," he told Wilson in 1920 (see Fitzgerald, *The Letters of F. Scott Fitzgerald*, ed. Andrew Turnbull [New York: Charles Scribner's Sons, 1963], 325). Therefore, the oft-made assertion that the billboard eyes of Dr. T. J. Eckleburg represent God, or the more subtle argument that Fitzgerald's pride-before-the-fall denouement of his major characters (Gatsby, Diver, Stahr) is a remnant of his Catholic upbringing, is not entirely compelling.

20. Fitzgerald's ten-page letter to Hemingway (June 1926) about the draft of *The Sun Also Rises* presents an excellent example of Fitzgerald the critic; he made Hemingway revise the opening, essentially cutting the first fourteen or fifteen pages (see Fitzgerald, *Correspondence of F. Scott Fitzgerald*, ed. Matthew Bruccoli and Margaret M. Duggan [New York: Random House, 1980], 193–96).

21. See Literary Notes, *The Writer's Almanac, with Garrison Keillor,* July 24, 2003, https://writersalmanac.publicradio.org/index.php%3Fdate=2003%252F07%252F24.html. See also William Elliott Hazelgrove, *Writing Gatsby* (Guilford, CT: Lyons, 2022), 234.

22. Fitzgerald, *The Crack-Up*, 84.

23. Lillian Ross, "How Do You Like It Now, Gentlemen? The Moods of Ernest Hemingway," *New Yorker,* May 13, 1950.

24. James R. Mellow, *Invented Lives: Scott and Zelda Fitzgerald* (New York: Ballantine, 1986), 179.

25. The remark appears in Fitzgerald's essay "What Kind of Husbands Do Jimmies Make?" (March 1924) (see Ruth Prigozy, ed., *The Cambridge Companion to F. Scott Fitzgerald* [Cambridge: Cambridge University Press, 2001], 172).

26. Fitzgerald, *A Life in Letters,* ed. Bruccoli, 352.
27. Ronald Berman, *The Great Gatsby and Modern Times* (Champaign: University of Illinois Press, 1994), 180.
28. Ibid.
29. Notebook E, http://fitzgerald.narod.ru/notes/notebooks_e.html.
30. F. Scott Fitzgerald, *The Last Tycoon* (London: Penguin, 1971), 25.

The Reputation

1. Raymond Chandler, *Selected Letters of Raymond Chandler,* ed. Frank MacShane (New York: Columbia University Press, 1981), 239.
2. Edmund Wilson, "F. Scott Fitzgerald," in *The Shores of Light* (New York: Vintage, 1961), 27.
3. Ibid.
4. John Peale Bishop, review of *The Beautiful and Damned, New York Herald,* March 5, 1922, sec. 8, p. 1.
5. H. L. Mencken, review of *The Great Gatsby,* by Fitzgerald, *Chicago Sunday Tribune,* May 3, 1925.
6. Ibid.
7. Glenway Wescott, "The Moral of F. Scott Fitzgerald," in *F. Scott Fitzgerald: The Man and His Work,* ed. Alfred Kazin (New York: Collier, 1966), 121.
8. Andrew Wanning, "Fitzgerald and His Brethren," in *F. Scott Fitzgerald: The Man and His Work,* ed. Alfred Kazin (New York: Collier, 1966), 162, 164.
9. Tom Burnam, "The Eyes of Dr. Eckleburg: A Re-Examination of the Great Gatsby," *College English,* October 1952, 8.
10. Malcolm Cowley, "FSF: The Romance of Money," in *Fitzgerald: Modern Critical Views,* ed. Harold Bloom (New York: Chelsea House, 1985), 60.
11. Leslie Fiedler quoted in Marius Bewley, "Great Scott," *New York Review of Books,* September 16, 1965.
12. Alfred Kazin, "An American Confession," in *F. Scott Fitzgerald: The Man and His Work,* ed. Kazin (New York: Collier, 1966), 180.
13. Ibid., 175.
14. Fitzgerald to Scottie, August 3, 1940. In F. Scott Fitzgerald, *A Life in Letters,* ed. Bruccoli (New York: Simon and Schuster, 1995), 460.
15. Ibid., 357.
16. F. Scott Fitzgerald, "How to Waste Material—A Note on My Generation," *Bookman* 63 (May 1926): 262–65.
17. David S. Brown, *Paradise Lost: A Life of F. Scott Fitzgerald* (Cambridge, MA: Belknap Press of Harvard University Press, 2017), 5.
18. Ibid.
19. Ibid., 259: "Dick's father belonged to a genteel tradition comprising Protestant purity, paternal rule, and liberal politics. For several

decades, it set the cultural tempo, suggesting an orderly civilization founded on a sense of shared values."

20. Ibid., 166.

21. Kazin, "Hemingway & Fitzgerald: The Cost of Being American," *American Heritage* 35, no. 3 (April/May 1984).

22. See Matthew Bruccoli's introduction to *The Notebooks of F. Scott Fitzgerald,* ed. Bruccoli (New York: Harcourt Brace Jovanovich, 1978).

23. Brown, *Paradise Lost,* 1.

24. Ibid., 281.

25. From a letter to Edmund Wilson, dated "Probably, spring, 1928," reprinted in Fitzgerald, *The Crack-Up,* 273.

26. F. Scott Fitzgerald, *The Last Tycoon* (London: Penguin, 1971), 16.

27. F. Scott Fitzgerald, *My Lost City: Personal Essays 1920–1940,* ed. James L. W. West III (Cambridge: Cambridge University Press, 2005), 109.

28. F. Scott Fitzgerald, "Echoes of the Jazz Age," *Scribner's Magazine* 90, no. 5 (November 1931).

29. F. Scott Fitzgerald, *Tender Is the Night,* paperback ed. (New York: Charles Scribner's Sons, 1962), 32.

30. Even Hemingway came round to the book's merits, writing to Perkins: "A strange thing is that in retrospect his *Tender Is the Night* gets better and better. I wish you would tell him I said so" (Matthew J. Bruccoli, *Fitzgerald and Hemingway: A Dangerous Friendship* [New York: Carroll and Graf, 1994], 183).

31. Alfred Kazin, *F. Scott Fitzgerald: The Man and His Work* (New York: Collier, 1967), 15.

32. See Mary McCarthy, *Ideas and the Novel* (New York: Harcourt Brace Jovanovich, 1980), 6.

33. Fitzgerald to Scottie, October 3, 1940, in Fitzgerald, *A Life in Letters,* ed. Bruccoli, 465.

34. Fitzgerald to Zelda, March 19, 1940, in Fitzgerald, *A Life in Letters,* ed. Bruccoli, 439. And in October, he writes to Zelda, "I don't suppose anyone will be much interested in what I have to say this time."

35. His last royalty check was for $13.13 in 1940, proceeds from the sale of seventy-two books (Brown, *Paradise Lost,* 338).

36. F. Scott Fitzgerald, *The Cambridge Edition of the Works of F. Scott Fitzgerald,* ed. James L. W. West III, Variorum ed. (Cambridge: Cambridge University Press, 2019), xiii.

37. Alexandra Alter, "New Life for Old Classics, as Their Copyrights Run Out," *New York Times,* December 29, 2018.

38. Quoted in "Edmund Wilson's Letters: To and about F. Scott Fitzgerald," *New York Review of Books,* February 17, 1977.

39. Wilson to Christian Gauss, September 8, 1941, quoted in Jeffrey Meyers, *Edmund Wilson: A Biography* (New York: Cooper Square, 2003), 226.

40. Included were *The Last Tycoon, Gatsby,* and four stories: "May Day," "The Diamond as Big as the Ritz," "Absolution," and "Crazy Sunday."

41. Stephen Vincent Benét, "Fitzgerald's Unfinished Symphony," *Saturday Review of Literature,* December 6, 1941.

42. Yoni Appelbaum, "Publishers Gave Away 122,951,031 Books during World War II," *Atlantic,* September 10, 2014.

43. Kathryn Schulz, "Why I Despise *The Great Gatsby,*" *New York Magazine,* May 6, 2013.

44. Jesmyn Ward, "Jay Gatsby: A Dreamer Doomed to Be Excluded," *New York Times Book Review,* April 12, 2018.

45. Once again I shamelessly borrow from one of my own essays: "A Pleasure to Read You," *American Scholar,* Winter 2019.

46. Fitzgerald to Maxwell Perkins, July 1922.

47. Min Jin Lee, introduction to *The Great Gatsby* (New York: Penguin Classics, 2021).

48. Wesley Morris, "Why Do We Keep Reading *The Great Gatsby*?," *Paris Review,* January 11, 2021; introduction to *The Great Gatsby* (New York: Modern Library, 2021), viii.

49. Matthew Bruccoli, *Some Sort of Epic Grandeur: The Life of F. Scott Fitzgerald,* 2nd rev. ed. (Columbia: University of South Carolina Press, 2002), 494, 492.

Final Impressions (for the Moment)

1. See "A Conversation by Scottie Fitzgerald and Matthew Bruccoli," recorded in 1977 for *Some Sort of Epic Grandeur,* Montgomery, Alabama, included in *Scottie Fitzgerald: The Stewardship of Literary Memory,* exhibition catalogue, Matthew J. and Arlyn Bruccoli Collection of F. Scott Fitzgerald, Thomas Cooper Library, University of South Carolina, 2007. "Valencia," composed by José Padilla in 1924.

2. Arthur Mizener, introduction to F. Scott Fitzgerald, *Afternoon of an Author: A Selection of Uncollected Stories and Essays* (London: Bodley Head, 1958), 11.

3. Midge Decter, "Fitzgerald at the End," *Partisan Review* 26 (Spring 1959): 303–12.

4. Ibid.

5. Ibid.

6. Fitzgerald to Dr. Robert S. Carroll, March 4, 1938, in F. Scott Fitzgerald, *A Life in Letters,* ed. Bruccoli (New York: Simon and Schuster, 1995), 350.

7. Fitzgerald to Scottie, undated, in *The Crack-Up,* ed. Edmund Wilson (New York: New Directions, 1993), 305.

8. Fitzgerald to Zelda, September 21, 1940, in *Dear Scott, Dearest Zelda: The Love Letters of F. Scott Fitzgerald and Zelda Fitzgerald,* ed.

Jackson R. Bryer, Cathy W. Barks, and Eleanor Lanahan (New York: Scribner, 2002), 367.

9. Lionel Trilling, *The Liberal Imagination* (New York: Anchor/Doubleday, 1953), 242.

10. Fitzgerald, *The Crack-Up*, 84.

11. Scott Fitzgerald to Zelda Fitzgerald, in Fitzgerald and Fitzgerald, *Dear Scott, Dearest Zelda*, ed. Bryer, Barks, and Lanahan, 193.

12. F. Scott Fitzgerald, *Correspondence of F. Scott Fitzgerald*, ed. Matthew J. Bruccoli and Margaret M. Duggan (New York: Random House, 1980), 494.

13. *Notebooks*, No. 1362, 204.

14. Fitzgerald, *A Life in Letters*, ed. Bruccoli, 350.

15. Fitzgerald to Scottie, Spring 1940, letter reprinted in *The Crack-Up*, 291.

INDEX

Callaghan, Morley, 70, 197n83
Camus, Albert, 34
Carson, Tom, 13
Cather, Willa, 65, 96, 97
Chandler, Raymond, 1, 7, 44–45, 80, 156
Chanler, Ted, 63–64
Chapman, John Jay, 39–40
Chaucer, Geoffrey, 177, 178
Cheever, John, 83, 169
Ciorin, E. M., 209n13
Cline, Sally, 61, 65, 108, 109, 124
Cohan, George M., 60
Collier's Weekly, 57, 90, 129, 130
Collins, William, 62–63, 196n48
Colum, Mary, 117
communism, 145, 148, 159, 211n8. *See also* Marxism
Conrad, Joseph, 9, 60, 100, 134, 168, 175, 176
"Count of Darkness, The" (unfinished novel), 113
Cowan, Lester, 130–31
Cowley, Malcolm, 31, 91, 158, 167, 201n31, 201–2n33, 203n47
Crack-Up, The, 14–15, 38, 116–19, 121, 134–39, 161, 166, 209n13
Crane, Stephen, 51
"Crazy Sunday," 57, 103
Cukor, George, 141
"Curious Case of Benjamin Button, The," 31, 186n5
Curnutt, Kirk, 21, 74

Dance, Beatrice, 114, 116
Dardis, Tom, 122
Davies, John, 27
Declaration of Independence, 48, 150, 211n12
Decter, Midge, 172–73
"Diamond as Big as the Ritz, The," 31, 43, 125, 189n25
"Dice, Brassknuckles & Guitar," 66
Dickens, Charles, 49, 50, 171
Dickstein, Morris, 147
Dixon, Wheeler Winston, 207n85
Doctorow, E. L., 135
"Dog" (song), 102–3
Donaldson, Scott, 92, 200n19

Dos Passos, John, 50, 117, 166, 202n44
Dostoevsky, Fyodor, 158; Fitzgerald as the Karamazov brothers, 1, 5, 29, 122–23, 124–25, 161, 162, 169, 180
Dreiser, Theodore, 50, 56, 96, 97, 111, 202n44
Duncan, Isadora, 62
Dyer, Leonides, 44
Dylan, Bob, 12

Eastwood, Clint, 112
"Echoes of the Jazz Age," 44, 200n19
Edison, Thomas, 47, 193n42, 200n7
Elevator Repair Service, 15
Eliot, T. S., 2, 63, 85, 99, 124, 179, 196n49; Fitzgerald meets, 105
Emerson, Ralph Waldo, 37, 49, 50, 79
Esquire essays. See *Crack-Up, The*
ethnic and racial issues, 41–44, 94, 100, 190n1, 192n30

Farrell, James T., 149
Faulkner, William, 50, 56, 92, 99, 121, 149, 175
Fay, Cyril Sigourney Webster, 18, 53, 152, 187n24
Fiedler, Leslie, 2, 158
film techniques, 66, 89, 207n85
Fitzgerald, Annabel, 16, 17–18, 24
Fitzgerald, Edward, 15–17, 24, 25, 38, 65, 101, 119, 136, 160, 203n1
Fitzgerald, F. Scott: alcoholism of, 1, 3, 23, 57, 62, 64–65, 69, 73, 102–3, 109, 116, 125, 128–29, 173, 177; Catholicism and, 18–19, 152, 212n19; death of, 132; early years of, 15–23, 33; European years of, 60–65, 68–73; extramarital affairs by, 61, 65, 84, 114, 123–25, 197n62, 199n31; football and, 26–27, 138; happiness obsession of, 30, 32, 34, 77, 79, 150–53, 177, 212n16; height/weight of, 184n12; Hollywood and, 33, 66–67, 101–4, 111, 120–32, 140–44, 175–76; homophobia of, 47, 62, 68; illnesses of, 114, 116, 118–19, 131–32; politics and, 148–49; posthumous

Index